P.E. GAMES & ACTIVITIES KIT

for Grades 6-12

KEN LUMSDEN

PARKER PUBLISHING COMPANY
Paramus, New Jersey 07652

Library of Congress Cataloging-in-Publication Data

Lumsden, Ken.
    P.E. games & activities kit for grades 6–12: over 250 games to put new variety
and challenge into your physical education program / Ken Lumsden.
      p.   cm.
    ISBN 0-13-041066-7
    1. Physical education and training—Study and teaching (Secondary)—United States.
2. Games—Study and teaching (Secondary)—United States. I. Title: Physical education games &
activities kit for grades 6–12. II. Title: P.E. games and activities kit for grades 6–12. III. Title.

GV365 .L84 2001
796'.071'273—dc21   00-064249

© 2001 *by* Parker Publishing Company

Acquisitions Editor: *Connie Kallback*
Production Editor: *Marian Hutlak*
Interior Design/Formatting: Pine Tree Composition

Printed in the United States of America

10 9 8 7 6 5 4 3 2 1

ISBN 0-13-041066-7

PARKER PUBLISHING COMPANY
Paramus, New Jersey 07652

www.phdirect.com

DEDICATION

This book is dedicated to my mother, Shirley,
and in memory of my father, Lou.

ABOUT THE AUTHOR

Ken Lumsden has been a secondary physical education teacher and coach at Ashland Middle School in Ashland, Oregon since 1976. He received his Master's degree in Physical Education and Health from Southern Oregon University in 1981. Parker, A Prentice Hall imprint, published Ken's physical education curriculum book, *Ready-to-Use P.E. Activities and Tournaments for Grades 6–12*, co-authored with Sally Jones, in 1996. Parker published Ken's basketball drills book, *Complete Book of Drills for Winning Basketball*, in 1999.

Ken was presented with the Ashland Rotary Club Outstanding Teacher Service and Achievement Award in 1997. He has also created several games, a unique method of organizing students, and a grading procedure based on student accountability.

Ken and Elaine, his wife of 30 years, have one son, Chris. In his spare time, Ken enjoys fishing, boating white water rivers, agate hunting, and traveling.

ABOUT THIS RESOURCE

The purpose of this resource is to enhance existing physical education programs. It is loaded with a vast array of fun and challenging activities, diverse organizational plans, an expanded assessment method, additional tournament formats, and other enhanced ready-to-use forms to facilitate the expansion and growth of any physical education curriculum. The following descriptions give an idea of what each section contains:

Part I, **Unit Activities,** encompasses a vast array of traditional as well as new easy-to-read games and activities which were incorporated to put interest, excitement, and challenge into any program while genuinely helping players to experience success, self-confidence, and enthusiasm. No longer does the same unit of slow-pitch softball need to be repeated year after year. The games are not loaded with official rules but instead have been adapted and modified to ensure safety and success. The information should be used as a follow-up after the students have learned the basic rules, court and field dimensions, skills, and strategies of the many games and activities included in this book. Each activity follows a similar format that includes the name, objectives, equipment needed, safety issues (when necessary), how to play, student tasks or goals, and variations or modifications that can be applied to the particular game. The text is relatively short, simple, and to the point. The diagrams are clear and easy to interpret. Each activity can be altered or adjusted to allow success for the varying degrees of age, ability, and skill within individuals or teams.

Part II, **Organization,** offers several exceptional and highly successful methods for organizing and dispersing students. One important benefit of these methods is to allow fast and simple organization with increasing excitement and decreasing boredom by creating a new composition of teams daily. Eliminating the loser syndrome by allowing students to be with various other classmates during any unit or competition, expanding practice and playing time by expediting the team choosing process, and providing for multiple activities are also worthy dividends. Newly created user-friendly reproducible forms, instructions, and easy-to-read illustrations are also provided.

Part III, **Assessments,** features the criteria, explanations, directions, and forms for several new and improved methods of "Student Accountability" grading. This section too, is complete with reproducible forms.

The use of this valuable resource can help teacher and student alike to realize an increase in excitement, motivation, and achievement. This resource should prove to be a valuable asset for every physical education program, instructor and student. I sincerely hope that everyone involved has a great experience.

Ken Lumsden

CONTENTS

Lacrosse—199

Large Group Games—203

Medicine Ball—221

Obstacle Course—231

Relays—249

PART II
ORGANIZATION FOR TOURNAMENTS

Tournaments—448

Team Organizer—453

PART III
EASY ASSESSMENTS

Assessment Format—457

Sample Roll Call—460

    10-Day Inverted Grade Scale   464
    15-Day Inverted Grade Scale   465

Sample Final Term Grade—466

    Final Term Grade Sheet   467

Unified Units Grade Scale—468

About Accountability Statement—469

    Accountability Statement Form   470

About Deficiency Report—471

    Physical Education Deficiency Report   472

Motivators—473

    Ticket Takers   473
    Lunch Bunch   475

PART 1
GAMES & ACTIVITIES

Aquatics to wrestling – 37 alphabetically organized units including over 250 games and activities for the secondary P.E. curriculum.

Aquatics	Lacrosse
Badminton	Large Group Games
Balancing and Juggling	Medicine Ball
Basketball	Obstacle Course
Bocce	Relays
Bowling	Shuffleboard
Cricket	Soccer
Croquet	Softball
Cross Country	Table Tennis
Cycling	Tennis
Darts	Tetherball
Dodgeball	Tug-of-War
Field Hockey	Volleyball
Floor Hockey	Wall Ball
Flying Disc	Wall Climbing
Football	Washers
Golf	Weight Training
Horseshoes	Wrestling
Korfball	

BRICK BRAWL*

Objectives:

- ◆ Score points by pushing a brick beyond the opponent's goal line.
- ◆ Score three points before the opposition does.
- ◆ Develop the ability to hold one's breath.

Essentials:

- ◆ Swimming pool
- ◆ Rubber pool brick or indoor shot put
- ◆ 4 floor cones to mark the goal line
- ◆ Stopwatch
- ◆ Scoreboard

How to Play:

1. Divide the pool in half and play from side to side in the shallow end.
2. Place cones about five feet away from the sides to establish each team's goal line.
3. Form teams composed of seven players each.
4. To start the game, each team will line up on opposite sides with everyone touching the side of the pool. The brick is then tossed into the middle. Play begins as soon as it hits the water.
5. Players will dive under water and attempt to push or tumble the brick past the opposition's goal line. One point is awarded for doing so.
6. Only the hands may be used to propel the brick.
7. It is illegal to grab or lift the brick off of the bottom of the pool.
8. Holding on to or pulling back another player is prohibited.
9. After a score, both teams will return to the start position. The team that was scored upon will gain an advantage by starting even with their goal line.
10. First team to score three points is the winner.

Student Tasks:

1. Prevent a score.
2. Push the brick at least ten feet across the bottom.
3. Take the brick away from an adversary.
4. Push the brick three different times during play.

*By Dustin Asher, 1998.

© 2001 Parker Publishing Company

Variations:

1. Play timed quarters.
2. Use two bricks.
3. Use a vinyl-covered indoor shot put.
4. Use goggles and swim fins.
5. Everyone must touch the brick before a score will count.
6. Use handheld hockey sticks (scooter board) and a heavy puck.
7. Use the other half of the pool (if not too deep), make four teams and play a round-robin tournament.

Example of Player Positioning for the Start of Brick Brawl

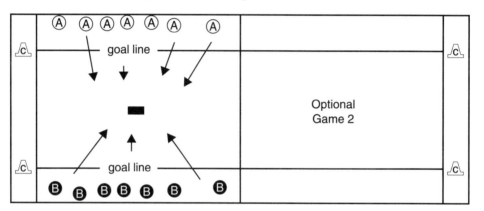

WATER BASKETBALL

Objectives:

◆ Outscore the opposition by throwing a ball through the basket.
◆ Promote team play and cooperation.

Essentials:

◆ Swimming pool
◆ Rubber basketball
◆ Swim caps for players (a different color for each team)
◆ 2 basketball hoops and backboards

◆ 6 floor cones
◆ Stopwatch
◆ Scoreboard

How to Play:

1. Use the cones and divide the pool into four sections (see illustration).
2. Create teams composed of six players each.

3. The game is composed of four quarters that last six minutes each.

4. Teams will switch ends at halftime.

5. To start play, both teams line up on their respective halves. The ball is then tossed into the middle of the pool.

6. Players can attempt to advance the ball by either passing it to a teammate or by constantly pushing the ball ahead (dribbling).

7. A player who has dribbled the ball and picked it up is not allowed to dribble again (double dribble). That player must pass or shoot the ball.

8. The ball can only be touched with both hands when passing or shooting.

9. A player can hold the ball for only five seconds when attempting a pass or score.

10. Players may not use the bottom or sides of the pool in order to gain an advantage over the opposition.

11. Scoring is the same as in basketball, except that a shot made from beyond the quarter mark is worth three points.

12. After a score, play is initiated in the same manner as basketball.

13. No defender is allowed to full pool press. Players may play defense as soon as the ball or the person they are guarding crosses the midline.

14. Once in possession of the ball, a team has 30 seconds in which to shoot at the basket.

15. Any shot or pass that leaves the playing area is given to the opposition.

16. The ball is turned over to the opposition for minor violations such as:

    a. Intentionally shoving and holding the ball underwater.

    b. Hitting the ball with a fist.

    c. Carrying the ball while swimming.

    d. Double dribbling.

    e. Hitting the arm or body of a player who is passing the ball.

    f. Throwing the ball out of bounds.

    g. Pushing off of a defensive player.

    h. Impeding the route of a player who is not in possession of the ball.

17. Two free throws are given for major fouls such as:

    a. Intentionally contacting another player.

    b. Holding or pulling on an opponent.

    c. Pushing a player underwater.

    d. Hitting the arm or body of a player who is shooting the ball.

18. Any player receiving three major violations will foul out of the game.

19. The team with the most points at the end of the contest is crowned the winner.

Student Tasks:

1. Take the ball away from two different players.

2. Block a shot attempt.

3. Get an assist.

4. Dribble past two opponents.

5. Pass to three different teammates.

6. Do not foul out of the game.

Variations:

1. Two different games can be played simultaneously (diagonally).

2. Eliminate all of the lines except the midline.

3. Allow players to use flotation apparel or apparatus.

Illustration of a Water Basketball Layout

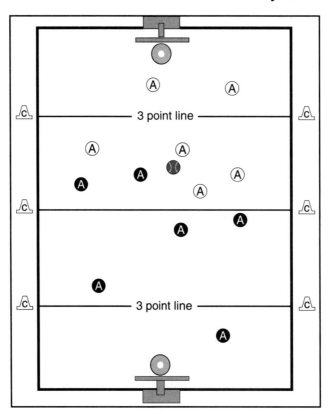

WATER POLO

Objectives:

◆ Score more points than the opposition by throwing a ball into the goal.

◆ Enhance cardiovascular endurance.

◆ Develop team play.

Essentials:

- ◆ Swimming pool
- ◆ Ball
- ◆ Swim caps for players (a different color for each team)

- ◆ Goals
- ◆ 14 floor cones (line markers)
- ◆ Stopwatch

How to Play:

1. Water polo rules are used with several modifications.
2. Divide the pool into sections using the floor cones (see illustration).
3. Create two teams composed of 14, 16, 18, or 20 players each. Divide each team equally into an A group and a B group. (Only half of a team's members will be in the water during play.)
4. The game is comprised of four quarters that last six minutes each. The A group will play the first three minutes followed by the B group the last three minutes. Teams will switch ends at halftime.
5. To start play, both teams line up on opposite ends and the ball is tossed into the water at the middle of the pool.
6. Players attempt to advance the ball by passing it to a teammate, swimming with it, or constantly pushing the ball ahead (dribbling).
7. The ball can only be touched with one hand during play.
8. A player can only hold the ball for two seconds when attempting a pass or score.
9. Players should not use the bottom or sides of the pool in order to gain an advantage over the opposition.
10. A goal is scored if the entire ball crosses the goal line between the goal posts.
11. A player cannot score from beyond the midline.
12. After a score, play is started with each team located anywhere on its respective half. The team that was scored against will put the ball into play. Play resumes as soon as the ball leaves the initiator's hand.
13. Once in possession of the ball, a team has 30 seconds in which to throw at the goal.
14. Any shot that is wide of the goal and leaves the playing area is given to the goalie to be put back into play.
15. No player may be inside of the red line when the ball is behind her/him (offside).
16. A neutral throw (indirect) is given for minor fouls such as:
    a. Shoving or pushing the ball underwater.
    b. Hitting the ball with a fist.
    c. Touching the ball with both hands at the same time.
    d. Hitting the arm or body of a player who is in possession of the ball.
    e. Throwing the ball out of bounds.

f. Pushing off of a defensive player.

g. Impeding the movement of a player that is not in possession of the ball.

17. A penalty throw (direct) is given for major fouls such as:

a. Intentionally contacting another player.

b. Holding or pulling on a player.

c. Intentionally pushing an opponent underwater.

18. Major fouls will result in the guilty person being suspended from play for 30 seconds. Any player receiving two major fouls will be ejected from the contest.

19. All direct throws will be thrown from behind the yellow line. All other players must be at least six feet away. The thrower cannot fake the toss at the goalie but instead must throw with one continuous motion.

20. The goalie can always use both hands.

21. The team with the most points at the end of the contest is declared the winner.

Student Tasks:

1. Take the ball away from two different players.

2. Be a goalie.

3. Cause a shutout.

4. Block a shot attempt.

5. Dribble the ball past two lines.

6. Pass to three different teammates.

7. Never receive a major foul.

Variations:

1. The ball can *only* be touched with the feet.

2. The ball must be splashed and never touched. Play this game from side to side.

3. Remove the goals and have the other half of the players protect their end of the pool by preventing a thrown ball from contacting the wall. Rotate mini teams after a given amount of time.

4. Two different games can be played simultaneously (diagonally). Use only the two- and four-meter lines.

5. Eliminate all of the lines except the midline, place half of each team on each end as goalies, and score by throwing the ball against the end wall.

6. Require that both hands must be used when controlling or throwing the ball.

7. Allow players to use flotation apparel or apparatus.

Diagram of a Water Polo Layout

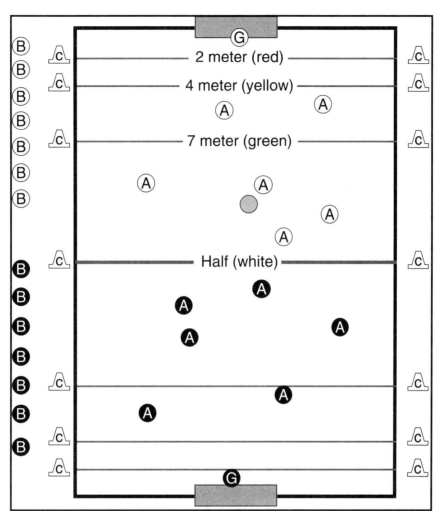

BAD DOG

Objectives:

- ◆ Eliminate the opponent by making fewer mistakes.
- ◆ Develop a game strategy with proper shot selection.

Essentials:

- ◆ Badminton court (indoor or outdoor)
- ◆ 1 racket for each student
- ◆ 3–4 shuttlecocks per court

How to Play:

1. The rules of badminton apply to this game with a few modifications.
2. Form teams composed of six players each.
3. Teams assemble opposite each other in a straight line and send the first two players to their court.
4. Each time any player hits the shuttlecock, he or she must immediately exit the court and return to the end of the team's line. The first player in line will replace the exiting player.
5. Any player who makes an error during play is eliminated.
6. The team that loses a player will always begin serve.
7. When a team has only one player remaining on the court, the opposition must hit all shots to the singles court.
8. Play until either team is eliminated to determine the winner.

Student Tasks:

1. Eliminate two of the opponents.
2. Use two different strokes during play.

Variations:

1. Alter the size of the teams.
2. Form two lines at each end as in doubles (see illustration).
3. A team may elect to bring back a player instead of having the other team lose one.
4. Use the "expedited" method of scoring. The receiving team counts out loud each returned stroke. After seven good returns, the receiving unit earns one point.
5. Make several teams and create a tournament format.

Diagram of Floor Play for Bad Dog Doubles

COURTS IN SESSION

Objectives:

- ◆ Get the entire team onto one side of the court and win the succeeding point.
- ◆ Refrain from making mistakes.

Essentials:

- ◆ Badminton court
- ◆ A racket for each participant
- ◆ 1 shuttlecock

Safety:

1. Be careful when swinging the racket if several players are on one side.
2. Remain spread out and cover a specific area.

How to Play:

1. The basic rules of badminton apply to this game.
2. Divide into teams composed of four players each.
3. Each team will go to opposite sides of the court and line up at the baselines.
4. To begin the play, one player from each team will occupy the court.
5. If a player makes a mistake, she/he will go to the end of her/his team's line and be replaced by the first person.
6. The team that does not make an error gets to add the first person in line to the team's side of the floor.
7. All serves must be regulation.
8. When only one adversary is on the floor, the opposition must hit all shots to the singles court.
9. After a team finally gets their last player on the court, they must win the next point in order to win the game.

Student Tasks:

1. Put two different players out.
2. Never go out.
3. Serve an ace.
4. After being down by two or more players, come back and win.

Variations:

1. Players must use the off hand.
2. A team must win two out of three games.
3. Use the "expedited" method of scoring. The receiving team counts out loud each returned stroke. After seven good returns, the point goes to the receiving group.
4. Have a round-robin tournament with several teams. The team with the best record wins.

Example of Courts in Session

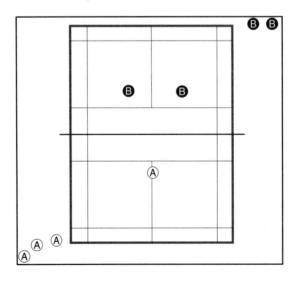

FOUR SEASONS

Objectives:

- ◆ As a team, score 15 points first.
- ◆ Eliminate the opposition and move up to the top position.

Essentials:

- ◆ Side by side badminton courts or a large open area
- ◆ 4 nets attached at a common center
- ◆ 1 racket for each student
- ◆ Shuttlecocks

How to Play:

1. The rules of badminton apply to this game with a few modifications.
2. Form groups of 12 participants. Students now join to form teams composed of two players each.
3. Teams A, B, C, and D will go to one of the designated courts of #1 (*Spring*), #2 (*Summer*), #3 (*Fall*), and #4 (*Winter*). Teams E and F will wait at the far corner of the *Spring* court.
4. Teams will try to eliminate any higher team in order to advance to the top *Winter* court.
5. Any team making an error during play is eliminated and must go to the end of the line at the *Spring* court. All of the other teams will advance one court if there is a vacancy ahead of them.
6. Any team that sends the bird into an opponent's court and causes that team to commit any error will receive one point.
7. Any team that causes the *Winter* team to make an error will receive two points.
8. The *Winter* court team will always receive two points for eliminating an opponent.
9. The *Spring* court will always begin serve.
10. First team to score 15 points is the winner.

Student Tasks:

1. Eliminate two opponents.
2. Use two different strokes during play.
3. Get rid of the top team.
4. Remain in the *Winter* court while three other teams are discharged.

Variations:

1. Play the game using one player in each court.
2. Play for a predetermined amount of time. The team that is in the *Winter* court when time expires is victorious.

Illustration of the Floor Plan for Four Seasons

HIGH NETS

Objectives:

- Score 15 points before the opposition does.
- Develop teamwork and cooperation.

Essentials:

- Volleyball court (indoors or outdoors)
- 1 racket for each student
- Shuttlecocks

Safety:

1. Be careful when swinging the racket if several players are on one side.
2. Remain spread out and cover a specific area.

How to Play:

1. The rules of badminton and volleyball apply to this game with a few modifications.
2. Form teams composed of four players each.
3. Disperse to the volleyball court and establish a rotation order.
4. Participants will serve from anywhere behind the 10 feet line.
5. Players must rotate positions after a player serves three points in succession.

© 2001 Parker Publishing Company

6. The shuttlecock may be hit up to three times on a side although no player may hit it twice in a row.

7. It is illegal to hit the net with the racket during play.

8. Anytime an error is made the opposition receives one point and the serve.

9. First team to score 15 points wins.

Student Tasks:

1. Score three points in a row.

2. Serve an ace.

3. Pass the shuttlecock to a teammate.

4. Involve three different teammates during one play.

5. Include all four teammates in any long rally.

Variations:

1. Using floor cones or tape split a volleyball court down the middle. Play two different games.

2. Use the "expedited" method of scoring. The receiving team counts out loud each returned stroke. After seven good returns, the point goes to the receiving team.

3. Teammates can defend any section of the floor.

4. Use two, three, or six players on a team.

5. Make several teams and create a tournament format.

Illustration of High Nets

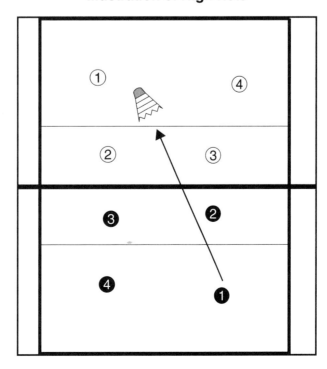

HIT 'N' GET

Objectives:

◆ Score 15 points before the opposition does.

◆ Keep track of a partner's total number of hits.

Essentials:

◆ Badminton court (indoors or outdoors)

◆ 1 racket for each student

◆ 3–4 shuttlecocks per court

How to Play:

1. The rules of badminton apply to this game with a few modifications.
2. Form teams composed of four players each. The four players will now pair-up.
3. Each team will have two players on the court and two players out-of-bounds at all times.
4. Pairs will defend either the right/left half or the front/back half.
5. After any player hits the shuttlecock for the second time, she or he must immediately exchange positions with a partner standing out-of-bounds.
6. First team to score 15 points wins.

Student Tasks:

1. Use several types of strokes during play.
2. Vary the speed and placement of the shuttlecock during a rally.
3. Score two or more points in succession.
4. Defend the net successfully.

Variations:

1. Partners must exchange after hitting the bird once.
2. Use the "expedited" method of scoring. The receiving players count out loud each returned stroke. After seven good returns, the point goes to the receiving players.
3. Teammates can defend any section of the floor.
4. Use six players on a team. Form two lines at each end as in doubles. The triplets must always defend one of the halves.
5. Make several teams and create a tournament format.

Diagram of Floor Play for Hit 'n' Get

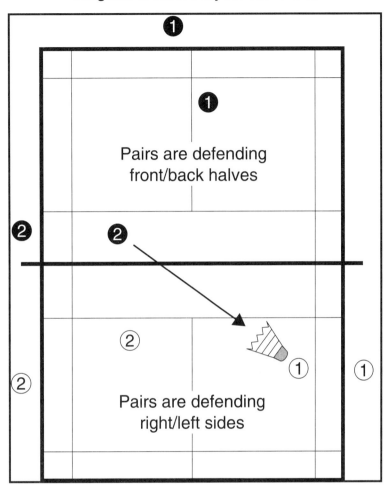

BALANCE AND JUGGLING CIRCUIT

Objectives:

- ◆ Score more points than the competition.
- ◆ Complete each assigned task successfully.
- ◆ Enhance concentration and focus.

- ◆ Develop hand-and-eye coordination.
- ◆ Develop personal balance.
- ◆ Challenge every participant.

Essentials:

- ◆ Large open area
- ◆ Objects to juggle (rings, rubber deck tennis rings, clubs, beanbags, scarves, balloons, shuffle boxes, etc.)
- ◆ Several items to balance (peacock feathers, brooms, dowels, pipe insulation, cardboard boxes, plastic bowling pins, spinning plates, hula hoops, etc.)
- ◆ A variety of balls (soccer ball, basketball, volleyball, tennis ball, football, etc.)

- ◆ Balance points (balance boards, floor beams, unicycle, bicycle, etc.)
- ◆ Safety equipment (helmets, pads, and floor mats)
- ◆ Stopwatch
- ◆ Skill statement cards
- ◆ Scorecards and pencils

How to Play:

1. Set up enough stations so that the entire class is active.
2. Players will pair up and obtain a scorecard and pencil.
3. Disperse the groups to a different station (shotgun start). (Note: It is not necessary for each group to rotate to every station.)
4. The instructor will signal the time periods (two minutes) for rotation, practice, and competition.
5. Each participant will have one minute at each station, forty seconds of practice time and twenty seconds of performance time. After the first player has performed, players will switch roles and score for their partners.
6. Record the scores and rotate on the next whistle.
7. Scoring:
   a. One point is awarded for each completed catch.
   b. When balance is required, one point is given for each successful second.
8. Sample Stations: (The following tasks can be written on 3″ x 5″ skill statement cards to explain each activity.)
   a. Balance one basketball on top of another.

b. Spin a ball on the finger.

c. Balance a broom on the foot.

d. Remain on a balance board.

e. Balance a wooden dowel on the forehead.

f. Juggle scarves in a figure eight.

g. Spin two plates.

h. Spin around three times and then walk the floor beam.

i. Juggle two clubs. *hockey pucks or beanbags*

j. Bounce the "Chinese juggling stick" back and forth.

k. Roll on a football blocking pad three revolutions in either direction.

l. Remain on a unicycle.

m. Juggle rings.

n. Stand on one foot and juggle beanbags.

o. Juggle three objects of different sizes and weights.

p. Use shuffle boxes and flip the center box 180 degrees each time.

q. Juggle batons with a partner.

r. Walk a floor balance beam backwards.

s. Juggle three beanbags.

t. Bicycle 15 feet, as slowly as possible.

u. Balance a broom on a balance board.

v. Keep a scarf dancing in the air.

w. Close the eyes and remain on a floor balance beam. *Bleachers*

x. Balance two different objects at once.

y. Juggle three volleyballs in a figure

z. Spin a hula hoop on a leg and arm simultaneously.

9. After a given amount of time, tally the scores to confirm the winner of each pair.

Student Tasks:

1. When everyone finishes every circuit, wind up in the top 50% of the class.

2. Finish in the top 10% of the class after everyone has finished the circuit.

3. Come from behind and defeat the partner.

4. Successfully complete and receive full points on three straight tasks.

5. Score ten points at seven different stations.

Variations:

1. Combine the team scores to determine a winning group.

2. Extend the competition time to 30 seconds.

3. Do not score the contest. Students will rotate every two minutes.

BALANCING AND JUGGLING

4. Make teams composed of four players each and extend the time. All four scores will be combined to determine the champions.

5. Allow the students to design and create a balance and juggling circuit.

Sample Scorecards for the Balance and Juggling Circuit
(Copy and distribute to each group)

Name: _____	Name: _____	Name: _____	Name: _____
Station:	Station:	Station:	Station:
Total _____	Total _____	Total _____	Total _____
Name: _____	Name: _____	Name: _____	Name: _____
Station:	Station:	Station:	Station:
Total _____	Total _____	Total _____	Total _____

Illustration of a Balance and Juggling Circuit Floor Layout

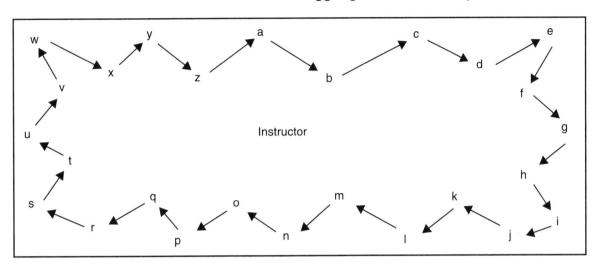

BALANCING BODIES

Objectives:

◆ Complete an assigned task without making an error.

◆ Concentrate and remain focused.

◆ Do not fall or touch the floor.

Essentials:

◆ Large open area

◆ Floor balance beams or lengths of lumber

◆ Balance boards

◆ Round football-blocking pads

◆ Floor mats

◆ Bicycle (safety helmets and pads)

◆ Unicycle

◆ Field cones

How to Play:

1. Pair up with another classmate and share the equipment.

2. Alternate turns after two successive errors.

3. Attempt to balance the body for five seconds without touching the floor or the ground.

4. Skills:

   a. While solely on the balance beam, walk, hop, skip, traverse backwards or sideways, sit down and stand back up, touch one knee, close the eyes, remain on one foot, jump and turn 180 degrees, balance an object, or create a stunt.

   b. With a partner on the balance beam, exchange ends, hold hands and balance on one foot, sit down and get back up, both walk backwards with the leader's hands placed on her/his partner's shoulders, spin 180 degrees simultaneously, create a tandem routine, or invent a group stunt.

c. When standing on the balance board, remain motionless, rock from side to side, or juggle anything.

d. While on the hands and knees on top of a football blocking pad, remain motionless, roll the bag three times to the left or right, roll three turns to the right then return to the start, or rotate the body 180 degrees (swap ends).

e. While on a unicycle, remain stationary, ride a given distance, navigate around cones, or pedal backwards.

f. While on a bicycle, travel 15 feet in the longest time possible, remain stationary, balance on the back tire while stationary or riding, negotiate an obstacle course, or create a stunt.

Student Tasks:

1. Complete three or more skills.
2. Improve in two or more skills.
3. Give a partner advice for improvement.

Variations:

1. Challenge another group to a timed competition. A task is specified and the combined times are used as a score.
2. Make teams composed of four players each, establish a short distance, and compete in relay races.

Illustration of Balancing Bodies

BALANCING OBJECTS

Objectives:

◆ Complete a task without making a mistake.
◆ Develop hand-and-eye coordination.
◆ Enhance concentration and focus.

BALANCING AND JUGGLING

Essentials:

- ◆ Large open area
- ◆ Several items to balance (large feathers, brooms, dowels, pipe insulation, cardboard boxes, plastic bowling pins, hula hoops, etc.)
- ◆ A variety of balls (soccer ball, basketball, volleyball, tennis ball, football, etc.)

How to Play:

1. Pair up with another classmate and share the equipment.

2. Alternate turns after every two successive mistakes.

3. Attempt to balance any item for 10 seconds.

4. Skills:

   a. Take an object and balance it from various points on the body such as the finger, thumb, back of the hand, elbow, forehead, or the top of the foot. Conceive a novel steady point.

   b. Attempt to balance two items simultaneously. These might include two dowels or a broom and a peacock feather. Move a poised object around the body, between the legs, or under the arms.

   c. Stabilize one ball on top of another ball or use two unmatched items, or invent a skill.

   d. Try spinning a ball on the finger, then transferring the ball from one finger to another, or tossing it to the forehead and back to a finger. Spin two balls simultaneously, stand on one foot, or transfer the ball to a partner. Come up with an innovative stunt.

Student Tasks:

1. Complete three or more skills.

2. Improve in two or more skills.

3. Give a partner advice for improvement.

Variations:

1. Challenge another group to a timed competition. A task is specified and the combined times are used as a score or the sum of the times is used.

2. Balance items while staying inside a hula hoop placed on the floor.

3. Make teams composed of four players each, establish a short distance, and compete in relay races while balancing like objects.

Illustration of Balancing Objects

BALLS OR BEANBAGS

Objectives:

- ◆ Complete a task without making a mistake.
- ◆ Develop hand-and-eye coordination.
- ◆ Enhance concentration and focus.

Essentials:

- ◆ Large open area
- ◆ Beanbags
- ◆ Low-bounce or non-bouncing juggling balls (shorter retrieval time)

How to Play:

1. Pair up with another classmate and share two or three beanbags.

2. Alternate turns after two successive errors.

3. When tossing and catching the bags, try to keep the elbows in, palms up, and look slightly upward as the hands make small U-shaped movements.

4. Attempt to make 10 successful grabs and tosses without a mistake.

5. Skills:

   a. Clockwise and counterclockwise circles with R/L hand.

   b. R/L alternating ups and downs. (Objects stay in the same location.)

   c. Figure eight in the air.

   d. Figure eight off of a wall.

   e. Create a stunt at the beginning or end of a routine. Examples might be to start by tossing the first ball under the leg or from behind the back, or catching the last object on the back of the neck or behind the back.

f. Stand on one foot and juggle.

g. Stand shoulder to shoulder with partner and perform a task.

h. Face the partner and exchange the objects back and forth.

Student Tasks:

1. Complete three or more skills.

2. Improve in two or more skills.

3. Give a partner advice for improvement.

Variations:

1. Use balls of various sizes and weights.

2. Juggle while standing inside a hula hoop placed on the floor.

3. Juggle while walking or running.

4. Toss objects between three or more individuals.

5. Form the "Harlem Globetrotter Circle" and pass a ball using any trick method.

6. Challenge another group to a competition. A discipline is specified and the combined number of catches in 30 seconds is used as a score.

7. Make teams composed of four players each, establish a short distance, and compete in relay races while juggling.

Illustration of Juggling Balls and Beanbags

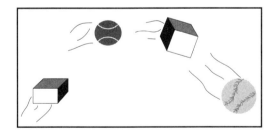

BOX SHUFFLE

Objectives:

◆ Complete a task without making a mistake.

◆ Develop hand-and-eye coordination.

◆ Enhance concentration and focus.

Essentials:

◆ Large open area

◆ Small reinforced cardboard boxes or blocks of wood about the size of a cigar box

How to Play:

1. Pair up with another classmate.

2. The couple will need to share three boxes.

3. Alternate turns after two successive errors.

4. Attempt to make 10 successful catches or exchanges without a mistake.

5. Skills:

   a. Catch the center box after it has rotated 180 degrees.

   b. Capture the center box after it has rotated 360 degrees.

   c. Seize the center box after it has rotated 720 degrees.

   d. Exchange the right or left box with the center box. Do the same feat but spin around one time before catching it.

   e. Perform a figure eight with the outside boxes.

   f. Stand on one foot and switch the boxes.

   g. Swap the left and right boxes with the hands returning to the original grip.

   h. Switch the left and right boxes without letting go of them. (The arms will now be crossed.)

   i. Catch the center box under one raised leg.

Student Tasks:

1. Complete three or more skills.

2. Improve in two or more skills.

3. Give a partner advice for improvement.

Variations:

1. Challenge another group to a competition. A discipline is specified and the combined number of catches in 30 seconds is used as a score.

2. Toss one box back and forth between partners.

Examples of Stunts for Box Shuffle

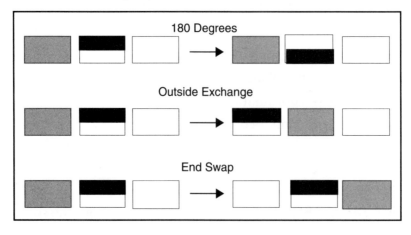

CHINESE STICKS

Objectives:

- ◆ Complete a task without making a mistake.
- ◆ Develop hand-and-eye coordination.
- ◆ Enhance concentration and focus.

Essentials:

- ◆ Large open area
- ◆ Chinese juggling sticks (also called Angel-Stik™ or Devil Sticks™)
- ◆ Plastic or rubber deck tennis rings

How to Play:

1. Pair up with another classmate.
2. The couple will need to share one set of sticks. The center stick is manipulated with the two smaller handheld sticks.
3. Alternate turns after two successive errors.
4. Attempt to perform a task 10 successful times without a mistake.
5. Skills:
   a. Pick the center stick up from the floor without touching it with the hands.
   b. Balance the center stick on one of the handheld sticks.
   c. Bounce the center stick back and forth.
   d. Rotate the center stick in a circle with the same end always up.
   e. Catch the center stick after it has rotated 180 degrees. Perform this task in both directions of rotation.
   f. Capture the center stick after it has rotated 360 degrees in either direction.
   g. Catch the stick after it has rotated 720 degrees either to the right or left.
   h. Rotate the stick around one of the handheld manipulators.
   i. Create a new stunt.
   j. Develop a routine.

Student Tasks:

1. Master three different skills.
2. Create a new stunt.
3. Improve in a new skill.
4. Give advice that improves the skill of another person.

Variations:

1. Challenge another group to a competition. A discipline is specified and the combined number of catches in 30 seconds is used as a score.

2. Toss one stick back and forth between two or more participants.

Illustration of Chinese Juggling Sticks

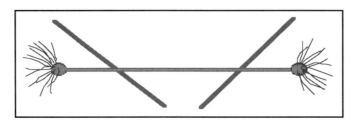

CLUBS AND RINGS

Objectives:

◆ Complete a task without making a mistake.

◆ Develop hand-and-eye coordination.

◆ Enhance concentration and focus.

Essentials:

◆ Large open area
◆ Juggling clubs (plastic or foam work well)
◆ Plastic or rubber deck tennis rings
◆ Juggling rings

How to Play:

1. Pair up with another classmate.

2. The couple will need to share two or three clubs or rings.

3. Alternate turns after two successive errors.

4. Attempt to keep the elbows in, palms up, looking forward and slightly up, as the hands should make small U-shaped movements when tossing and catching the objects.

5. Attempt to make 10 successful grabs and tosses without a mistake.

6. Skills:

   a. Figure eight in the air with one, two, and three clubs.

   b. Up and backs with one, two, and three rings.

   c. Perform a stunt at the beginning or end of a routine such as beginning with a toss from under the leg or from behind the back.

d. Stand on one foot while performing a routine.

e. Face the partner and toss the objects back and forth.

Student Tasks:

1. Complete three or more skills.

2. Improve in two or more skills.

3. Give a partner advice for improvement.

Variations:

1. Juggle while standing inside a hula hoop placed on the floor.

2. Juggle while walking or running.

3. Challenge another group to a competition. A discipline is specified and the combined number of catches in 30 seconds is used as a score.

4. Make teams composed of four players each, establish a short distance, and compete in relay races while juggling.

Illustration of Clubs and Rings

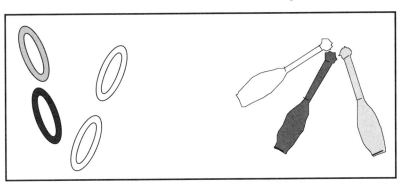

EQUILIBRIUM

Objectives:

◆ Win two out of three contests.

◆ Develop balance.

◆ Complete a task without making a mistake.

◆ Enhance concentration and focus.

Essentials:

◆ Large open area

◆ Floor balance beam

◆ Floor mats

◆ 1 track relay baton

How to Play:

1. Place a floor balance beam over a floor mat.

2. Players will challenge each other.

3. Players must maintain balance while simultaneously holding onto a track relay baton.

4. The first player who either lets go of the baton, or touches any part of the body to the floor, loses.

5. The player who wins two out of three battles is declared the victor.

Student Tasks:

1. Defeat three players in a row.

2. Win a contest after losing the first match.

3. Defeat a past champion.

Variations:

1. Use a rope instead of a baton (see illustration).

2. Use two parallel floor beams placed at opposite ends of the mat and a rope.

3. Participants must stand on one foot during the entire skirmish.

4. A player who continues to win gets to stay and take on new challengers.

5. Attempt to defeat five different players in a row.

Portrayal of Equilibrium Using a Rope

SCARF DANCE

Objectives:

◆ Score 21 points first.

◆ Keep a juggling scarf in the air by throwing a beanbag repeatedly into it.

◆ Develop hand-and-eye coordination.

◆ Enhance concentration and focus.

Balancing and Juggling

Essentials:

- Large open area
- 1 juggling scarf
- 1 round or square beanbag

How to Play:

1. Pair up against another classmate.
2. Each couple will need one scarf and a beanbag.
3. Determine which player begins by enacting rock, paper, and scissors. The winner may choose to begin or go last.
4. The first player will place the beanbag into the center of the scarf, pull the scarf back over the bag, and toss it into the air. As the bag falls out of the scarf and returns back to the floor, the player will attempt to catch the bag, toss it back up and into the scarf over and over in an effort to keep the juggling scarf from hitting the floor.
5. The bag can be tossed and caught with the same hand repeatedly.
6. Players are not permitted to replay a dropped beanbag.
7. One point is awarded for each time the beanbag hits the scarf and is subsequently caught.
8. If and when the player who started the game reaches 21 or higher, the opponent will have one last attempt to tie or win the contest. All ties will result in a sudden death playoff.

Student Tasks:

1. Hit the scarf four or more times in a row.
2. Come from behind and win.
3. Win in three or fewer turns.

Variations:

1. Give each player only five errors. Alternate tosses as before. After both players have bombed out, the highest score wins.
2. Try using a softball, a handball, or a large wiffle ball.
3. Increase the number of hits needed to win.
4. Participants must alternate hands with each new catch and toss.
5. Playing a dropped bag is permitted so long as the scarf does not hit the floor.
6. Make boundaries that the participants must stay within.
7. Perform a contest while sitting, from the knees, or standing on one leg.
8. Challenge another group to a competition. The combined number of catches in 30 seconds is used as a score.

BALANCING AND JUGGLING

Illustration of a Beanbag being Tossed During Dancing Scarf

SCARVES AND BALLOONS

Objectives:

◆ Complete a task without making a mistake.

◆ Develop hand-and-eye coordination.

◆ Enhance concentration and focus.

Essentials:

◆ Large open area

◆ Juggling scarves

◆ Small balloons

How to Play:

1. Pair up with another classmate.

2. The couple will need to share two or three scarves.

3. Alternate turns after two successive errors.

4. The palms are usually facing the floor (pawing) when grabbing and releasing the floating scarves.

5. The balloons can be volleyed in any manner desired.

6. Attempt to make 10 successful grabs and tosses without a mistake.

7. Skills:

   a. Clockwise and counterclockwise circles with R/L hand.

   b. R/L alternating ups and downs. (Scarves stay in the same location.)

   c. Perform a figure eight several times.

   d. Create a new stunt.

   e. Create a routine with a partner.

BALANCING AND JUGGLING

Student Tasks:

1. Master three different skills.
2. Improve in a new skill.
3. Help a teammate improve.

Variations:

1. Use four scarves or balloons.
2. Set a class record for the most balloons that can be kept airborne for 30 seconds.
3. Juggle while staying inside a hula hoop placed on the floor.
4. Challenge another group to a competition. A specific task is performed and the total number of catches (30 seconds) is used as a score.

Illustration of Scarves and Balloons

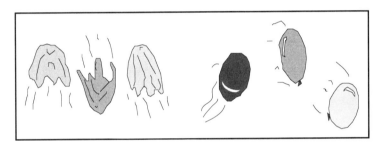

SPINNING PLATES AND HOOPS

Objectives:

◆ Complete a task without making a mistake.
◆ Develop hand-and-eye coordination.
◆ Enhance concentration and focus.

Essentials:

◆ Large open area
◆ Several hula hoops
◆ Plates
◆ Wooden dowels
◆ 4″ X 4″ wood timber with five holes drilled in it to hold the dowels

How to Play:

1. Set up several areas comprised of hula hoops at some and plates at others.
2. Pair up with another classmate and report to either the hula hoop area or the spinning plate area.
3. Alternate turns after every two successive errors.

4. Attempt to make all of the plates or hoops spin at the same time for 30 seconds.

5. Skills:

    a. Spin two plates for 30 seconds.

    b. Transfer a spinning plate from one dowel to another.

    c. Spin a plate while walking around.

    d. Move a plate around the body, through the legs, or under the arms.

    e. Spin three or more plates at once.

    f. Face the partner and transfer or toss a plate back and forth.

    g. Spin several hula hoops from the arms, legs, and body.

    h. While spinning a hoop from the ankle, hop over it with the other leg 15 or more times.

    i. Transfer a spinning hula hoop to a partner. (This can be accomplished by either a direct exchange or passing the hoop through the air.)

Student Tasks:

1. Master three different skills.

2. Improve in a new skill.

3. Help a teammate improve.

Variations:

1. Spin a flying disc or a ring on the wooden dowel.

2. Challenge another group to a competition. A discipline is specified and time is used as the score.

Illustration of Spinning Plates and Hoops

TOLL BRIDGE

Objectives:

♦ Eliminate the competition.

♦ Develop balance.

♦ Enhance concentration and focus.

Essentials:

- ◆ Large open area
- ◆ 1 floor balance beam
- ◆ 2 large beach balls
- ◆ Floor mats

How to Play:

1. Place a floor beam over a floor mat.
2. Make two teams composed of three players each of about the same size. Each team will line up at opposite ends of the beam.
3. The first two opponents, with beach ball in hand, will scale the beam and try to force each other from the beam by whacking the opponent with the ball.
4. Hitting a player above the shoulders is not allowed.
5. Players must keep both hands on the ball at all times.
6. Touching the opponent with anything other than the ball is illegal.
7. The first player to touch the floor is eliminated from further competition, even when both challengers fall simultaneously.
8. The winner remains in the contest but must return to the back of the team's line.
9. The next two players enter the toll bridge and repeat the process.
10. A team wins by eliminating all of its rivals.

Student Tasks:

1. Defeat two players from the other team.
2. Win a contest after losing two players.

Variations:

1. One point is awarded for each opponent that is dislodged. Nobody is eliminated, though; they simply return to the end of the line. The winner gets to stay and take on a new challenger. Regardless of who wins the next dispute, the player must return to the end of the line after two contests. The first team to score 15 points is the winner.
2. Place five players on each team.

Illustration of Players with Beach Balls in Toll Bridge

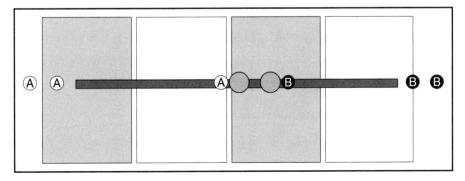

ALTER CATION

Objectives:

- Score more points within a given amount of time than the opposition.
- Develop shooting skills under pressure.

Essentials:

- Basketball half court
- 1 basketball
- 8 floor cones with visible numbers
- Paper and pencil to record points
- Stopwatch

How to Play:

1. This game is a modified version of "NBA 2Ball."
2. Place six cones at various locations on the court. Assign a different point value to each cone by attaching a piece of paper with the point value written on it.
3. Divide into teams composed of two players each.
4. The contest will last for 90 seconds.
5. Players must alternate shooting the ball.
6. Begin by having one player behind any cone and his/her teammate positioned to grab the rebound, made or missed.
7. All shots must be released from behind the cones.
8. A player may choose to shoot from the same spot each time or move around freely.
9. Each player is allowed one lay-up during the contest, worth one point.
10. When time has expired, the ball must be in the air in order to count.
11. At the end of the time period, tally the shot values made.
12. The team with the highest score wins.

Student Tasks:

1. Make a shot from three different cones.
2. Make a shot from behind the same cone three times.
3. Make three shots in a row.

Variations:

1. Form mixed-gender teams.
2. Reduce or increase the time allowed.
3. Play a tournament format.

Illustration of an Alter Cation Floor Layout

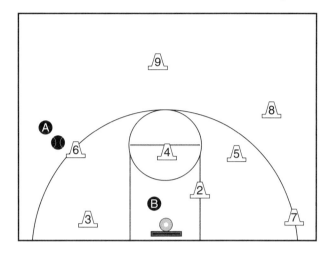

ALTER CATION II

Objectives:

◆ Score more points within a given amount of time than the opposition.

◆ Develop teamwork and cooperation.

◆ Develop shooting skills under pressure.

Essentials:

◆ Basketball half court

◆ 2 basketballs

◆ 8 floor cones with visible numbers

◆ Paper and pencil to record points

◆ Stopwatch

How to Play:

1. This game is a modified version of 2Ball.

2. Place the eight cones at various locations on the court. Assign a different point value to each cone by attaching a piece of paper with the point value written on it.

3. Divide into teams composed of three players each.

4. The contest will last for 90 seconds.

5. The team will establish a shooting order.

6. Begin by having two players, each with a ball, behind any cones and the third teammate positioned to grab the rebound, made or missed.

7. If the shooter misses the first shot attempt, the ball must be quickly returned for a second attempt before the next teammate is allowed to shoot.

8. All shots must be released from behind the cones.

9. A player may choose to shoot from the same spot each time or move around freely.

10. Each player is allowed one lay-up during the contest, worth one point.

11. When time has expired, the ball must be in the air in order to count.

12. After time has expired, total the shot values made.

13. The team with the highest score wins.

Student Tasks:

1. Only repeat the same shot twice.

2. Make a shot from three different cones.

3. Make a basket from behind the same cone three times.

4. Make three baskets in a row on the first try.

Variations:

1. Form mixed-gender teams.

2. Add more shooting locations.

3. Increase the time to two minutes.

Diagram of an Alter Cation II Floor Plan

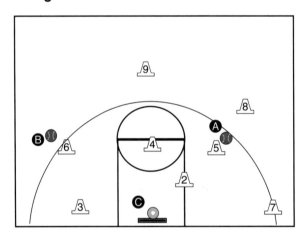

BASKET BOWLING

Objectives:

♦ Score more points than the opposition.

♦ Make free throws and lay-ins.

♦ Knock over the bowling pin.

Essentials:

- ◆ Gymnasium with four backboards
- ◆ 4 basketballs
- ◆ Scorecard
- ◆ 4 bowling pins (can be plastic)

How to Play:

1. Divide the class into four equal teams.
2. Place four bowling pins about two feet apart at center court.
3. Each team will go to the corners and get into a single file line behind the bowling scratch line.
4. On a given command, the first player in line will roll her/his ball at the pin in the middle. Only this person may enter the court to retrieve any balls that have missed. A ball must have gone past the bowling pin before it can be grabbed.
5. All return passes to the team bowling line must be bounced or rolled for safety reasons.
6. Players in each line will continue this process until the bowling pin is finally knocked over.
7. Each team will scamper to the middle to procure a ball.
8. The first team to cause one or more of the bowling pins to tumble will shoot lay-ins.
9. The three other teams will form a line and shoot free throws.
10. Scoring:
    a. Each knocked over pin is worth three points
    b. Each successful foul shot is worth two points.
    c. One point will be awarded for each successful lay-in.
    d. The first team to make three free throws will stop all action.
    e. Tally up each team's score for the frame.
    f. Teams will report back to their bowling scratch line, wait for the next signal, and continue the process until 10 frames have been completed.
    g. The team that is ahead after 10 frames is the winner.

Student Tasks:

1. Knock over the pin.
2. Make a free throw.
3. Make successive lay-ins.
4. Come from behind and win the match.

Variations:

1. Each player must bowl with her/his weak hand.
2. Shoot lay-ins from the left side.

3. Use a different type of a ball.

4. Teams will only shoot free throws and three-point shots.

5. Play a round robin by combining the scores from two different teams, each new game.

Sample Scorecards for Basket Bowling

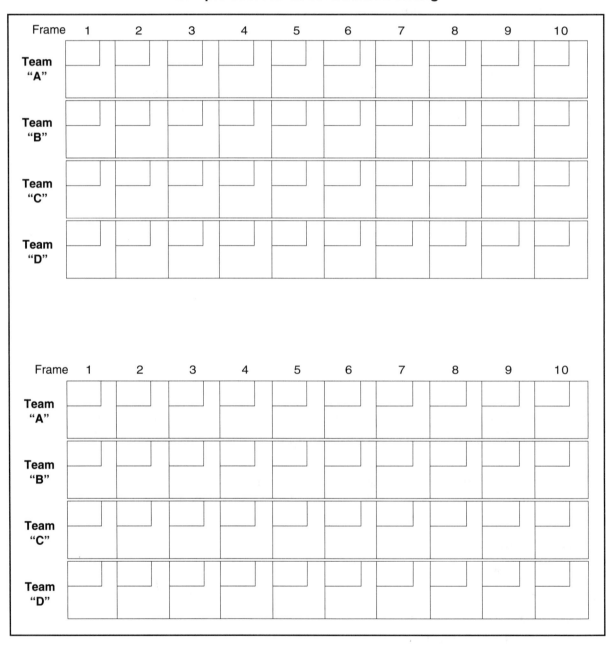

Illustration of the Floor Layout for Basket Bowling

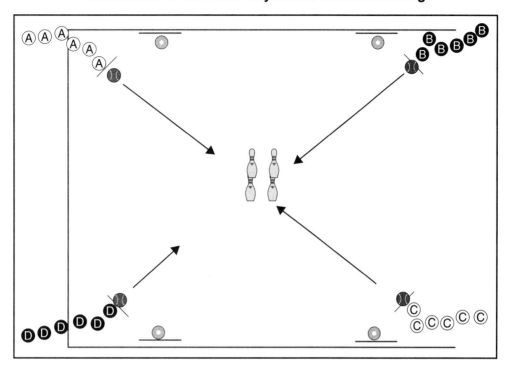

BASKETBALL GOLF

Objectives:

◆ Finish the circuit with the fewest number of shots.

◆ Make corrections from mistakes.

◆ Understand the terms of golf.

Essentials:

◆ Gymnasium with several baskets

◆ Basketball for each station

◆ Numbered floor cones with instructions

◆ Scorecards and pencils (See the section on "Golf" for scorecards.)

Terminology:

1. Shotgun start   Players start at different places

2. Bogey   Number of shots taken over the par

3. Par   Average number of shots

4. Birdie   1 under par

5. Eagle   2 under par

6. Hole in one	Make a pin with the first shot
7. Fore	Protect your head
8. Pin	Basket to be made
9. Away	Player farthest from the basket
10. Lie	At the point where the ball is rebounded
11. Putt	A short shot to the basket

How to Play:

1. Design a course with nine or more different shots. Establish a par for each shot. Depending on difficulty, 18 might be the established par for a nine-pin course.

2. Create an array of shots and stunts such as:

   a. Shoot from various spots such as the corner, foul line, or three-point arc.

   b. Dictate that a shot must hit the backboard, be a granny, or be a hook.

   c. Require trickery and luck by bouncing the ball to the floor then into the basket, shooting from behind the backboard, or using the weak hand.

   d. Add a skill prior to the shot such as a reverse pivot, dribbling behind the back, circling the ball around the body, or double clutching the ball.

   e. Invoke creativity by allowing participants to design a shot at a specific cone.

3. After receiving a score card and pencil, shotgun-start the groups.

4. After establishing a shooting order, each player will shoot from behind the same cone, until she/he makes the shot. Record the number of times needed to make the shot.

5. After everyone has finished, the entire group moves to the next basket.

6. The lowest scorers of the previous basket will go first.

7. The winner is the person who completes the course with the fewest shots.

Student Tasks:

1. Make three baskets on the first attempt.

2. Win three holes.

3. Beat the course par.

Variations:

1. Limit the number of attempts that a player may take before having to stop.

2. Allow the students to design the entire circuit.

3. Place a different type of ball at each cone. Examples might be a tennis ball, football, volleyball, soccer ball, softball, nerf ball, etc.

4. Create a tournament format.

Illustration of Basketball Golf Floor Layout

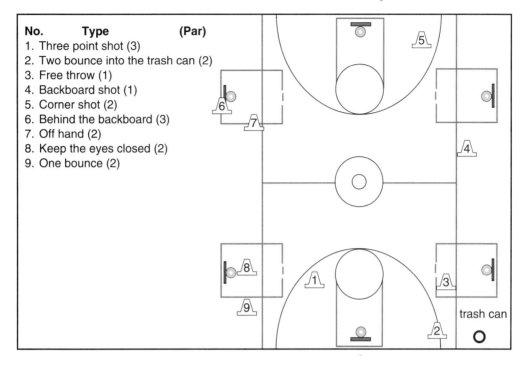

No.   Type   (Par)
1. Three point shot (3)
2. Two bounce into the trash can (2)
3. Free throw (1)
4. Backboard shot (1)
5. Corner shot (2)
6. Behind the backboard (3)
7. Off hand (2)
8. Keep the eyes closed (2)
9. One bounce (2)

trash can

BASKETBALL GOLF II

Objectives:

◆ Complete the circuit with the fewest shot attempts possible.

◆ Quickly procure the rebound on any missed shot.

Essentials:

◆ Basketball at each basket

◆ Numbered floor cones with instructions

◆ Scorecards and pencils (See the "Golf" section for scorecards.)

How to Play:

1. The terms and rules for this game are the same as Basketball Golf with a few modifications.

2. Design a course with nine or more different shots. Establish a par for each shot.

3. After receiving a score card and pencil, shotgun-start the groups.

4. After establishing a shooting order, each competitor must shoot her/his first shot from behind the same cone.

5. Immediately after any shot attempt, the shooter must spin around in a circle one time before retrieving the ball, whether the shot is made or missed.

6. The away ball (farthest from the basket) will always shoot first.

7. Any additional shot attempt/s will be taken from where the rebound is seized.

8. Repeat this procedure until everyone has made the basket.

9. Record the total number of shots taken at each basket (pin).

10. The player with the lowest score is the winner.

Student Tasks:

1. Make three baskets on the first attempt.

2. Win three holes in succession.

3. Beat the course par.

Variations:

1. Change the routine that must be done before retrieving the ball. Examples could be a sit-up, a push-up, two jumping jacks, or touch the cone.

2. Every initial shot attempt must be from behind the three-point arc.

3. The backboard has to be used with each or every other shot.

4. Make teams with two players each. Teammates must shoot every other shot.

5. Make teams composed of two players. When both individuals miss the first attempt, they will pick the best location of the two rebounds, and shoot their second shot from there.

6. Allow students to develop and initiate a course.

7. Groups will create their own shot at each basket.

8. Create a tournament format.

Example of a Player Retrieving the Rebound after a Missed Shot

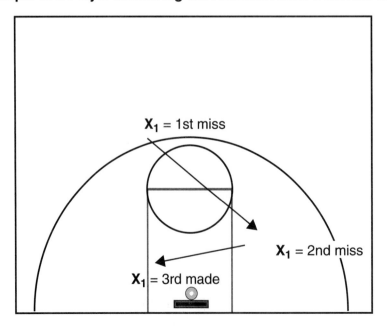

X_1 = 1st miss

X_1 = 2nd miss

X_1 = 3rd made

Illustration of Champs or Chumps Floor Layout

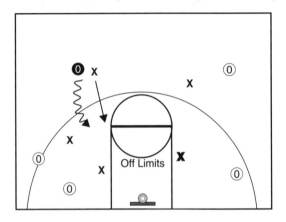

GAMBLER

Objectives:

◆ Be the first person to make a basket from every spot.

◆ Develop shot confidence from a variety of locations.

Essentials:

◆ Basketball floor

◆ 10 marked shooting spots

◆ 2 or 3 basketballs

How to Play:

1. Create units with five or six players each.

2. Determine a shooting order so that only one person shoots at a time.

3. Each player starts at #1 and attempts to finish at #10.

4. When the first shot is made, the player moves to the next number and continues shooting.

5. A player who misses the first shot can either shoot again or stop and relinquish the ball. She/he will begin at this spot on the next go around.

6. When the second shot is made, the player moves to the next number and continues shooting.

7. When the second shot is missed, the player must forfeit the ball and start at #1 the next time up.

8. After the first player reaches #10, everyone *behind* that player in the shooting order has one last chance to tie the game. If they cannot, then the first person wins.

Student Tasks:

1. Make three or more spot shots in a row.

2. Come behind any player and tie or go ahead.

3. Make three backboard shots.

Variations:

1. Alternate shooting between the right and left hand on the first six shots.

2. Form teams and alternate shooting.

3. Players must go from #1 to #10 and then back to #1 before winning.

4. Use a different type of ball.

Illustration of Floor Layout for Gambler

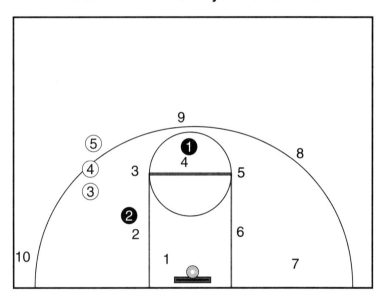

KICK BASKET

Objectives:

◆ Score more points than the opposition by kicking the ball against the wall or by making a basket.

◆ Develop team play and cooperation.

Essentials:

◆ Indoor basketball court

◆ Indoor soccer ball or vinyl-covered foam ball

◆ Flip scoreboard

◆ Pinnies or flags

How to Play:

1. Both basketball and soccer rules apply to this game.

2. Split the entire group into two teams. Send each team to the opposite ends of the arena. Once there, each player is a goalie and helps to defend the entire wall.

3. To begin the game, the first four players will enter the arena. The ball is tossed into the air or thrown on the floor.

4. Stop play every two minutes and rotate in four new members from each team. Players leaving will go to the end of the goalie line.

5. When the ball last touches the floor, ceiling, or a wall, the rules of soccer apply.

6. Heading is not allowed for safety reasons.

7. Offense:

   a. When the ball is lifted or kicked into the air with the foot, any player may grab the ball. Basketball rules will now apply.

   b. Dribbling is prohibited.

   c. Players may not travel or take steps once in possession of the ball although one step is allowed when trying to stop or when shooting.

   d. Any rebound grabbed prior to hitting the floor, may be passed or shot again.

8. Defense:

   a. A goalie can kick or throw the ball to his or her teammates via the air or floor.

   b. Goalies will always initiate play after any score.

   c. Fouls will result in free throws or penalty shots depending in which mode the ball was being played when the infraction occurred.

9. Scoring:

   a. One point is awarded for kicking the ball past the goalies and against the wall below a given height.

   b. Free throws are valued at one point.

   c. Making a basket inside the three-point arc is credited for two points.

   d. Making a basket outside the three-point arc is worth four points.

   e. The team that is ahead after a given amount of time will win the game.

Student Tasks:

1. Block or deflect a ball from hitting the wall.

2. Assist in two types of scoring.

3. Lift the ball to three different players during class.

4. Lift the ball to yourself.

Variations:

1. Allow the goalies to place one or two plastic bowling pins, at any location, in between the wall and the baseline. When a bowling pin is knocked over, award 2 extra points.

2. Increase or subtract the number of floor players allowed.

3. A team may not score until all four players are on the scoring side of the floor.

4. When side baskets are available, allow teams to score at them, too.

Team Positioning for Kick Basket

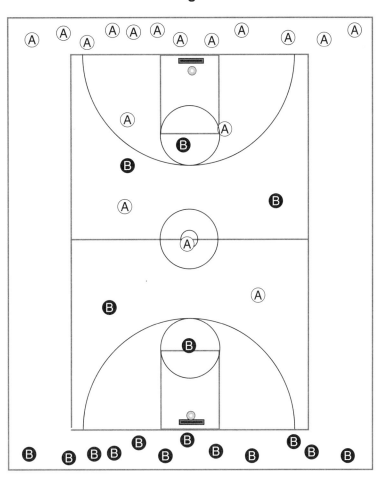

MAKE IT TAKE IT

Objectives:

- ◆ Reach a predetermined number of points before the opposition.
- ◆ Develop shooting concentration under pressure.

Essentials:

- ◆ Half court of a basketball floor
- ◆ Basketball
- ◆ Pinnies or flags

How to Play:

1. The rules of basketball apply to this game with a few modifications.

2. Make teams composed of two players each.

3. Play a half-court game.

4. Each time a team scores, it retains possession of the ball.

5. Play is restarted beyond the three-point arc each time a basket is scored or after any defensive rebound.

6. When the shooter is fouled, she/he may elect to shoot foul shots or retain the ball.

7. If a ball is intercepted or stolen, it can instantly be taken to the basket without having to bring it out beyond the three-point arc.

8. When a shot misses the rim and backboard (air ball), it is considered a pass and can be shot by the player who grabs it first.

9. All fouls and violations are to be called by the players. (Arguing is not allowed.)

10. The same scoring method as basketball is used.

11. Attempt to be the first team to rack up a predetermined number of points.

Student Tasks:

1. Make three shots in a row.

2. Come from six or more points behind and win.

3. Grab three rebounds.

4. Grab an offensive rebound and put it back up for a score.

Variations:

1. Increase the number of players on each team.

2. Use a different type of ball.

3. Create a tournament format.

Illustration of Make It Take It

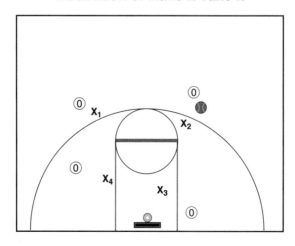

MARCH MADNESS

Objectives:

◆ Pick the final four for the NCAA men's and women's tournaments.

◆ Choose the overall winner of each championship.

◆ Reach a group consensus through dialog and discussion.

Essentials:

◆ Sixteen team bracket

◆ Answer sheet

◆ Pencils

How to Play:

1. Create a "Sweet Sixteen" bracket with the teams involved (see bracket sheet on the next page).

2. Create groups composed of four or five individuals and pass out a bracket sheet.

3. Have the groups discuss and come to a consensus as to which teams will likely make each open bracket slot and then list them.

4. Collect the worksheets. As the tournament unfolds, return the sheets and keep track by drawing a line through any wrong choices.

5. One point is provided for each correct answer.

6. The group with the most correct choices is the winner.

Student Tasks:

1. Pick the winner.

2. Score five or more points.

Variations:

1. Use this format with any sport.

2. Use this format with the high school playoffs.

3. Have only boys pick the women's bracket and the girls pick the men's.

Illustration of a Championship Bracket

Event: _____

Names:
1. _____
2. _____
3. _____
4. _____
5. _____
6. _____

Directions: Place the selected team's number on the open bracket.
One point is awarded for each correct answer.

```
1  _____
2  _____
3  _____
4  _____
5  _____
6  _____
7  _____
8  _____
9  _____
10 _____
11 _____
12 _____
13 _____
14 _____
15 _____
16 _____
```

Final Score _____

NOTHING BUT NET

Objectives:

◆ Make a shot from each of the various locations before the opposition does.

◆ Develop a strategy in which players may gain an advantage.

Essentials:

◆ Half-court area of a basketball floor

◆ 2 basketballs at each area

◆ 10 marked spots or cones to designate each shot location (floor tape also works)

How to Play:

1. Set up the floor spots (see illustration below).

2. Create groups with four or five individuals each.

3. Send each group to a different basket with one or two basketballs.

4. After determining a shooting order, the first shooter starts at spot #1.

5. A player will always restart from where his or her last shot was missed.

6. Intermediate procedure:

    a. When the shot is made and hits nothing but net, the shooter moves up two spots and continues shooting.

    b. The shooter advances one spot and shoots again when the shot is made, but hits the rim or backboard in doing so.

    c. Anytime the shot is missed, the next player is up.

    d. After the first player reaches spot number 10, everyone behind that player in the shooting order has one last opportunity to tie the leader. If they are unsuccessful, the first player wins.

7. Advanced methodology:

    a. A player must always shoot the ball twice when starting, and after a made basket.

    b. When the first shot is made and hits nothing but net, the shooter moves up two spots and receives two more shots.

    c. If the second shot is made but did not swish, the shooter goes back one spot and continues shooting.

    d. When the second shot touches nothing but net, the shooter advances only one spot.

    e. If the second shot is missed, then there is a loss of turn and that player must start over at #1.

8. The game is over when any player goes up to #10 and back to number #1. The winner must give everyone behind her or him in the shooting order one last chance to tie.

Student Tasks:

1. Make three shots in a row.

2. Make two nothing-but-cord (NBC) shots in a row.

3. Advance five spots in one turn.

4. Overtake any player, after being down three or more positions.

5. Pass two different players in one go around.

Variations:

1. Allow the players to determine the shooting spots.

2. Use a different type of ball.

Illustration of Shooting Spot Locations for Skip One

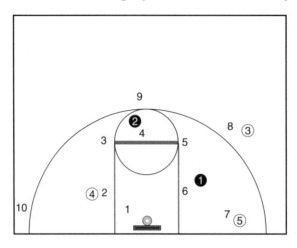

ORGANIZED CHAOS*

Objectives:

- ◆ Accumulate fewer points than the opposition does, in a given amount of time.

- ◆ Develop team play and court awareness.

- ◆ Prevent other teams from scoring at the team's basket.

- ◆ Form an alliance with another team and defeat the leading group.

Essentials:

- ◆ Two basketball courts
- ◆ 3 basketballs
- ◆ Different colored pinnies or flags for each team

- ◆ 2 flip scoreboards
- ◆ Timing device

How to Play:

1. The general rules of basketball will apply to this game.

2. Form four teams. Send each team to defend a different basket with everyone lining up against the wall directly behind it. Three players from each team enter the court.

3. Place the flip scoreboards on opposite sides of the court and in between the waiting teams. Inactive participants will become scorekeepers.

4. Begin the game by placing the three balls at the center. One player from each team will form a circle around the "pumpkins" while facing outward. On the sound of the whistle, each player will attempt to gain possession of a ball.

5. Stop the action every two minutes and rotate in three new players.

Created by Ken Lumsden, 1997.

6. Teams attempt to score in any of the other three baskets.

7. A team may possess more than one basketball at a time.

8. After a made basket, only the scored-upon team may put that ball back into play.

9. For minor infractions of the rules, the ball will be put back into play from where the violation took place (indirectly), by the nearest opponent. Shooting fouls, however, will be taken out under the nearest basket.

10. Each time a shot is scored in a team's basket, one point is posted.

11. The team with the lowest score, after a predetermined number of sessions, is declared the winner.

Student Tasks:

1. Grab a given number of rebounds.

2. Make two baskets.

3. Steal the ball.

4. Assist in a score.

5. Successfully prevent two different players from scoring at the team's basket.

Variations:

1. Start each team with a given number of points. Each time a team is scored upon, one point is removed. The game is over when any team reaches zero. The winner would have the highest number.

2. Use three different types of balls. Make one of the balls worth two points when scored.

3. Allow only two players from each team to be on the floor at one time.

Illustration of Organized Chaos

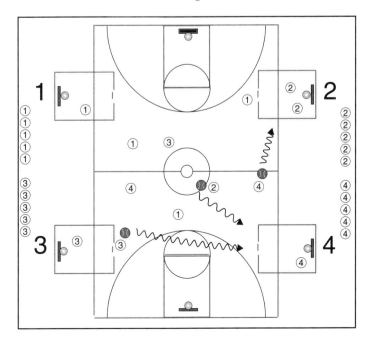

ORGANIZED DISORDER*

Objectives:

- ◆ Score more points in a given amount of time.
- ◆ Develop team play and court awareness.
- ◆ Prevent other teams from scoring at the team's basket.

Essentials:

- ◆ 2 side-by-side basketball courts
- ◆ 3 basketballs
- ◆ Different colored pinnies or flags for each team
- ◆ 2 flip scoreboards

How to Play:

1. The rules of basketball apply to this game.
2. Form four teams. Send each team to defend a different basket with everyone lining up against the wall directly behind it. Three players from each team enter the court.
3. Place the flip scoreboards on opposite sides of the court and in between the waiting teams. Inactive participants will keep score.
4. Begin the game by placing all three balls at the center. One player from each team will form a circle around the balls while facing outward. On the sound of the whistle, each player will attempt to gain possession of a ball.
5. After scoring, the player must return to the end of her or his team line. The first person in line now enters the contest. This variation is a nonstop continuous action game.
6. Teams may score in any of the other three baskets.
7. Any team may be in possession of more than one ball.
8. After a made basket, only the scored-upon team may put that ball back into play.
9. Teams may form alliances and gang up against any team that is ahead.
10. Participants will call all fouls and violations. (There is no arguing.)
11. When scoring, use the same point values as in basketball although there are no free throws.
12. The first team to reach a predetermined score wins.

Student Tasks:

1. Grab a given number of rebounds.
2. Make two baskets.

---

*Created by Ken Lumsden, 1997.

© 2001 Parker Publishing Company

3. Steal the ball.

4. Assist in a score.

5. Successfully prevent two different players from scoring at the team's basket.

Variations:

1. Be ahead after a given amount of time.

2. Use three different types of balls and possibly assign different point values to each. For example, a football would be worth one extra point when made.

3. Allow only three players from each team to be on the floor.

4. Blow the whistle every 90 seconds. Four new players will rotate in and resume play. (This too, is a continuous scoring contest.)

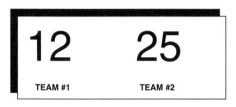 

ORGANIZED PANIC*

Objectives:

◆ Eliminate the other teams first.

◆ Develop team play and court awareness.

◆ Prevent other teams from scoring at the team's basket.

Essentials:

◆ 2 side-by-side basketball courts

◆ 3 basketballs

◆ Different colored pinnies or flags for each team

◆ 3 floor cones for each team

How to Play:

1. The rules of basketball apply to this game.

2. Form four teams. Send each team to defend a different basket with everyone lining up against the wall directly behind it.

3. Four players from each team enter the court. The remaining players will rest, watch, and become scorekeepers.

Created by Ken Lumsden, 1997.

4. Begin the game by placing all three balls at the center. One player from each team will form a circle around the balls while facing outward. Players attempt to grab a ball on the whistle.

5. Set cones up near each team's basket. Each time a shot is made in the team's basket, one of the team's cones is knocked over.

6. When all of the team's cones have been tumbled, its players must immediately leave the floor.

7. The session is over when only one team remains.

8. Each team will reset its cones and rotate four new players into the next contest.

9. Offense:

   a. Teams may score in any of the other three baskets.

   b. Any team may be in possession of more than one ball.

   c. Only the scored-upon team may put that ball back into play.

10. All violations of rules will be initiated back into play from where the infraction took place. However, shooting fouls will be taken out under the basket.

11. Each time a team wins a session, one point is awarded.

12. After several games, the team with the most points wins.

Student Tasks:

1. Grab a given number of rebounds.

2. Steal the ball.

3. Assist in a score.

4. Successfully prevent two different players from scoring.

Variations:

1. Give every team five cones. Any three-point shot is worth eliminating two of that team's cones.

2. Allow for a knocked over cone to be set back up when a player scores a three-point shot.

3. Allow only two or three players from each team to be on the floor.

PIG STY

Objectives:

◆ Score more points than the opposition does in a predetermined amount of time.

◆ Develop passing and catching skills.

◆ Play a game by combining the rules and skills of ultimate disc, basketball, and football.

BASKETBALL

Essentials:

- ◆ Basketball floor
- ◆ Nerf-type football
- ◆ Pinnies or flags
- ◆ Flip scoreboard

How to Play:

1. Divide into two equal teams with five or six players on each.

2. Use an entire basketball court.

3. Teams will attempt to advance the football down the court and make a basket.

4. As in basketball, the ball can be rebounded by either team on a missed shot. If the ball hits the floor off of a rebound, any player may grab it since the ball is still alive.

5. Offense:

    a. Teammates will attempt to throw and catch the football inside the boundaries. If the ball is dropped or lands out-of-bounds, the defensive team will take possession at that point.

    b. The football may be thrown to another player in any manner.

    c. The football must be shot like a basketball when attempting to score.

    d. The football may not be handed from one player to another.

    e. Players may not take steps once they are in possession of the ball. However, momentum must be taken into consideration when a player catches the ball and takes a step or two in order to stop.

    f. A player in possession of the ball may use one foot as a pivot.

    g. The thrower may not push the defensive person out of the way.

    h. The thrower may not catch her/his own pass.

    i. The thrower will have only five seconds of possession time.

    j. When playing co-ed, a boy and a girl must touch the ball before scoring.

    k. When fouled in the act of shooting, two free throws shall be awarded. Any other participants may stand anywhere they desire during the free throws, as long as they do not interfere with the shooter.

    l. A player may not score more than five points in a row.

6. Defense:

    a. Only one person may guard the player with the football and must be at least one step back. The guard's main objective is to alter the throw.

    b. The ball may not be forcefully taken or knocked away from the offense.

    c. If the defense deflects the ball to the floor, the offense retains possession.

    d. The defense will make all the calls and is always right.

7. Use the same scoring method as in basketball.

8. Play for a predetermined number of minutes to determine a winner.

Student Tasks:

1. Block a shot.
2. Grab two rebounds.
3. Catch three balls.
4. Intercept a thrown pass.
5. Make a two-point shot.
6. Make a three-point shot.

Variations:

1. Play to a set number of points to decide a winner.
2. Insert the rule that there are no out-of-bounds lines.
3. Use any type of a ball other than a basketball. Examples might include volleyball, softball, small beach ball, or a soccer ball.
4. Use a flying disc.
5. Play the game at half court. The ball must be taken beyond the three-point arc on defensive rebounds or after a basket.
6. Every time a person has possession of the ball, she/he must make pig noises.
7. Create several teams and play a round-robin tournament.

Pig Sty

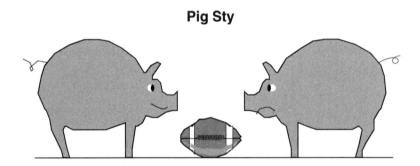

SEVEN ELEVEN

Objectives:

◆ Win two out of three contests.
◆ Score 11 points when on offense.
◆ Score seven points when on defense.
◆ Develop teamwork and cooperation.

Essentials:

◆ Half-court basketball court
◆ Basketball
◆ Pinnies or flags

BASKETBALL

How to Play:

1. Create teams with five players each.

2. The goal is for the offense to get to 11 points before the defense gets to seven.

3. Every time the offense succeeds with the 11 passes, one point is awarded.

4. The defense will attempt to gain possession either by intercepting a pass, causing a turnover, or creating a jump ball. When successful, one point will be awarded.

5. The ball may be dribbled for two consecutive bounces.

6. No player may hold the ball for more than five seconds.

7. Play a second game with the offense and defense switching roles.

8. The first unit to win two out of the three games, is the champion.

Student Tasks:

1. Score five consecutive points while on offense.

2. Score three consecutive points while on defense.

3. Come from behind and win the contest.

Variations:

1. Authorize the defensive team to have one extra player.

2. Do not allow any dribbling.

3. Reduce the boundaries to be inside the three-point area.

Illustration of a Smaller Court Boundary for Seven Eleven

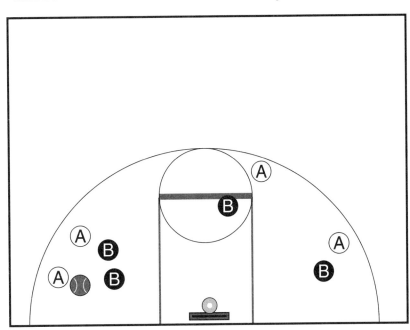

SPACE INVADERS*

Objectives:

- ◆ Outscore the opponent before time runs out.
- ◆ Develop teamwork and cooperation.

Essentials:

- ◆ Basketball floor
- ◆ 1 basketball
- ◆ Pinnies or flags
- ◆ Scoreboard

How to Play:

1. Basketball rules apply to this game with a few modifications.
2. Divide into teams composed of eight players each.
3. Each team will send an equal number of players to each zone.
4. Competitors must stay within their zone during play.
5. The ball may not be passed completely over the top of an adjoining zone. It must be controlled in each zone before being advanced.
6. The offense must constantly attempt to maneuver the ball down the floor in the direction of the basket. The ball may not be passed or dribbled back into the preceding zone (opposite direction).
7. Scoring is the same as in regular basketball.
8. Team members must rotate to a new zone following a score or after a predetermined amount of time. Opposing teams will rotate one zone in opposite directions.
9. Play for a predetermined amount of time. The team that is ahead will receive a standing ovation and a gold medal.

Student Tasks:

1. Do not allow the opposition to score.
2. Complete three or more passes.
3. Make an assist.
4. Block a shot attempt.
5. Intercept a pass.

Variations:

1. Play a half-court game with four players comprising each team.
2. Play until a team reaches a given number of points.

Created by Ken Lumsden, 1999.

© 2001 Parker Publishing Company

3. Play three games by combining two different teams for each contest. Each team will have four players. The first game will involve A + B taking on C + D, the second incorporates A + C opposing B + D, and the third will consist of A + D against B + C.

4. Use a round-robin format and play several short games.

Illustration of the Space Invaders Zones

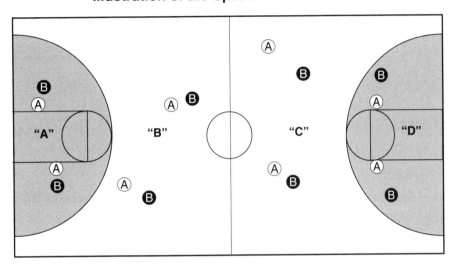

SPACE INVADERS TWO BALL*

Objectives:

◆ Score more points than the opponents do before time expires.

◆ Develop teamwork and cooperation.

Essentials:

◆ Basketball floor

◆ 2 basketballs

◆ Pinnies or flags

◆ Scoreboard

How to Play:

1. Basketball rules apply to this game with a few exceptions.

2. Create teams composed of eight players each.

3. Each team will send an equal number of players to each zone.

4. To begin the game, both balls are started at the middle by opposing teams. Each team will concurrently attack in opposite directions.

*Created by Ken Lumsden, 1999.

5. Competitors must stay within their zone during play.

6. The ball may not be passed completely over the top of an adjoining zone.

7. The ball must be controlled in each zone before it can be advanced.

8. The offense must constantly attempt to move the ball down the floor in the direction of the basket. The ball may not be passed or dribbled back into the preceding zone (opposite direction).

9. Scoring is the same as in regular basketball. However, when either ball scores it is eliminated from action. Play continues until the second ball scores. At that time, both teams rotate one zone in the opposite direction. The balls are again started simultaneously from the center.

10. Play for a predetermined amount of time to determine a winner.

Student Tasks:

1. Do not allow the opposition to score.

2. Score both balls during a possession.

3. Make an assist.

4. Intercept a pass.

Variations:

1. Play a half-court game with four players per team.

2. Play until a team reaches a given number of points.

3. Play three games by combining two different teams for each contest. Each team will have four players. One player from each team will occupy a zone.

Illustration of the Space Invaders Two Ball

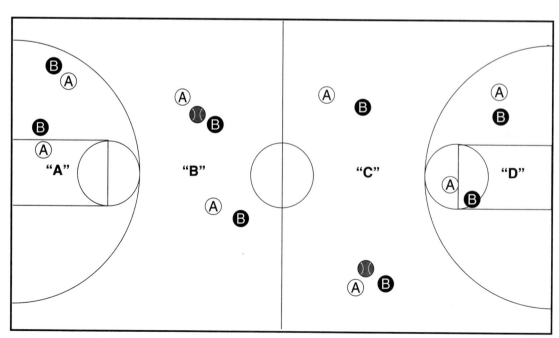

THREE SQUARED

Objectives:

- ◆ Score more points than the opposing teams.
- ◆ Develop teamwork and cooperation.

Essentials:

- ◆ Basketball half court
- ◆ 1 basketball
- ◆ 3 pinnies or flags (three different colors)

How to Play:

1. All of the rules of basketball apply to this game with a few exceptions.
2. Divide into three teams composed of three players each.
3. Two teams take the half court and begin the game. The extra team waits near middle court.
4. Each time a team scores, they retain the ball and take on the awaiting team.
5. The defense can immediately score on any missed basket by the offense. The ball does not have to be brought back out to the foul line or three-point arc to initiate play.
6. There are no boundaries.
7. All jump balls will result in alternating possessions.
8. Shooting fouls result in two free throws, unless the basket was made.
9. All other fouls result in possession of the ball.
10. The players are also referees and will make all offensive and defensive calls.
11. The first team to score four baskets in a row is the winner. (To accomplish this feat, a team would have to score eight successive points.)

Student Tasks:

1. Make a basket.
2. Grab a rebound and immediately score.
3. Intercept an offensive pass.
4. Get an assist.

Variations:

1. The first team to score three baskets in a row wins.
2. Play for a predetermined amount of time. Keep score for the entire session. The team with the most points is declared the winner.
3. Make new teams and play the game again. Players will keep individual records for the most wins.

Diagram of Three Squared

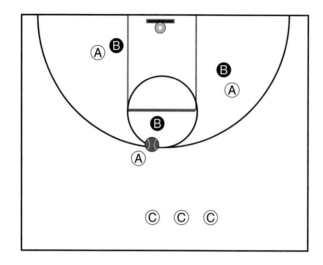

TIPS

Objectives:

◆ Obtain 11 points before the opposition does by making baskets.

◆ Develop ball control and shooting accuracy while in the air.

◆ Develop teamwork and cooperation.

Essentials:

◆ Half-court playing area

◆ Basketball

How to Play:

1. Make teams composed of two players each. Team A will go to the three-point line and team B will assume the key area.

2. The game is scored just like table tennis in that the offense and defense switch places after five points (in any combination) have been scored.

3. Team A will begin by shooting a three-pointer. If the basket is made, they will receive one point and shoot again. Team A will alternate the initial shot attempts.

4. Team B will rebound. If any shot by team A is missed, team B has three attempts to tip the ball into the basket. Team B may tip the ball to each other in order to get a closer tip, but must never be touching the floor when in possession of the ball. If the shot is made within the three tips, team B will receive one point. If team B misses a tip or fails to score, team A gets the ball back and the score remains the same.

5. First team to score 11 points is the winner.

Student Tasks:

1. Make three long distance shots.
2. Tip the ball into the basket on the first or second tip.
3. Win by a margin of five or more points.

Variations:

1. Alter the shooting distance of the initial shot.
2. Play a game to 21.
3. Play a second game. The winner is determined by the biggest margin of victory in either game.
4. Create a tournament format.

Illustration of Tips

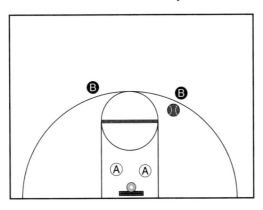

TIPS 2 BOUNCE

Objectives:

◆ Accumulate 15 points before the opposition does by making baskets.
◆ Develop ball control and shooting accuracy while in the air.
◆ Increase foul shooting accuracy.

Essentials:

◆ Half-court playing area
◆ Basketball

How to Play:

1. Create groupings composed of three players and one basketball.
2. The group will establish a shooting order.

3. Players may never be touching the floor when in possession of the ball or while attempting a shot.

4. Any player who makes a field goal will immediately go to the free-throw lane and shoot foul shots until she or he misses.

5. To start the contest, player A bounces the ball off of the floor from inside the free-throw circle, jumps up, grabs the ball, and shoots a shot while in the air. If the shot is missed, player B retrieves the ball and attempts to score next.

6. Scoring:

   a. Making a basket on a rebound before the ball bounces to the floor is worth three points.

   b. Making a basket after the ball bounces one time on the floor is worth two points.

   c. Making a basket after the ball bounces two times on the floor is awarded one point.

   d. Free-throws are worth one point.

7. First player to accumulate 15 points is the winner.

Student Tasks:

1. Score five or more points in a row, inclusive of foul shots.

2. Score twice on three point put backs.

3. Come from five or more points back and win the contest.

4. Win by a margin of five or more points.

Variations:

1. Play a game to 21.

2. Use four players in each group.

3. Create a tournament format.

Illustration of Tips 2-Bounce

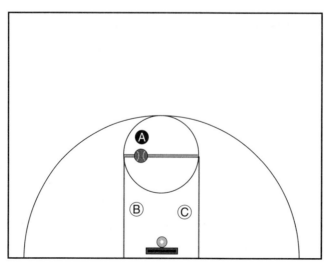

TWENTY-ONE

Objectives:

- ◆ Be the first player to score exactly 21 points.
- ◆ Follow the missed shot and quickly grab the rebound.

Essentials:

- ◆ Half-court basketball floor
- ◆ 1 basketball for each group
- ◆ Floor cones

How to Play:

1. Form groups composed of four to six players each.
2. Set the cone at any desired location and line up behind it. All competitors are to shoot the first shot from behind this cone.
3. If the shot is made, two points are awarded. The ball is then recovered and passed to the next person in line.
4. When the shot is missed, the shooter will attempt to rebound the ball before it touches the floor, and with only one step, shoot a second shot. If the second shot is made, one point is obtained. If the second shot is missed, no points will be credited.
5. The first player to score exactly 21 points (cannot go over) is the winner.

Student Tasks:

1. Make three two-point field goals.
2. Grab three rebounds and make the second shot.
3. Come from five points behind and win the contest.

Variations:

1. Create teams with four or five players and play the game at several baskets. After each game, teams rotate one cone clockwise and begin another game (see illustration below).
2. Any player who ends up with exactly seven or fifteen points must subtract five points from his/her score and return to the end of the line.
3. Use a different type of ball.
4. The first shot must be attempted from behind the three-point arc.

Illustration of a Twenty-One Team Competition

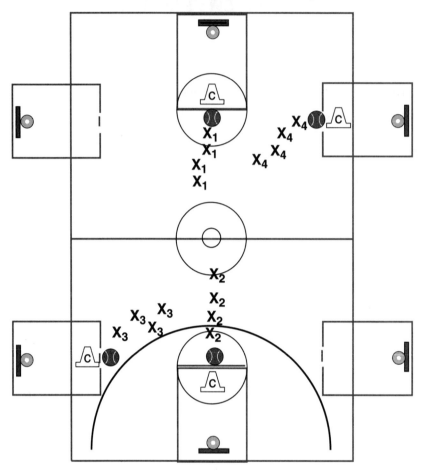

Illustration of Twenty-One Played with Teams

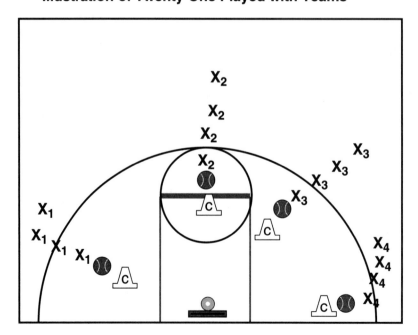

TWO-WAY TRAFFIC

Objectives:

◆ Score more points than the opposition.

◆ Develop court awareness.

Essentials:

◆ Full court basketball floor

◆ Pinnies

◆ 2 basketballs

◆ Flip scoreboard

How to Play:

1. The rules of basketball apply to this game.

2. Create equal teams of three, four, or five players.

3. Use two basketballs at the same time.

4. When team A scores against team B, only B may put that ball back into play.

5. A team may possess both basketballs at once.

6. A player may only score two baskets in a row. Someone else on the same team must score before she or he can score again.

7. When a foul occurs, both teams must freeze on the whistle. The shooter and any players on that end will line up for a foul shot. Play continues after the ball hits the rim or is made.

8. Play to a predetermined number of points or for a given amount of time.

Student Tasks:

1. Score two baskets in a row.

2. Capture four rebounds during a game.

3. Pass to two different players for an assist.

Variations:

1. Make three or more teams. Each game will last for four minutes. The winners will remain and take on a new group of challengers.

2. Use two basketballs of different sizes or colors. One may *not* be dribbled and is worth three points on any field goal.

3. Substitute another type of ball for one of the basketballs.

Illustration of Two-Way Traffic Using a Basketball and Soccer Ball

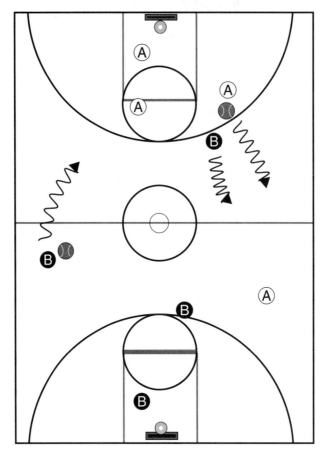

WASP

Objectives:

◆ Become the last player tagged.

◆ As a wasp, tag as many runners as possible.

◆ Enhance dribbling skills by not looking at the ball.

Essentials:

◆ Large open floor

◆ 1 basketball for each participant

How to Play:

1. This game is a take-off of "Octopus."

2. Use the entire playing surface.

3. Every player is a "fly" and has a basketball. All "flies" are to report to one endline.

4. Ask for a volunteer to be the "wasp."

5. The wasp will start the flies by yelling "wasp." The wasp dribbles after the flies and attempts to tag or force them to lose control of the ball.

6. On the command from the wasp, the flies attempt to dribble to the other end and avoid the wasp or "stingers."

7. Any tagged fly will become a "stinger." Each stinger will stand in one place, constantly dribble the ball, and when a fly passes by, attempt to tag her/him with the free hand. Stingers are allowed to use either foot as a pivot.

8. Repeat this process until only one fly remains.

Student Tasks:

1. Tag two players.

2. Finish in the top five.

3. Tag two or more players in one series while being the wasp.

Variations:

1. Designate two players to be the wasps.

2. The wasp does not use a ball.

3. Change the safe zone to be inside the opposite free-throw lane.

Illustration of Wasp

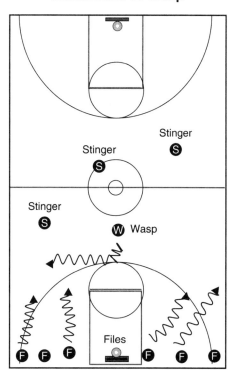

CLOSED BOCCE

Objectives:

- ◆ To be the first team to score 15 points.
- ◆ Roll the ball so that it stops closer to the jack ball than your opponent's ball.
- ◆ Hit the opponent's ball away from the jack ball, leaving your own ball nearer.

Essentials:

- ◆ Any open area (does not have to be level)
- ◆ Field cones are needed if lines are not available to mark boundaries. (five-yard lines on a football field work well)
- ◆ 1 target object (field cone, poly spot, softball base, etc.)
- ◆ 8 matching balls (rubber basketballs, softballs, soccer balls, etc.) (mark four with an "A" and four with a "B")

How to Play:

1. The rules of "Open Bocce" apply to this game with a few exceptions.
2. A member of team A places the target ball (jack) anywhere from side to side on the midline. The same player now rolls or throws two balls as close to the target as possible.
3. Next, a player from team B attempts to roll two balls nearer to the jack.
4. The second player from team A rolls, and finally the last player from team B.
5. A player may not step past the end line before releasing the ball.
6. The ball may be rolled, bowled, or thrown in any manner.
7. Measure the balls from their outer distance. (Use heel-to-toe steps to measure the distances if two balls are close.)
8. Any ball that is closer than the opposition's scores one point.
9. Ties between two balls of opposing teams will cancel each other.
10. The team that scores will toss the jack to begin the next frame. This gives the advantage (hammer) to the opposition.
11. Any ball that rolls or is hit out-of-bounds is eliminated.
12. First team to attain 15 is declared the winner.

Student Tasks:

1. Place three or more balls closest to the jack.
2. Hit an opponent's ball out of play.
3. Score three or more points in one frame.

Variations:

1. Play the game indoors by dividing a basketball court into lanes (diagonally). Use wiffle balls or objects that will slide such as plastic hockey pucks, beanbags, flying discs, etc.

2. If the jack is moved, one point is deducted.

3. Play with three players and each player has two balls.

4. Play one against two, two against three, etc. Each team has the same number of objects.

Illustration of a Fixed Bocce Outdoor Field

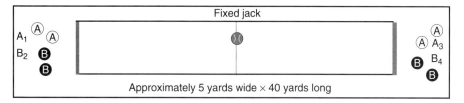

NEAREST BALL BOCCE

Objectives:

◆ Secure 15 points before the opposition does.

◆ Roll the ball so that it stops closer to the jack ball than your opponent's ball.

◆ Knock the jack away if your opponent's ball is closer.

◆ Hit the opponent's ball away from the jack ball, leaving your ball nearer.

Essentials:

◆ Any open area with any type of surface

◆ 8 matching balls (rubber basketballs, softballs, soccer balls, etc.) (mark four with an "A" and four with a "B")

◆ Target ball (different from the rest)

How to Play:

1. The general rules of Open Bocce apply to this game with a few modifications.

2. The first player tosses the jack, then rolls or tosses the first ball only and steps aside. That player does not roll again until the opposing side has gotten one of its balls closest to the jack.

3. The side whose ball is the closest to the jack is called "Inside" and the opposing side "Outside."

4. Whenever a team gets "Inside" it steps aside and lets the "Outside" team bowl.

5. This continues until one side has used all its balls and the opposing side is then entitled to toss its remaining balls.

6. Measure the balls from their outer distance. (Use heel-to-toe steps to measure the distances if two balls are close.)

7. Any ball that is closer than the opposition's scores one point.

8. Ties between two balls of opposing teams will cancel each other.

9. Game is to 15 points.

Student Tasks:

1. Place two or more balls closest to the jack.

2. Hit the jack so that your team scores instead of the opponent.

3. Roll the first ball so close that the opposition never beats it.

Variations:

1. Ties between two balls of opposing teams may be played over.

2. Play mixed doubles.

3. Play with three players and each player has two balls.

4. Play one against two, two against three, etc. Each team has the same number of balls.

5. Form teams of three or four players. When there are four individuals on a team, two players on each team take positions at about the same distance from the jack on opposite ends of the field and play alternate rounds.

6. Build a tournament format for any of the above.

7. After each game, switch partners and tally individual records.

Illustration of Nearest Ball Bocce with Two Players

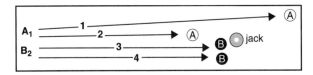

OPEN BOCCE

Objectives:

♦ Roll the ball so that it stops closer to the jack ball than your opponent's ball.

♦ Hit the jack away from your opponent's ball when it is closer.

♦ Knock the opponent's ball away from the jack, leaving your ball nearer.

♦ Hit your team ball closer to the jack.

♦ Acquire 18 points first.

BOCCE

Essentials:

- Any open area with any type of surface
- 8 alike balls (rubber basketballs, softballs, soccer balls, etc.) (mark four with an "A" and four with a "B")
- Target ball (different from the rest)

How to Play:

1. Form teams of two players and challenge any other team.
2. Move to any area desired on a field.
3. The jack may be tossed any distance and in any direction. The same player now rolls two balls as close possible to the jack. A player from team B tries the same, followed by the second player from team A, and finally the last player from B.
4. All tosses are from the same general area.
5. A player may take one step before releasing the ball.
6. The ball may be rolled, bowled, or thrown in any manner.
7. Measure the balls from their outer distance. (Use heel-to-toe steps to measure the distances if two balls are close.)
8. Any ball that is closer than the opposition's ball scores one point.
9. Ties between two balls of opposing teams will cancel each other.
10. The team that scores will toss the jack to begin the next frame. This gives the advantage (hammer) to the opposition.
11. First team to reach 15 points is declared the winner.

Student Tasks:

1. Place three or more balls closest to the jack.
2. Hit the jack so that your team scores instead of the opponent.
3. Block a scoring ball from the opposition.

Variations:

1. Make teams composed of singles or with three players (two balls each).
2. Play one against two, two against three, etc. Each team has the same number of balls.
3. Play mixed doubles.
4. Form teams of three or four players. When there are four individuals on a team, two players from the same team take positions at about the same distance from the jack at opposite ends of the field. These two will play alternate rounds. Game is 18 points.
5. Build a tournament format.

Illustration of Open Bocce with Two Players

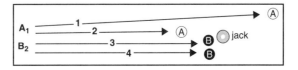

Illustration of Open Bocce with Four Players

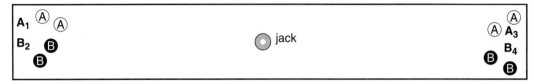

PÉTANQUE

Objectives:

◆ Win two out of three rounds.

◆ Be the first side to score 13 points.

◆ Throw a ball as close to the target as possible.

◆ Displace an opponent's ball.

Essentials:

◆ Outdoor area

◆ 4 to 6 throwing balls (shot puts, golf balls, tennis balls, ball bearings, etc.)

◆ Target object (any small type of ball or object dissimilar to the throwing balls)

◆ Measuring device (tape, yardstick, string)

Terminology:

1. Boule	Throwing balls (The game is officially played with metal balls between 705 and 800 mm in diameter and weighing between 650 and 800 grams)
2. Cochonnet	"Jack" (target ball) (made entirely of wood and the diameter is between 25 mm and 35 mm)
3. Tête-à-tête	One player against another
4. Doublet	Two against two
5. Triplet	Three against three
6. Holding	Player or team with the closest ball to the jack

How to Play:

1. These rules have been slightly modified.

2. Choose singles or team competition. In singles and doubles, each player receives three boules. In triplets, each player receives two.

3. The playing surface should be relatively flat and approximately 10 to 15 feet wide by about 40 feet long.

4. To begin a game, an 18 to 24 inch wide circle is drawn. The jack is then hurled 20 to 30 feet away. The jack must rest at least three feet from any obstacle and be visible from the throwing circle.

5. Next, one player from either side tosses a boule as close to the jack as possible. This player is closest (holding) since this ball is the only one thrown so far. Play now transfers to the opposition.

6. When playing a ball, the feet must be entirely inside the circle and maintain contact with the ground until the ball lands.

7. Any type of delivery is permitted.

8. A player from the opposing side attempts to lag a ball closer to the jack and must continue doing so until she or he either holds or has run out of balls to throw.

9. Participants can attempt to displace the ball of the opposing team or the jack so that their ball is closer.

10. After all the balls have been played, the side with the closest number of balls to the jack scores one point for each. If there are no more balls to be played and two opposing balls are at an equal distance from, or touching the cochonnet (jack), the game is negated. The side that won the previous game then throws the jack.

11. If, during measuring, one of the players moves the cochonnet or a ball being measured, the player's team loses the point.

12. The winning side will draw a circle around the jack and start the next game from this location.

13. The first team to reach 13 points is the winner of the first round.

14. Matches are played until either side wins two out of three rounds.

Student Tasks:

1. Score with all of the balls.

2. Eliminate either a portion of or all of the opponent's points.

3. Toss the first ball so that it winds up being the closest after everyone has thrown.

Variations:

1. Play on an area that is hilly or uneven. (This can be quite challenging.)

2. Pit one person against two, so long as each side has an equal number of balls.

3. Organize a round robin tournament.

Illustration of a Pétanque Field

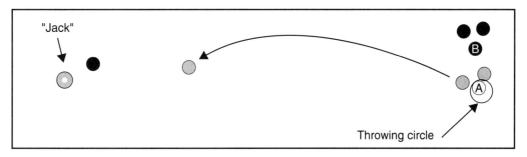

CANADIAN FIVEPIN

Objectives:

◆ Score more points than the opposition.

◆ Knock over as many pins as possible.

Essentials:

◆ Large open area or gymnasium

◆ 5 bowling pins (wood or plastic) for each lane (60 ft. long by 3 ft. 6 in. wide)

◆ Softballs or any type of ball approximately five inches in diameter

◆ 1 score sheet and pencil

Terminology:

1. Strike   Knock over all five pins with the first throw
2. Spare   Knock down all five pins with two rolls within a frame
3. Open   One or more pins remain standing after three throws

How to Play:

1. The game is played with two players.
2. The game consists of 10 frames.
3. The head pin is worth five points, the two pins immediately behind it are worth three each, and the last two pins are valued at two points each (see example below).
4. Players take turns (frame) rolling a ball down the lane in an attempt to knock over as many pins as possible.
5. Each player receives three attempts to knock over all of the pins.
6. It is illegal to cross the foul line (scratch) during or after the release of the ball. When the player scratches, all of the pins knocked down will score but a penalty of 15 points is subtracted from the final score.
7. A player is eliminated from competition after committing a fourth foul line violation.
8. Scoring:
   a. A strike is worth 15 points for that frame plus the score from the first two balls of the next frame/s.
   b. A spare (first two balls only) is worth 15 points plus the score from the first ball of the next frame.
   c. A strike on the 10th frame will result in two extra throws.
   d. A spare on the 10th frame will result in one extra bonus toss.

BOWLING

9. After the completion of the 10th frame (including bonus throws), tally the scores. The highest score wins.

Student Tasks:

1. Never have an open frame.
2. Bowl a strike.
3. Make three or more strikes.
4. Make two spares during a contest.
5. After being behind at the conclusion of the fifth frame, rally to close the gap or win the game.

Variations:

1. Make two or three member teams.
2. Allow for four throws per frame.
3. Create a tournament format.

Illustration of Pin Values for Canadian Fivepin

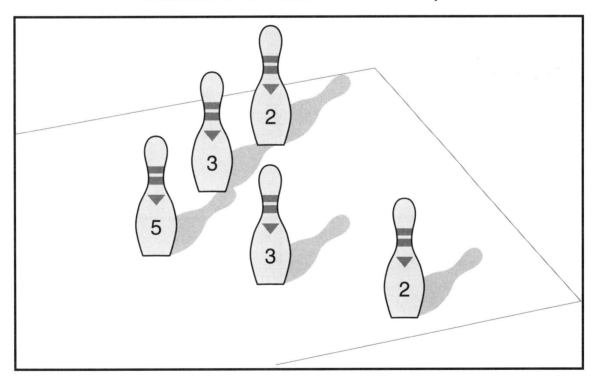

© 2001 Parker Publishing Company

81

Canadian Fivepin Score Cards

Scoring

    1. Strike   15 plus the next two rolls.

    2. Spare   15 plus the next roll.

    3. Open   Total of the displaced pin values.

Name/s	1	2	3	4	5	6	7	8	9	10
_____										
_____										
_____										
_____										
_____										
_____										
_____										
_____										
_____										
_____										

FIVE MEMBERS

Objectives:

♦ Score more points than the opposition.

♦ Develop teamwork by alternating frames.

Essentials:

♦ Bowling alley

♦ Gymnasium (plastic bowling pins and balls)

♦ Score cards and pencils

Terminology:

1.	Scratch	Participant crosses the foul line
2.	Strike	10 plus the next two balls
3.	Spare	10 plus the next ball
4.	Open	Failure to knock down all 10 pins within two throws

How to Play:

1. This is a modified version of the "Baker Format," used to determine the Oregon high school team bowling championships.

2. Make teams composed of five players each.

3. Each player is assigned a number and a set of frames.

    a. #1   1 and 6.

    b. #2   2 and 7.

    c. #3   3 and 8.

    d. #4   4 and 9.

    e. #5 (anchor)   5 and 10.

4. Each team will line up in single file on adjoining lanes.

5. Teams will alternate throws no matter what the pin action was from the opposing bowler. For example, if a player on team A knocks down seven pins, she/he will not bowl for a spare until a player from team B has thrown a ball. Any team that rolls more strikes during a match could finish way ahead of a non-striking team.

6. A competitor has 10 to 15 seconds to bowl a ball, after the opposition has thrown.

7. Player #5 will bowl three balls on the tenth frame if earned.

8. Each team will bowl 10 frames on one lane, tally their scores, switch lanes, and then bowl 10 more.

9. At the conclusion of 20 frames, the two 10 frame scores are added together to determine a winner.

Student Tasks:

1. Pick up two spares or throw one strike.

2. Come from behind after the fifth frame and defeat the opposition.

Variations:

1. Create a single or double elimination tournament format.

2. First shot by player #1 on team A must be off-handed, the second shot (if needed) from the same player must be with the dominant hand.

Illustration of Five Members

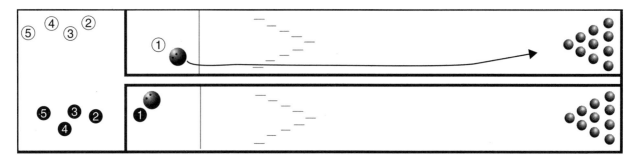

BOWLING

Bowling Score Cards

Scoring

1. Strike	10 plus the next two rolls.
2. Spare	10 plus the next roll.
3. Open	Total number of pins knocked down.

Name/s   1   2   3   4   5   6   7   8   9   1 0

TAG ALONG

Objectives:

◆ Score more points than the opposition.

◆ Develop teamwork by alternating frames.

Essentials:

◆ Bowling alley

◆ Gymnasium (plastic bowling pins and balls)

◆ Score cards (see "Five Members")

◆ Pencils

Terminology:

1. Scratch   Participant crosses the foul line

2. Strike   10 plus the next two balls

3. Spare   10 plus the next ball

4. Open   Failure to knock down all 10 pins within two throws

How to Play:

1. Make teams composed of five players and assign a bowling order.

2. Challenge another team to a contest (10 frames).

3. Each team will line up in single file.

4. Each team will alternate throws in sequence no matter what the pin action was from the previous bowler. For example, if the first player knocks down five pins, she or he will not bowl for the attempted spare. Instead, the second bowler on the same team will throw for the spare. The third person will throw the first ball of the second frame. Proceed in this manner until all ten frames have been completed.

5. The team with the most points after 10 frames have been completed is the winner.

Student Tasks:

1. Make a spare.

2. Make three or more spares during a match.

3. Bowl a strike.

4. Obtain three or more strikes in a contest.

5. Come from behind after the fifth frame and defeat the opposition.

Variations:

1. Place only three players on a team.

2. Players must alternate hands with each new toss.

3. Create a single or double elimination tournament format.

Illustration of Tag Along

ABOUT CRICKET

Objectives:

- ◆ Score more runs than the opposition.
- ◆ Be safe before the wicket is broken.
- ◆ Eliminate 10 of the 11 players with outs.

Essentials:

- ◆ Large open field (use the inside of a football or soccer field)
- ◆ 1 restricted flight softball
- ◆ 2 softball bats (optional: wooden softball bats with an area shaved flat)
- ◆ 2 wickets (see diagram below)
- ◆ Catcher mask

Terminology:

1.	Bails	Dowels that rest on top of the wicket stumps
2.	Creases	Lines designating the pitch area
3.	Bowl	Pitch the ball
4.	Bowler	Pitcher
5.	Non-striker	Runner located at the opposite wicket
6.	Over	Six fair pitches to a striker
7.	Popping crease	Front edge of home plate or safe area
8.	Pitch area	Infield consisting of the pitching and hitting areas
9.	Run out	Put out
10.	Striker	Batter
11.	Stump	Wicket post
12.	Wicket-keeper	Catcher

How to Play:

1. The concepts are similar to softball although the rules are quite different. These rules have been modified.
2. Divide into two teams composed of 11 players each.
3. Two players of the batting team go to opposite wickets of the pitch area and assume positions at each home plate (popping crease).
4. The fielding side consists of a pitcher (bowler), a catcher (wicket-keeper) who is located at the opposite wicket, and nine other fielders dispersed over the entire field.
5. There are no foul balls and the entire field is playable.

6. Offense:

   a. The batter farthest from the pitcher is the hitter (striker); the other is the runner (non-striker). Each batter will possess a bat at all times.

   b. The striker may attempt to hit the ball with the bat. If the ball is missed, and the wicket-keeper catches it, the ball is dead. If the striker hits the ball, the striker and non-striker may attempt to score runs. (The challenge is to hit the ball in between the fielders.)

   c. Returning for another run is accomplished by touching the ground beyond the popping crease with an outstretched bat.

   d. The hitter and runner do not have to run when the ball is hit.

   e. If the hitter misses a ball and the catcher fails to control it, the runners may take off and attempt to score.

   f. The runner and batter may not interfere with the fielders at any time.

   g. Only one runner may be put out and is replaced by a teammate waiting off field.

   h. The ball is dead after any out.

   i. When ten batters have been put out, the inning is over and the teams switch sides. (There must always be two base runners.)

7. Defense:

   a. A fielder may break the wicket with the hand that holds the ball, or by throwing the ball directly against it.

   b. After the pitcher has completed six good pitches (an over), a teammate from the fielding team will pitch the next over from the opposite wicket.

   c. The pitcher must give a good pitch or the batting team will receive one run and an extra pitch during the over.

   d. The ball is live when the pitcher begins to step toward the striker.

   e. The pitcher must release the ball over-handed from behind the popping crease. The arm must be straight and locked during the entire delivery.

   f. The pitcher should try and bounce the ball a short distance in front of the hitter. (The bounce is not required but makes the ball much harder to hit, especially when spin is added to the ball during the release.)

8. Outs:

   a. Preventing a delivered ball from hitting the wicket by stopping it with any part of the body. The bat may be used, also. (LBW—leg before wicket).

   b. Whenever a fielder catches a fly ball (caught).

   c. Missing the pitch and the ball then dislodges a bail from the wicket (bowled).

   d. Missing the pitch and being out of the popping crease when the wicket-keeper catches the ball and breaks the wicket (stumped).

   e. When attempting to score runs, a runner is not behind the popping or return crease line when her/his wicket is broken (run out).

   f. When the striker, for any reason, hits the wicket and dislodges a bail.

9. Scoring:

    a. The hitter (striker) and runner (non-striker) score each time they both run to the opposite popping crease before a fielder can knock off a bail with the ball. They may return for another run immediately.

    b. After scoring one, three, or five runs, the striker/non-striker roles are reversed for the next pitch unless it is an over.

    c. When a striker hits the ball and it rolls or bounces across the boundary line, four runs are automatically tallied without having to run (four).

    d. When a striker hits a fly ball over the boundary line, six runs instantly scored without having to run (a six).

    e. A pitched ball that is out of the reach or wide of the striker automatically scores one run. The striker and non-striker may elect to obtain additional runs before the ball is returned.

    f. Additional runs can be attempted on all overthrows. If the ball reaches the boundary on an overthrow, four runs (a four) are scored in addition to any runs accumulated before the overthrow.

    g. Whenever the pitcher illegally throws or releases the ball beyond the popping crease, one run is scored and an extra pitch awarded.

    h. After each team has batted one or two innings, the team with the most runs wins.

Student Tasks:

1. Break a wicket with a thrown ball and put a runner out.
2. Hit a four.
3. Score three runs after hitting the ball.
4. Catch a fly ball.
5. Pitch the ball and have it break the wicket.
6. Break two wickets while being the wicket-keeper.

Variations:

1. Use three bowling pins for each wicket. If a pin is knocked over, the wicket is broken.
2. Allow only three pitches during the over.
3. After five players are out, the teams switch places.
4. The game ends after a predetermined number of players are put out, instead of complete innings.

Explanation and Diagram of a Wicket for Cricket

1. Stumps: Three wooden posts (1″ diameter by 28″ high) that are driven into the ground just close enough together that a softball will not pass between them.

2. Bails: Two wooden cross pieces (1/2″ diameter) that sit in small grooves on top of the adjoining pairs of stumps.

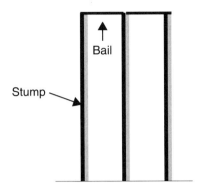

Illustration of a Cricket Pitch Area Layout

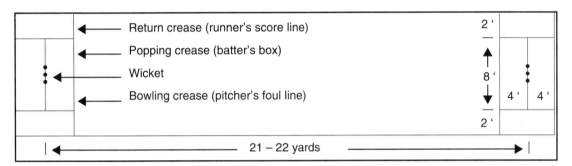

Illustration of the Player Positioning in the Pitch Area

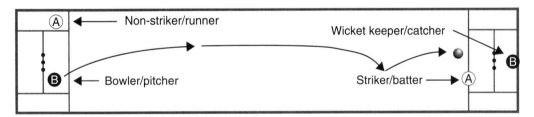

INDOOR CRICKET

Objectives:

◆ To score more runs than the opposition.

◆ To be safe before the wicket is broken.

Essentials:

◆ Large indoor area or gymnasium

◆ Plastic bat

◆ 6 bowling pins

◆ Tennis ball or small vinyl-covered foam ball

◆ Catcher's mask

◆ Floor tape

Terminology:

1. Creases   Lines designating the pitch area
2. Bowl   Pitch the ball
3. Bowler   Pitcher
4. Non-striker   Runner at opposite wicket
5. Over   Three fair pitches to a striker
6. Popping crease   Front edge of home plate or safe area
7. Pitch area   Infield consisting of the pitching and hitting areas
8. Striker   Batter
9. Stump   Bowling pin
10. Wicket-keeper   Catcher

How to Play:

1. These rules have been modified from the official game of "Indoor Cricket."

2. Divide the entire class into two teams. One team is at bat; the other is distributed over the entire playing area.

3. Offense:

   a. Batters pair up and establish a batting order as in softball.

   b. Future batters may not interfere with the ball when it is in play.

   c. Two players of the batting team go to opposite wickets of the pitch area and assume positions behind each popping crease.

   The batter farthest from the pitcher is the hitter (striker); the other is the runner (non-striker).

   d. The striker attempts to hit the ball with the bat. If the ball is missed, and the wicket-keeper catches it, the ball is dead. If the striker hits the ball, the striker and non-striker may or may not endeavor to score.

   e. If the hitter misses a ball and the catcher fails to control it, the runners may take off and score.

   f. Additional runs are accomplished by touching the floor beyond the popping crease with the foot.

   g. After scoring one run, the striker/non-striker roles are reversed. If the pair score three runs, they stop and go to the end of the batting line and are replaced by a new crew.

   h. After four outs, the inning is over and the teams switch roles.

4. Defense:

   a. The fielding side consists of the pitcher (bowler), and the catcher (wicket-keeper) who also assume positions at opposite wickets. The other fielders disperse over the entire floor.

   b. Not including the wicket-keeper, a fielder cannot be closer than 15 feet from the batter prior to the ball being hit.

   c. A fielder may break the wicket (knock over any pin) with the hand that holds the ball, or by throwing the ball directly at it.

   d. The ball is in play from the time the pitcher begins her or his approach.

   e. After the pitcher has completed three good pitches (an over), the wicket-keeper rotates to the pitcher position and a fielder becomes the wicket-keeper.

   f. The pitcher must give a good pitch or the batting team will receive one run and an extra pitch. (This does not count as one of the three runs they are able to score before going out.)

   g. The ball is released under-handed from behind the popping crease.

   h. The pitcher should try and bounce the ball a short distance in front of the hitter. Only one bounce is permitted, though (The bounce is not required but makes the ball much harder to hit, especially when spin is added to the ball during the release.)

5. Outs:

   a. If the striker prevents a delivered ball from hitting the wicket by stopping it with any part of the body. The bat may be used, also. (LBW—leg before wicket).

   b. Whenever a fielder catches a fly ball (in the air, off a wall, from the ceiling, or any obstruction) before it hits the floor (caught).

   c. After missing the pitch, the ball knocks over a wicket pin (bowled).

   d. If the batter misses the pitch and is then totally in front of the batters box (popping crease) when the wicket-keeper catches the ball and breaks the wicket (stumped).

   e. When attempting to score runs, a runner has not touched behind the popping crease line when her or his wicket is broken (run out).

   f. The striker, for any reason, hits the wicket and dislodges a bail.

6. Scoring:

   a. The hitter (striker) and runner (non-striker) score each time they both run to the opposite popping crease before a fielder can knock over a pin with the ball.

   b. A pitched ball that is ruled out of the reach or wide of the striker scores one run. The striker and non-striker may attempt to obtain additional runs before the ball is returned.

   c. Additional runs can be attempted on all overthrows.

   d. After a given time or a predetermined number of innings, the team with the most runs wins.

Student Tasks:

1. Knock over a pin with a thrown ball and put a runner out.

2. Score three runs after hitting the ball.

3. Catch a fly ball.

4. Pitch the ball and have it break the wicket.

Variations:

1. Place a line at the middle of the pitching area. The batter and runner need to run to it and back in order to score.
2. Set one wicket at the three point arc and the other at half court.
3. After five players are out, the teams switch places.

Diagram of a Wicket for Indoor Cricket

Illustration of an Indoor Cricket Pitch Area Layout
(Note: Use floor tape to mark only the popping creases at both ends)

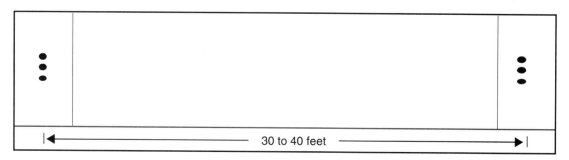

30 to 40 feet

Illustration of Indoor Cricket Using a Basketball Court

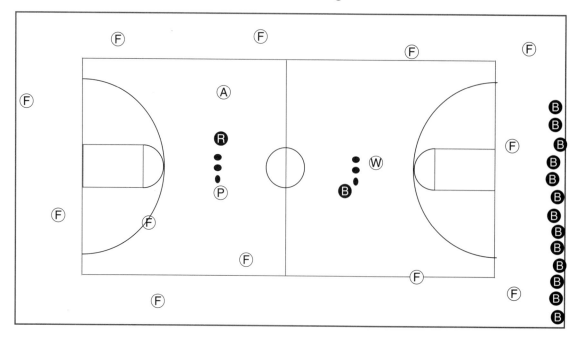

ABOUT CROQUET

Objectives:

- ◆ Finish the course first.
- ◆ Develop hand-and-eye coordination.

Essentials:

- ◆ Large open field (the field does not have to be flat if a more challenging course is desired)
- ◆ Croquet equipment

Terminology:

© 2001 Parker Publishing Company

1. Roquet	To strike one's own ball so that it comes in contact with another.
2. Croquet	To strike one's own ball when in contact with a roqueted ball. The player may place one foot on her or his own ball and whack it against the other, sending it in any direction.
3. Ricochet	Displace two or more balls with one hit of the mallet.
4. Rover	When a ball has been through all of the arches and hits the turning post, instead of striking the starting post and quitting, the player prefers to continue to play, making the ball roam around. The player may assist her or his own side and drive the opposition back.

How to Play:

1. The following rules have been modified.
2. Pick a color and always hit in the order of blue, red, black, yellow, green, and orange.
3. Begin by placing the ball one-third the distance between the starting post and the middle of the first arch. The ball must be struck (not pushed) with the face of the mallet. Every stroke counts, even if the ball is barely moved.
4. Extra strokes are allowed for passing through a wicket, hitting another ball, or hitting a stake.
5. A player who drives the ball through two arches is entitled to two extra strokes.
6. Playing out of turn or hitting the wrong ball will cause a forfeiture of that turn.
7. If a ball displaces another ball and then passes through an arch, the player can either croquet or continue.
8. If a ricocheting and croqueting ball both pass through an arch with the same stroke, only one extra stroke is awarded.
9. No ball can croquet the same ball twice, until the croquet has passed under an arch or hit a stake.

10. A player roqueting a ball is not forced to croquet it.

11. If a ball is driven from the play area, it is replaced one mallet length inside the outer boundary where it originally went out.

12. A ball has not passed an arch if the handle of the mallet is placed on the backside of the wicket and it touches the ball.

13. No matter how many balls are hit on a single stroke, only one additional stroke is given. The player must croquet all hit balls or none.

14. First player to complete the course is the winner.

Student Tasks:

1. Become a rover.
2. Hit the ball through three or more arches during a turn.
3. Croquet a ball, pass through an arch, and then croquet any ball again.
4. Croquet three different balls during any individual contest.

Variations:

1. Play singles (Blue / Red / Black / Yellow / Green / Orange).
2. Play with a partner (Blue + Yellow / Red + Green / Black + Orange).
3. Play teams (Blue + Black + Green / Red + Yellow + Orange).
4. Redesign a course.
5. Use different equipment. Try a softball bat, soccer ball, and two cones as a wicket. The ball must go between the cones without displacing either one.

Illustration of Dimensions for a Nine-Wicket Field

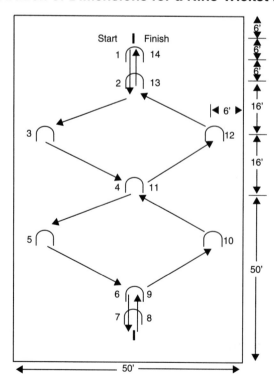

CROQUET GOLF

Objectives:

- ◆ Finish a course in the least amount of strokes.
- ◆ Develop hand and eye coordination.

Essentials:

- ◆ Large open space
- ◆ Croquet equipment
- ◆ Pencil and paper
- ◆ Scorecards and map (see the section on "Golf" for scorecards)

Terminology:

1. Bogey   Strokes taken over the par
2. Par   Average number of strokes needed to go under the arch
3. Birdie   1 stroke under par
4. Eagle   2 strokes under par
5. Hole in One   Make a pin with the first shot
6. Fore   Protect your head
7. Pin   Wicket that the ball is to pass completely under
8. Away   The player farthest from the pin
9. Lie   Position of a resting ball
10. Putt   Short shot to the pin

How to Play:

1. Set up a traditional six- or nine-wicket course.
2. Send a group of four players to each wicket (shotgun start).
3. Take turns, as in golf, to make each wicket.
4. Remove and replace any ball that impedes another player's shot.
5. Record the number of strokes taken at each arch.
6. Move to the next wicket after all players have finished.
7. Player with the least number of strokes needed to complete the course, wins.

Student Tasks:

1. Win a game by three or more strokes.
2. Shoot a lower score than your opponent on a predetermined hole.
3. Shoot from the middle of the course and score a birdie at the next pin.
4. Shoot a hole in one on a six-wicket course.

Variations:

1. Play on a hilly or uneven field.

2. Place various obstacles on the course.

3. Set up a course where obstacles already exist.

4. Make teams and combine the scores.

5. Make teams and after both players have shot, pick the best lie (best ball). Both players will now shoot from this location.

6. Make teams, use one ball, and alternate players each stroke.

Illustration of a Redesigned Croquet Golf Course

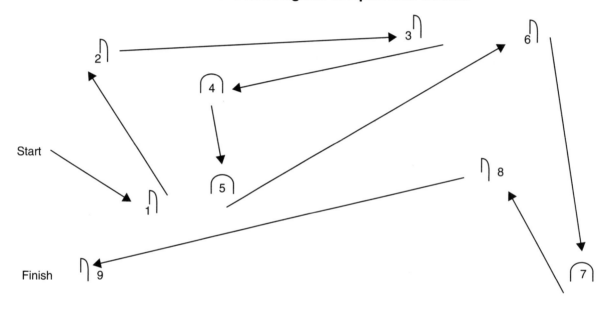

CROQUET KICKER

Objectives:

◆ Finish a course first.

◆ Develop foot-and-eye coordination by kicking a ball between two cones.

Essentials:

◆ Large open area

◆ 1 kicking ball per participant

◆ Field cones used as wickets (old hula hoops that are cut in half also work)

◆ 2 end stakes (optional: use additional field cones)

How to Play:

1. The basic rules of croquet are used for this game.

2. Allow six players per group or flight. Flights can start and finish at any wicket so long as they stay in order.

3. The game can be played in singles or as teams.

4. Determine a kicking order. Example: 1A - 1B - 1C - 2A - 2B - 2C - 1A - etc.

5. Extra or bonus strokes are allowed for passing through a wicket, hitting another ball, or hitting a stake.

6. A player kicking the ball through two wickets is entitled to two extra strokes.

7. The kicker is not allowed to hold his or her own ball when croqueting another ball.

8. Playing out of turn or kicking the wrong ball will cause a forfeiture of that turn.

9. If a ball ricochets off of another ball and then passes through a wicket, that player can either croquet or continue.

10. If a ricocheting and croqueting ball both pass through a wicket with the same kick, only one extra kick is given.

11. No ball can croquet the same ball twice, until the croquet has passed between the cones or hit a stake.

12. A player roqueting a ball is not forced to croquet it.

13. When a ball goes out of the play area, it is replaced one yard in from the exit point.

14. A ball has not passed a wicket if two or more people agree that it hasn't.

15. Only one additional smack is given no matter how many balls are hit on a single kick. The player must croquet all or none.

16. The first player or team to complete the course is the winner.

Student Tasks:

1. Kick the ball through three or more wickets during a single turn.

2. Croquet a ball, pass through an arch, and then croquet any ball again.

3. Croquet three different balls during any individual contest.

Variations:

1. Replace the end stakes with an additional wicket.

2. Redesign a course.

3. Play on a field that is hilly or uneven.

4. Players must use the weak leg when kicking the ball.

5. Switch the kicking leg with each new stroke.

Illustration of Soccer Croquet Field Using Cones

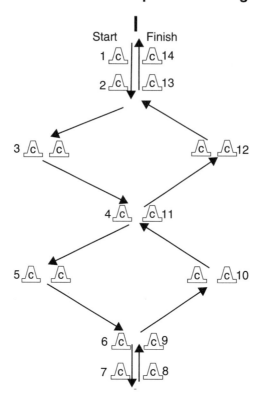

SIX-WICKET CROQUET

Objectives:

- ◆ Finish a course first.
- ◆ Develop hand and eye coordination.
- ◆ Develop and create a strategy.

Essentials:

- ◆ Large open field (84′ X 105′ is the official size but a smaller 50′ X 40′ playing area is recommended for beginners.)
- ◆ Croquet equipment

Terminology:

1.	Roquet	To strike one's own ball so that it comes in contact with another.
2.	Croquet	To strike one's own ball when in contact with a roqueted ball. The player may place a foot on her or his own ball and whack it against the other, sending it in any direction.
3.	Ricochet	Displacement of two or more balls with one hit of the mallet.

4. Rover　　　　　　　When a ball has been through all of the arches and hits the turning post, instead of striking the starting post and quitting, the player prefers to continue to play, making the ball roam around. The player may assist her or his own side and drive the opposition back.

How to Play:

1. The following rules have been modified from croquet.

2. Make groups composed of four players each. This game can be played in singles or pairs. Four balls are used. One player or team uses the blue and black balls while the other uses the red and yellow balls.

3. Begin by placing the ball three feet behind wicket #1. Stay in the hitting order of blue/red/black/yellow. The ball must be struck (not pushed) with the face of the mallet. Every stroke counts, even if the ball is barely moved.

4. Extra or bonus strokes are allowed for either passing through a wicket or hitting another ball.

5. A player who drives the ball through two arches is entitled to two extra strokes.

6. Playing out of turn or hitting the wrong ball will cause a forfeiture of that turn.

7. If a ball hits another ball and then passes through an arch, the player can either croquet or continue.

8. If a ricocheting and croqueting ball both pass through an arch with the same stroke, only one extra stroke is awarded.

9. No ball can croquet the same ball twice, until the croquet has passed under an arch or hit a stake.

10. A player roqueting a ball is not forced to croquet it.

11. If a ball is driven from the play area, it is replaced one mallet length inside the outer boundary where it originally went out.

12. A ball has not passed an arch if the handle of the mallet is placed on the backside of the wicket and it touches the ball.

13. Only one additional stroke is given no matter how many balls are hit on a single stroke. The player must croquet all or none.

14. First player or team to complete the course is the winner.

Student Tasks:

1. Hit a ball through three or more arches during any turn.

2. Croquet a ball, pass through an arch, and then croquet any ball again.

3. Come from behind and win.

Variations:

1. Play on a field that is hilly or uneven.

2. Use different equipment. An example would be a softball bat, soccer ball, and two cones as a wicket. The ball must go between the cones without knocking either one over.

Illustration of a Six-Wicket Field Layout

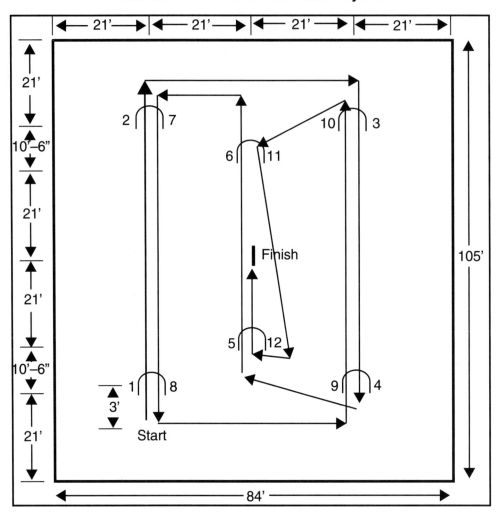

ABOUT CROSS COUNTRY

Objectives:

- ◆ Complete the course by running, jogging, walking or a combination of these within a given time limit.
- ◆ Improve fitness and cardiovascular endurance.
- ◆ Determine potential for distance running.
- ◆ Appreciate a life-long fitness activity.

Essentials:

- ◆ Large open area
- ◆ Field cones (for marking course)
- ◆ Stopwatch
- ◆ Recording sheets
- ◆ Clipboard

How to Play:

1. Designate the course by setting up cones.
2. Vary the terrain, distance, and elevations when possible.
3. Draw the course on the board for explanation to the class.
4. Stretch prior to and after running.
5. Prior to the start, the fastest runners will be up front.
6. Be aware of hazards on the course such as ditches, rocks, hills, etc.
7. A side stitch (ache) is not life-threatening.
8. Student hardships will be dealt with on an individual basis. These could include asthma, obesity, or injury.
9. A participant must pass on the same side of each cone when covering the course.
10. Students will write down their own times in the proper column on the score sheet.
11. Daily, weekly, and school records will be posted in a high-visibility area.
12. Awards can be given on the basis of effort and not time.
13. Scoring for a meet is established by finish. First place receives 1 point, second place receives 2 points, third place receives 3 points, and so forth. Lowest score wins.

Student Tasks:

1. Finish in the top ten in the class.
2. Finish the course each time within the time limit.
3. Run or jog the entire course.
4. Improve each time during three consecutive runs.
5. Pass six other runners while covering the course.

CROSS COUNTRY

Variations:

1. Form teams and tally the points of the group.
2. Form four-person teams, distribute evenly over the course, and run a relay.
3. Form six-person teams and allow no one to go faster than the slowest person. The fastest group wins.
4. Allow only speed or power walking.
5. Change the direction and length of a course.
6. Run the course on a given day of each week.
7. Record the distance covered and plot this measurement on a local, state, or country map.

Sample Cross-Country Time Sheet

Cross Country Period: Name	#1	#2	#3	#4	#5	#6	#7

BACK TO THE FUTURE

Objectives:

- ◆ To cover a course in the quickest time possible.
- ◆ Work cooperatively as a unit.

Essentials:

- ◆ Large field with a measured course
- ◆ Batons
- ◆ Stopwatch
- ◆ Time recording sheets

How to Play:

1. Make teams composed of six participants each.
2. Teams will line up in single file. The first person will have possession of a baton.
3. As each team begins walking or jogging over the course, the baton will be passed backward to each individual.
4. Once the last person receives the stick, she or he will hustle to the front of the line and pass the baton back.
5. Repeat this process throughout the entire course.
6. If the baton is dropped, the entire team must stop and reorganize before proceeding.
7. Record each team's time at the finish.

Student Tasks:

1. Pass two or more teams along the way.
2. Finish in the top three.
3. Do not finish last.

Variations:

1. Place an even number of girls and boys on each team.
2. Make larger or smaller teams.
3. Use a raw egg instead of a baton. If the egg is broken when the team finishes, figure out some sort of consequence. (The baton may also be carried in the event the egg is dropped.)
4. Shorten the distance to approximately 800 meters.

Illustration of Back to the Front

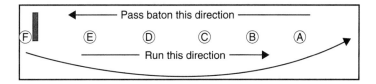

ROUTE 66

Objectives:

- ◆ Finish a predetermined cross-country course.
- ◆ Accumulate miles and reach a predetermined destination over a given period of time.

Essentials:

- ◆ Large field with a measured course
- ◆ Tally sheet for recording total distance
- ◆ Map of the region

How to Play:

1. Each participant will pick a destination, be it another city, county, across states, or across a country.
2. As a class, do the same as above.
3. Students will walk, jog, or run the predetermined course.
4. Record only those participants who complete the course.
5. Tally up the total distance and plot the mileage on a posted map. (For example, if 33 students finished the 1. 3-mile course, the total mileage would be 42.9 miles.)
6. Use several colors of ink or stickpins to differentiate the various classes.
7. After a predetermined amount of time, reward those individuals and groups that attain their goals.

Student Tasks:

1. Accomplish the distance desired.
2. Be part of a group that accomplishes its plan.
3. Beat a goal by 10 percent or more.

Variations:

1. Allow students to accumulate and record distances from walking, jogging, or running after school.
2. Allow entire families to add to the distance.
3. During the school year, combine the entire school body.
4. Pit grade levels against one another.

Illustration of a Route 66 Map

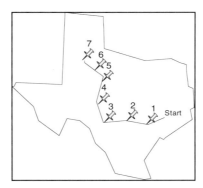

Sample of a Blank Route 66 Tally Sheet

Period:					Route 66 Tally Sheet:											
Name	1	2	3	4	5	6	7	8	9	10	11	12	13	14	15	Total
Daily Class Totals																

RURAL KICK BALL

Objectives:

- Finish ahead of the competition.
- Complete the course in the fastest time possible.
- Accumulate the lowest score possible.

Essentials:

- Measured course
- Stopwatch
- 1 tennis ball per participant (match roll call number to ball number to insure that the tennis balls are returned)
- Finish cards (deck of playing cards with numbers written on the backs)
- Time recording sheets (see "About Cross Country" for form)

How to Play:

1. Create a cross-country course.
2. Make teams composed of five to six players.
3. Each member of a team will acquire the tennis ball with the matching roll call number.
4. Participants must kick the tennis ball around the entire course.
5. It is illegal to touch the ball with any part of the body other than the feet.
6. Players are not allowed to kick another person's ball.
7. Pass out the placement cards at the finish line.
8. Each team will collect, tally, and turn in the final score to the instructor.
9. The team with the lowest score wins the meet.

Student Tasks:

1. Pass five or more opponents.
2. Come from behind and win.
3. Do not allow three competitors to pass by.

Variations:

1. Place all of the tennis balls in a bucket. Dump them on the ground. Before participants can begin the race, they must find the ball that corresponds to their roll call number.
2. Use a different type of ball, a can, or any similar object.

© 2001 Parker Publishing Company

Illustration of Player Kicking a Tennis Ball in Rural Kick Ball

SAMPLE COURSES

Objectives:

◆ Create enthusiasm.

◆ Reduce boredom.

◆ Enhance creativity.

Essentials:

◆ Large open area

◆ Field cones (for marking course)

◆ Stopwatch

◆ Recording sheets (see "About Cross Country" for form)

◆ Clipboard

How to Play:

1. Design several different courses.

2. Vary the terrain, distance, direction of travel, and elevations on each course.

3. Draw the course on the board for explanation to the class.

4. Determine and display the distance of each course.

5. Point out hazards on the course such as a ditch, rocks, hills, etc.

6. Students will write down their own times in the proper column on the score sheet.

7. Post the top runners of each course.

CROSS COUNTRY

Sample Cross-Country Courses for the Same Area

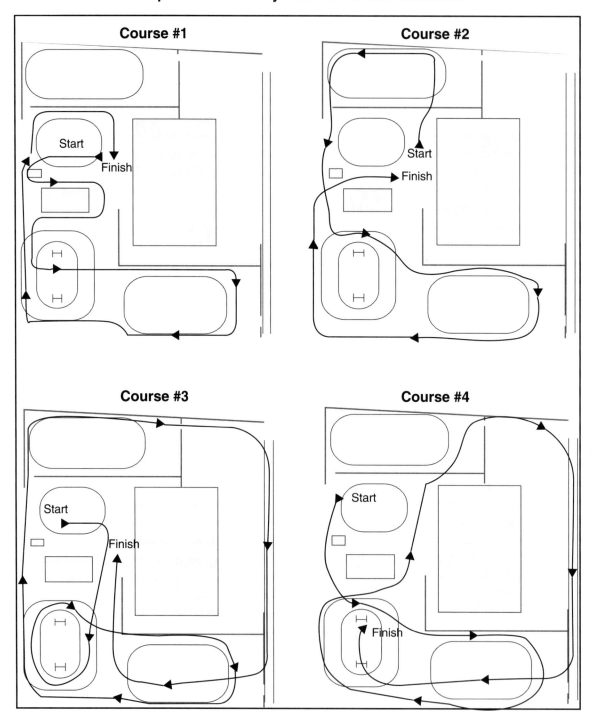

TEAM TRIATHLON

Objectives:

- ◆ Finish the course ahead of the competition.
- ◆ Complete the course in the fastest time possible.

Essentials:

- ◆ Measured course
- ◆ 2 field cones (used to designate sections)
- ◆ Stopwatch
- ◆ Segment objects (bikes, balls, hoops, etc.)
- ◆ Time recording sheets

How to Play:

1. Create a cross-country course and divide it into three distinct zones.
2. Make teams composed of three players each. Each member will compete in one section.
3. Send each participant to the beginning of her or his chosen zone.
4. Each zone will require that a participant run, roll a hula hoop, kick or dribble a ball, ride a bike, drag something, or whatever can be imagined, over the entire portion.
5. When a person finishes a segment, she or he will tag a teammate, who will then venture forth.
6. The first team to have its third participant cross the finish line will win the contest.
7. Record each team's finish time.

Student Tasks:

1. Pass two or more different teams during any segment.
2. Come from behind and win.
3. Do not allow three other competitors to go by during a segment.

Variations:

1. Transfer the same object as if it were a relay.
2. Make teams of four. Place the fourth person at the finish. The object must be transferred from teammate to teammate and wind up going around the course a given number of times.
3. Each person will have to cover the course and do each of the activities. (Plenty of equipment might be needed for this one.)

Illustration of a Team Triathlon Course

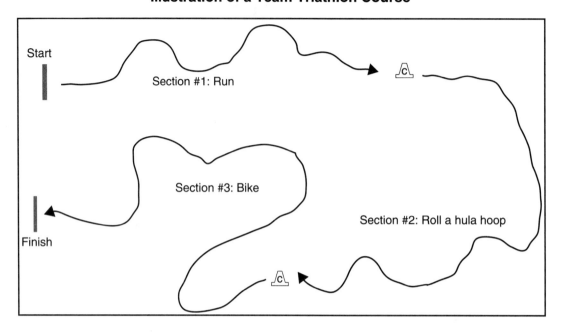

WORM WALKING

Objectives:

- Cover a course in the fastest time possible.
- Work together as a team.

Essentials:

- Large field with a measured course
- Stopwatch
- Time recording sheets (see "About Cross Country" for form)

How to Play:

1. Make teams comprised of four walkers each.
2. The first person is the leader. The others will form a line behind the leader with their hands on the shoulders of the person in front. Group members may never let go during the race.
3. Each team must walk in unison around a relatively short course. That is, all left feet will move forward at the same time, followed by the right.
4. Each time a team is out of sync, 10 seconds will be added to its final time.
5. At three or more predetermined points along the course, the leader will drop to the last position of the pack.

CROSS COUNTRY

6. Record each team's time at the finish, and add any penalty seconds.

7. The fastest team is declared the champions.

Student Tasks:

1. Pass two or more teams during the contest.

2. Finish in the top three.

3. Finish in the top 10 percent of the class.

Variations:

1. Place two boys and two girls on a team.

2. Increase the size of each group.

3. Allow teams to jog in synchronized movement.

4. Include an uphill or downhill slope in the course.

5. Start out with one person. At various points along the way, a new member will join in and take over the lead.

Representation of Worm Walking

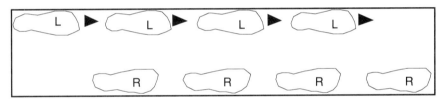

ROAD COURSE*

Objectives:

- ◆ Demonstrate the proper rules of the road while riding on public roads.
- ◆ Experience an enjoyable life-long activity.

Essentials:

- ◆ 1 bicycle for each student
- ◆ Personal safety equipment
- ◆ Cell phone for instructor

How to Play:

1. Every student must have successfully completed a bike repair lesson, possess safety gear, and know the rules of the road.
2. Design a road course in which everyone will follow the leader.
3. Periodically stop and let everyone regroup. (Intentionally hanging back is prohibited.)
4. Assign two or three different riders to alternate being the last in line (caboose).
5. Racing is not allowed.
6. Each student must be back on campus before time has expired.

Student Tasks:

1. Be a leader.
2. Be the designated last rider.
3. Always give the proper hand signals.
4. Return before time has expired.

Variations:

1. Allow several students to alternate leading the way.
2. Stop at a store along the way and allow each student purchase a treat. (Set a dollar amount if desired.)
3. Do not plan a specific route. Instead, travel away from school for half of the riding time, then turn around and head back to the campus by retracing the route.

---

*From Julie Ponder, 2000.

© 2001 Parker Publishing Company

Diagram of a Bicycle-Road Course

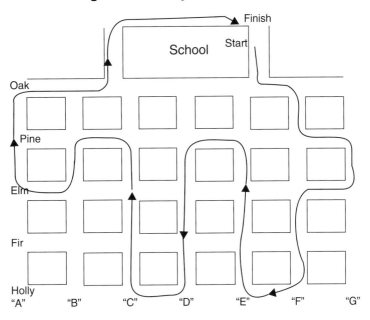

TURTLE RACES

Objectives:

◆ Be the last person to finish the race.

◆ Ride a bike across a course in the longest amount of time possible.

Essentials:

◆ Large indoor or outdoor area

◆ Bicycle for each rider

◆ Personal safety gear

◆ Field cones to depict start and finish

◆ Stopwatch

◆ Record sheet (see below)

How to Play:

1. Create two lines (start and finish) about 50 feet apart.

2. Every biker will set up with the front wheel on the starting line.

3. On the command "Go" each rider will travel in a straight line as slowly as possible to the finish.

4. Participants are disqualified when any part of the body touches the riding surface.

5. The last person left riding or the rider that took the longest amount of time to cross the finish line is the winner.

Student Tasks:

1. Never touch the surface.
2. Finish in the "Top 10."
3. Have four riders pass by.
4. Remain stationary for five or more seconds.

Variations:

1. Develop groups with six participants each. Top two in each round advance to the finals.
2. Form teams comprised of two riders each. Combine the times to establish a winner.
3. Everyone must cross the finish line. A competitor is not disqualified when a foot touches the ground. Instead, the rider must deduct 10 seconds (for each touch) from the finish time.
4. Set up several identical short obstacle courses. Riders will take turns competing.

Illustration of Turtle Races

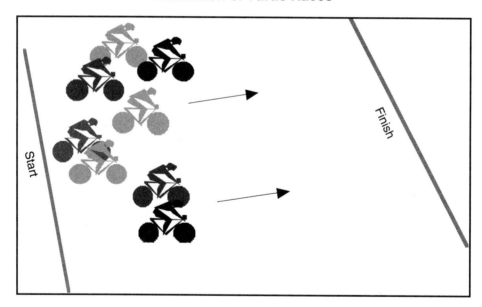

CYCLING

Sample Turtle Race Recording Sheet

Turtle Races							
Roll #	Time	−10's	Final Time	Roll #	Time	−10's	Final Time
1				21			
2				22			
3				23			
4				24			
5				25			
6				26			
7				27			
8				28			
9				29			
10				30			
11				31			
12				32			
13				33			
14				34			
15				35			
16				36			
17				37			
18				38			
19				39			
20				40			

First ——————————————————

Second ——————————————————

Third ——————————————————

ALL FIVES

Objectives:

- ◆ Obtain 51 points before the opposition does.
- ◆ Develop hand-and-eye coordination.

Essentials:

- ◆ Room or wall
- ◆ 1 dart board for every three to four players (carpet or padding around the boards is recommended)
- ◆ Scratch paper and pencils for scoring
- ◆ Desks (optional but helpful)
- ◆ 4 safety darts per board (teflon tipped)

How to Play:

1. Pick an adversary to compete against.
2. The first player will toss three darts in a row.
3. Any dart that does not stick in the board or strays outside of the double score band will result in forfeiture of that turn and any accumulated points earned during it.
4. The total of the three darts must be divisible by five.
5. Each five count results in one point. (For example, a 50 would receive 10 points.)
6. The first player to reach exactly 51 points is declared the winner.

Student Tasks:

1. Score four or more points within the allotted three throws.
2. Hit a bull's-eye.
3. Come from behind and win.

Variations:

1. Use only the off hand.
2. Alternate hands with each new toss.
3. Make outside of the triple band the out-of-bounds area.
4. The final score must be divisible by four or seven.
5. Make teams of two players and play a tournament.

Illustration of All Fives with a Triple Band Boundary

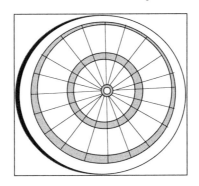

DART BASEBALL

Objectives:

◆ Score more runs than the opposition after nine innings.

◆ Develop hand-and-eye coordination.

Essentials:

◆ Room or wall

◆ 1 dart board for every three to four players

◆ Pencils

◆ Baseball diamond card (see below)

◆ 4 tokens to mark the runners that are on base

◆ Desks

◆ 4 safety darts per board

How to Play:

1. Pick an opponent, draw a baseball diamond on a piece of paper, grab four tokens, and begin play.

2. Scoring:

   a. A dart that lands anywhere inside segment 1 is worth a single hit.

   b. Stick the dart in segment 2 and receive a double.

   c. Wind up in section 3 and be rewarded with a triple.

   d. One that hits the bull's-eye is equal to a home run.

3. Any dart landing outside of segments 1, 2, or 3, is an out.

4. An inning is comprised of each player remaining at bat until she/he tosses three outs.

5. Play until a nine-inning game has been completed to determine the winner.

6. Use the baseball diamond to track the base runners (see sample below).

Student Tasks:

1. Score three or more runs in any inning.
2. Hit two home runs during the game.
3. Come from behind after seven innings and win.

Variations:

1. Shorten or lengthen the distance of the toss.
2. Do not allow the thrower to use the dominant arm.
3. Hitting outside of the required number but still landing in the double or triple band, is worth a double or triple also.

Illustration of a Baseball Diamond

(Copy and distribute.)

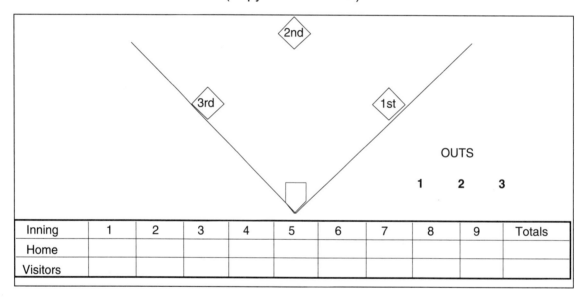

DART FOOTBALL

Objectives:

◆ Score 10 touchdowns before the opposition does.
◆ Develop hand-and-eye coordination.

Essentials:

◆ Room with wall
◆ 1 dart board for every three to four players
◆ Scratch paper and pencils
◆ Desks
◆ 3 safety darts per board

DARTS

How to Play:

1. Classmates will pair up and become opponents.

2. Each player will toss three darts in a row.

3. The first player who lands a dart in the bull's-eye will gain control of the ball. She or he may start scoring goals by throwing doubles.

4. To take the ball away, an opponent must score a bull's-eye.

5. The first player to score 10 goals will win the game.

Student Tasks:

1. Take the ball away from the opposition.

2. Score two goals during any possession.

3. Come from behind and win.

Variations:

1. Play for a predetermined amount of time. The player who is ahead when time expires, wins.

2. Play four timed quarters.

3. Create a tournament format (Super Bowl).

Example of Control and Scoring for Dart Football

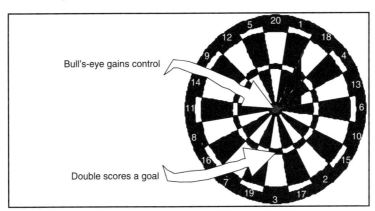

EYE DROPPER*

Objectives:

◆ Score more points than the opposition.

◆ Develop hand-and-eye coordination.

Created by Ken Lumsden, 1997.

Essentials:

- Gymnasium with bleachers
- 1 dart board for every three to four players
- Scratch paper and pencils
- Desks
- 4 safety darts per board

How to Play:

1. Pull out the first row of bleachers in the gymnasium.
2. Pick a partner then choose any dart game such as Cricket or 501.
3. Place the dartboard on the floor next to the first row of bleachers.
4. While standing on the first row, each player will hold the dart close to her/his nose, lean over slightly, and drop the dart onto the board.

Student Tasks:

1. Score with both darts on two consecutive turns.
2. Hit a bull's-eye.
3. Come from behind and win.

Variations:

1. Change the release point. The dart must be dropped from:
   a. Above the waist.
   b. The arm held straight out.
   c. Above the head.
   d. Behind and over the shoulder. (Players need to turn around for this one.)
2. Form teams and play another pair. The player doing the dropping will close her or his eyes and be told by a partner where to aim the dart.

Illustration of Eye Dropper

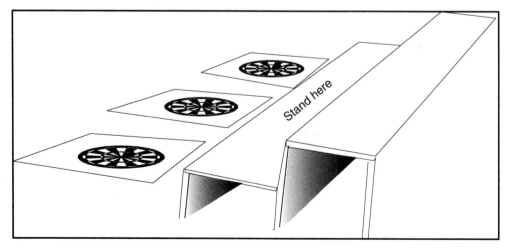

Stand here

FIGHTING FRIGATES

Objectives:

- ◆ Do not get hit with a ball (below the shoulders).
- ◆ Be hit the least number of times.
- ◆ Strike the opposition with a ball.

Essentials:

- ◆ Large indoor area
- ◆ 1 scooter for every two players (minus three)
- ◆ 3 vinyl-covered foam balls

How to Play:

1. Pair up all players with one being the captain (skipper) and the other the wind.
2. The captain sits on a scooter (frigate). The partner (wind) propels the vessel by continually holding on to the skipper's shoulders with both hands. The wind may not rapidly shove nor let go of the captain for safety reasons.
3. Each frigate attempts to eliminate (sink) the other frigates by hitting only the captain with the cannonball (below the shoulders).
4. Only the captain may pick up and throw a cannonball.
5. The pusher may not intentionally deflect a thrown ball with the head, arms, or legs. However, the ship may be maneuvered in such a way that the pusher's body becomes a shield.
6. Any captain that gets hit will relinquish the scooter, and along with her or his partner, report to the re-entry line.
7. Teammates in the re-entry line will wait to claim the first available scooter. Pairs will switch roles each time they re-enter.
8. Play for a predetermined amount of time.
9. The team that was sent to the bottom the least is victorious.

Student Tasks:

1. Sink three different vessels.
2. Prevent the skipper from being hit.
3. Eliminate a previously undefeated ship.

Variations:

1. Add more cannonballs.
2. Give each pair two football flags apiece. Each time the frigate is hit, one flag must be forfeited. A team is vanquished when all flags are lost.

Illustration of Fighting Frigates

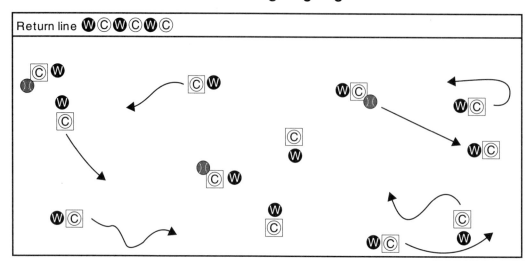

FRIGATE FLOTILLAS

Objectives:

◆ Eliminate the other team by hitting them with the ball.

◆ Do not get hit with a ball.

◆ Be the last team on the floor.

Essentials:

◆ Large indoor area

◆ 1 scooter board for every two players

◆ 3 vinyl-covered foam balls

◆ 4 different colored sets of pinnies or flags

How to Play:

1. Divide the entire class into four equal teams (flotillas). Pair up within the teams and have each pair procure a scooter board.

2. The captain sits on a scooter (frigate). The partner (wind) propels the vessel by continually holding on to the skipper's shoulders with both hands. The wind may not rapidly shove and let go of the captain for safety reasons.

3. Each individual flotilla of frigates attempts to eliminate (sink) the other flotillas by hitting only the skipper (below the shoulders) with a cannonball.

4. Only the skipper may pick up and throw a cannonball.

5. The pusher may not intentionally deflect a thrown ball with the head, arms, or legs. However, she or he may maneuver the ship in such a way that the body acts like a shield.

6. When the captain is hit (below the shoulders), the partners immediately switch places. When the new captain is pelted with a ball, the frigate is eliminated from further play.

7. Play until three of the four flotillas have been dismantled.

Student Tasks:

1. Sink three different vessels.

2. Destroy a frigate from each flotilla.

3. Never be expelled from the action.

Variations:

1. Add more cannonballs.

2. If the captain catches a thrown ball, the thrower is out.

3. If the captain catches a thrown ball, an eliminated frigate (from the same flotilla) is allowed to return.

Illustration of Frigate Flotillas

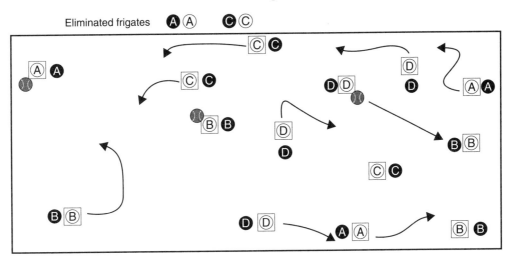

HORNET NEST

Objectives:

◆ Finish as the last person left within the boundaries.

◆ Re-enter the hornet nest after being eliminated.

Essentials:

◆ Large indoor area (basketball court)

◆ 3 vinyl-covered Nerf™ balls

DODGEBALL

How to Play:

1. Use the boundaries of the basketball court.

2. Divide into two groups, hornets and exterminators.

3. One group (hornets) disperses inside the boundaries (nest) and attempts to avoid being hit with the balls.

4. A hornet who is hit (below the shoulders) must go to the perimeter and assume the role of an exterminator.

5. Balls that bounce off of anything are neutralized.

6. A hornet can gain an extra life (honor system) by catching a thrown ball. The ball must be dropped or tossed back out immediately. Each time a hornet is hit, one extra life is used up.

7. The exterminators spread out along the perimeter and attempt to eliminate the hornets by whacking them with the ball (below the shoulders).

8. An exterminator must throw the ball from behind the boundary lines of the nest. Exterminators may enter the nest to retrieve a dead ball but must return to the outside before throwing it.

9. Exterminators may run around the outside of the court in order to obtain a better shot but may only possess a ball for 10 seconds.

10. After hitting three hornets, an exterminator will enter the nest and assume the role of a hornet.

11. Any violation by an exterminator will result in the forfeiture of all of that player's accumulated hits.

12. Individuals will be immediately removed from the game for consistently or intentionally throwing the ball with excessive force.

13. The game is over when one hornet remains.

Student Tasks:

1. Return to the nest two times.

2. Eliminate five hornets.

3. Accumulate two extra lives.

Variations:

1. Add more balls.

2. Require that an exterminator must hit five hornets before re-entering the nest.

3. When a hornet catches a ball, the thrower either sits down for a predetermined amount of time or does a given number of push-ups or sit-ups before continuing.

Representation of Hornet Nest

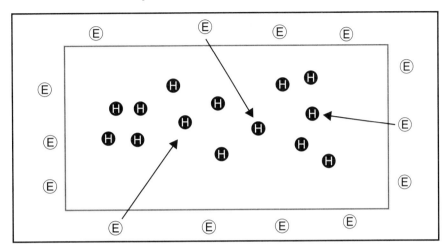

HOSPITAL DODGEBALL

Objectives:

- ◆ Eliminate the opposition first.
- ◆ Rescue the teammates who are out.

Essentials:

- ◆ Large indoor area or gymnasium
- ◆ 6 vinyl-covered Nerf™ balls (8-inch diameter)
- ◆ 2 folding floor mats

How to Play:

1. Divide into two teams and send each to opposite ends of the floor.
2. Place a floor mat (hospital) at each end.
3. Two members from each team act as doctors.
4. Any player hit with a thrown ball (below the shoulders) must immediately lie down.
5. The doctor(s) will drag any eliminated player to the emergency room.
6. Only three players are allowed in intensive care at any given time. When the fourth indisposed player arrives, the first person in line has healed and is allowed back into action.
7. If a doctor is hit, she or he, too, must lie down until saved by the other doctor.
8. When both doctors are down, then the ability to restore the other players has been nullified.
9. Play until an entire team is resting on the floor.

Student Tasks:

1. Be a doctor.

2. Save three downed players.

3. Eliminate a doctor.

Variations:

1. If a player throws a ball and the opposition catches it, she/he must lie down, too.

2. As soon as any downed player touches the hospital mat, she or he is allowed to return to the game.

3. A doctor who is hit with the ball, then later restored, is no longer allowed to drag eliminated players to the hospital.

4. Allow anyone to drag a downed teammate to the infirmary.

5. Individuals will be immediately removed from the game for consistently or intentionally throwing the ball with excessive force.

6. Form four teams. Play three different contests by combining two different teams each game. (Game #1; A + B vs. C + D) (Game #2; A + C vs. B + D) (Game #3; A + D vs. B + C) The team with the best overall record is declared the winner.

Diagram of Hospital Dodgeball

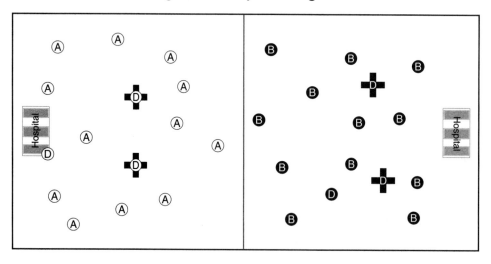

IN HOT WATER

Objectives:

- ◆ Put the opposing team in hot water.

- ◆ Avoid getting hit.

- ◆ Escape out of the hot water and return to cold water.

DODGEBALL

Essentials:

- Large indoor area or gymnasium
- 6 vinyl-covered foam balls (8-inch diameter)
- Floor cones (boundary markers)

How to Play:

1. Use the outside boundaries of a basketball court.

2. Divide the class into two equal teams. Send each team (with three balls) to the opposite cold-water area, within the basketball court.

3. Any player who is hit (below the shoulders) while in cold water must go to the hot water space, outside the boundaries. This is always true if the ball was not caught and then bounced onto the same cold water area.

4. An individual hit in cold water does not go to hot water when the ball ricochets through the air and onto any other water zone or against a wall. The ball can also be smacked while it is still in the air onto another water zone or wall, without that player having to leave.

5. If the ball is accidentally dropped or dribbled onto the same cold water zone that the player is standing in, that player must exit.

6. If a ball ricochets off of two players and lands in their cold water zone, both must depart.

7. If thrower A hits player B and the ball ricochets into the air and subsequently is caught by player C, only A must vacate since the ball never touched the floor.

8. When player A in hot water hits opponent B in the cold water, A must go back to her/his chilly water and B exits to boiling water. If B catches the ball, nothing happens.

9. Players may possess a ball for up to 10 seconds.

10. A player can use a held ball to deflect a thrown ball, so long as the deflected ball does not hit her or him anywhere below the shoulders before striking the floor, and does not knock the held ball out of her or his hand.

11. Participants may move around freely in the hot water.

12. Players may not reach or step over any boundary line to procure a ball.

13. Individuals will be immediately removed from the game for consistently or intentionally throwing the ball with excessive force.

14. The game is over when an entire team is in hot water.

Student Tasks:

1. Send four opponents to the hot water.

2. Catch a thrown ball.

3. Toss a ball to a teammate in the hot water who then hits an opponent and gets out.

Variations:

1. Students sent to the hot water must remain there. This method speeds the game up.
2. Use more or fewer balls.
3. Make four teams and play three games by joining two different teams each time.
4. Use the above format and play a best two out of three before switching teams.

Diagram of a Hot Water Dodgeball Layout

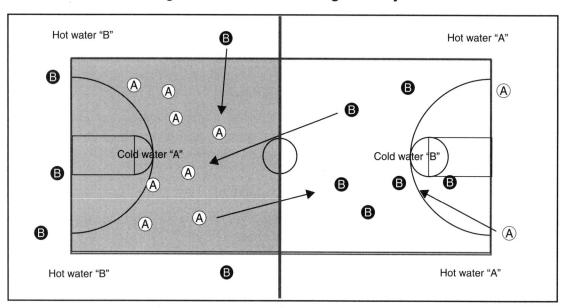

JAIL BREAK*

Objectives:

◆ Avoid being captured for the longest amount of time.

◆ Capture the escapees in the shortest duration of time.

◆ Develop teamwork and cooperation.

Essentials:

◆ Gymnasium

◆ 3 vinyl-covered Nerf™ balls

◆ 4 folding floor mats

◆ Stopwatch

---

*Created by Ken Lumsden, 2000.

DODGEBALL

How to Play:

1. Place the floor mats on end and stand them up in the center of the floor so they are at least 10 feet apart.

2. Divide the class into four groups.

3. Give the pinnies to one of the groups (fugitives) and send them into the middle (swamp).

4. Distribute the balls to the other three groups (guards) and send them to the outside.

5. Two guards will be designated as wardens and also reside in the swamp. They will retrieve and throw any dead balls back to their teammates.

6. Guards will attempt to capture all of the prisoners by thumping each one with the ball (below the shoulders). A bagged prisoner must quickly return to the jail.

7. Any guard stepping into the swamp to retrieve a ball or while throwing is eliminated until doing 15 push-ups.

8. When holding a ball, guards are no longer allowed to travel (as in basketball) because they are now "in the tower."

9. A guard may only hold onto a ball for five seconds.

10. The escapees can hide behind the mats or use them as shields but are not allowed to touch them since they are electrically charged.

11. If a fugitive catches a thrown ball, the first prisoner in the jail, if there are any, escapes back to the swamp.

12. After the first group has been captured, stop the timer, and send out a new group.

13. Individuals will be immediately removed from the game for consistently or intentionally throwing the ball with excessive force.

14. Whichever group takes the longest time to be captured, wins.

Student Tasks:

1. Hit two escapees.
2. Win by 10 or more seconds.
3. Catch a ball and release a player in jail.

Variations:

1. Do not allow captured fugitives to return to action after going to jail.
2. Add various other safe objects to be used for protection while in the swamp.
3. Add more balls.
4. Allow the guards to move outside the boundaries while in possession of a ball.
5. Set a time limit.

Example Jail Break Layout

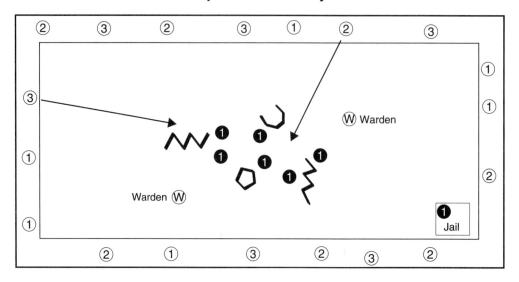

SCORPION

Objectives:

◆ Eliminate the scorpion.

◆ Develop teamwork and cooperation.

Essentials:

◆ Gymnasium

◆ 1 vinyl-covered Nerf™ ball for each group

◆ 1 jump rope for each group

How to Play:

1. Create groups of 9 to 10 people and form a large circle (electric fence).

2. Three players will go into the middle to form the scorpion. The first person represents its head, the second its thorax, and the third its tail and stinger.

3. The participants representing the scorpion must continuously hold on to the jump rope with one hand.

4. Each time the tail is hit, the scorpion members will rotate one position back. In other words, the tail would become the head.

5. The scorpion will move around freely within a predetermined area in order to protect its tail.

6. The first two members of the scorpion may temporarily halt any player on the outside by touching the player with a free hand. That player must recharge her or his battery by doing 10 push-ups or 10 sit-ups before re-entering the action.

© 2001 Parker Publishing Company

7. If the stinger touches any player on the outside, the player is eliminated from the contest until doing 10 push-ups and 10 sit-ups.

8. Members representing the electric fence will attempt to destroy the scorpion by hitting its tail six times (shocking it) with the ball. Only ten attempts are allowed to perform this feat.

9. Throwers must hit the last person below the shoulders in order for it to count.

10. Individuals will be immediately removed from the game for consistently or intentionally throwing the ball with excessive force.

11. A player may not take steps when in possession of the ball. When possible, players should pass it quickly to another teammate for a better shock attempt.

12. The scorpion wins if not destroyed within the 10 attempts.

13. Create a new scorpion from within the group and play again.

Student Tasks:

1. Never get hit while being the tail.

2. Hit the tail twice.

3. Sting two or more electric fence members.

Variations:

1. Add players to the scorpion.

2. Create two scorpions with one large outside group.

3. Add one more ball and let the scorpion throw, too.

4. Change the number of hits needed to conquer the scorpion.

5. Create smaller or larger boundaries in which everyone must remain except to retrieve a ball.

Illustration of Scorpion

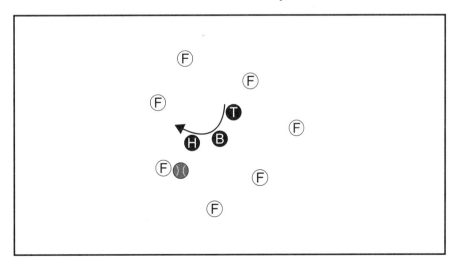

TANDEM TAG II

Objectives:

- ◆ Score more runs than the other team.
- ◆ Throw and pass the ball with accuracy.
- ◆ Develop teamwork and cooperation.
- ◆ Avoid being hit with the ball.

Essentials:

- ◆ Gymnasium
- ◆ 1 vinyl-covered Nerf™ ball
- ◆ 2 floor mats
- ◆ Flip scoreboard

How to Play:

1. For safety reasons, do not place the two bases close to the walls.
2. Players need to move under control and be aware of teammates traveling in the opposite direction.
3. Make two equal teams.
4. The offensive team will line up at center court and attempt to reach either of the bases located at opposite ends and then return home for one point.
5. There are always two runners on the court at any given time.
6. A runner may travel in any method, speed, or direction desired.
7. To initiate play, the first person in line will throw the ball anywhere onto the court and both she/he and the second teammate in line will take off simultaneously.
8. When either player scores or is hit (below the shoulders) with the ball, the next person in line begins. The eliminated runner should immediately move to the side of the court and return home.
9. The ball is considered poison and if it hits a runner in any way, shape, or manner, the runner is out.
10. A player may seek shelter in one of two safe zones for a maximum of 15 seconds. Once the runner has left a safe zone, she or he may not return to it, though.
11. The inning is over when everyone has attempted to run down and back twice.
12. The defense may not interfere with the runners.
13. An outfielder may only be in possession of a ball for three seconds.
14. Any defender in possession of the ball is not allowed to travel (take steps).
15. The team with the most runs after a set time or number of innings wins.

Student Tasks:

1. Avoid being hit two different ways.
2. Make two outs in a row.
3. Put out four players in one game.

© 2001 Parker Publishing Company

Variations:

1. The inning is over after three or more outs.

2. Allow each runner three attempts.

3. Form four teams. Play three different contests by combining two different teams for each game. (Game #1; A + B vs. C + D) (Game #2; A + C vs. B + D) (Game #3; A + D vs. B + C) The team with the best overall record is declared the winner.

Illustration of Tandem Tag II

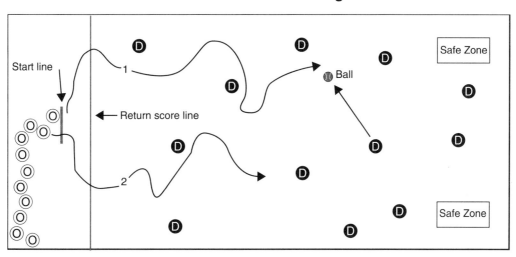

TIME OUT

Objectives:

◆ Stay within the boundaries the longest amount of time.

◆ Eliminate the inside players.

Essentials:

◆ Large indoor area

◆ 4 vinyl-covered Nerf™ balls

◆ Stopwatch

◆ Tally sheet

How to Play:

1. Use the boundaries of the basketball court.

2. Make four teams and play four games, sending a different team to the inside for each game.

3. The mission of the "inside" team is to remain in the middle as long as possible.

4. Stop the clock when the last person has been eliminated. Record that team's time.

5. A player who is hit below the shoulders must go to the return line.

6. If an insider catches a thrown ball, she or he signals for the first person in the return line to re-enter the contest.

7. Balls that bounce or ricochet from the floor or off of another player do not count.

8. The "outsiders" apportion themselves around the perimeter. They will throw the balls at the inside team and try to eliminate it as fast as possible.

9. Outsiders must throw all balls from behind the boundary line. They may enter the inside to retrieve a dead ball but must return to the outside before throwing it.

10. Outsiders may run around the outer boundary of the court in order to obtain a better shot but may only possess a ball for five seconds.

11. Individuals will be immediately removed from the game for consistently or intentionally throwing the ball with excessive force.

12. Whichever team remains in the center the longest, wins.

Student Tasks:

1. Eliminate two or more players from the inside.
2. Catch a thrown ball.
3. Toss the ball to a teammate who then hits a player on the inside.
4. After being eliminated, return to the floor and catch a ball.

Variations:

1. Use more balls.
2. Each team will enter the middle twice. Their times are then added for determination of the winner.
3. Form four teams. Play three different contests by combining two different teams for each game.

Illustration of Time Out

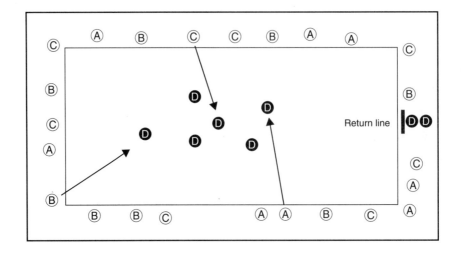

TWICE AROUND

Objectives:

◆ Score more runs than the opposition.

◆ Safely scamper around the bases twice.

Essentials:

◆ Gymnasium

◆ 1 vinyl-covered Nerf™ ball

◆ 4 folding floor mats to be used as bases

◆ Pinnies

How to Play:

1. For safety reasons, do not place the bases close to a wall. (The bases are placed 45 to 50 feet apart.)

2. Divide into two equal teams.

3. The pitcher will roll the ball on the floor to the opponent.

4. The kicker will remain until she or he boots a playable ball.

5. Bunting (slow or checked kick) is not allowed.

6. Any number of base runners may inhabit a base.

7. Runners must be touching the base once the pitcher starts the delivery and until the kicker makes contact with the ball.

8. Runners do not have to tag up on caught fly balls.

9. Sliding is prohibited for safety reasons.

10. A base runner must advance once she or he has left or run past a base.

11. Any stranded base runner will return to the same base at the beginning of the next inning.

12. The kicker is out if the defense catches a fly ball, even if it hits the wall, ceiling, or an obstruction first, before touching the floor.

13. Base runners are put out if hit or tagged with the ball (below the shoulders) while off base, or when forced out at any base.

14. A team is retired after three outs.

15. Fielders may not be in front of the pitcher until the ball has been kicked.

16. The defense may not interfere with the base runners.

17. The defense makes all of the calls and is never wrong.

18. One point is scored each time a player goes around the bases twice. The runner will then return to the end of the kicking line.

19. Individuals will be immediately removed from the game for consistently or intentionally throwing the ball with excessive force.

20. Play for a predetermined number of innings to determine a winner.

Student Tasks:

1. Be involved in a double play.
2. Catch a deflected ball.
3. Kick a home run.
4. Assist in a play at first base.

Variations:

1. Use a bat instead of kicking the ball.
2. Play this game outdoors. Place the bases 60 feet apart.
3. Use the 10-run rule. (A team may score only 10 runs an inning. If a team is behind by more than 10 runs though, they may score as many runs as needed to go ahead by one run.)
4. Designate a few objects in the area that would equal a home run when hit by a fly ball.
5. Make four teams; combine two different teams for each game. Best record wins.

Illustration of Twice Around

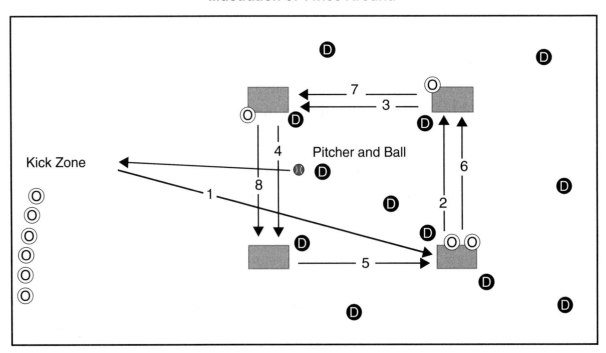

ABOUT FIELD HOCKEY

Objectives:

◆ Hit the ball into the opponent's goal.

◆ Score more goals than the opposition does.

Essentials:

◆ Large field (100 yards by 60 yards)

◆ 2 goals (12 feet wide by 7 feet high)

◆ Marked striking circle 16 yards out from each goal post

◆ Field hockey sticks

◆ Pinnies or flags

◆ Field hockey ball (8 to 10 inches in circumference)

◆ Shin guards

◆ Goalie face masks

Terminology:

1. High Stick — Holding or swinging the blade above the knees
2. Slashing — Hitting with the stick
3. Hooking — Placing the stick between feet or legs
4. Body checking — Slamming into an opponent to gain an advantage
5. Lofting — Intentionally hitting the ball into the air

How to Play:

1. This is a modified version of Field Hockey.

2. Divide into teams with 11 players each.

3. Begin the game with a backward hit at the center of the field. Teams must be on sides.

4. A player may not shield or obstruct the ball by using the body. All participants have an equal opportunity to gain control of the ball during the dribble or the pass.

5. The goalie can attempt to stop the ball from crossing the goal line in any manner.

6. A player will not intentionally use the feet (or body) to control the ball.

7. It is illegal to high stick, slash, body check, hook, or intentionally loft the ball.

8. Violations outside the semi-circle will result in a free or indirect hit from the point of the infraction.

9. Violations inside the 25-yard line or semi-circle will result in a penalty corner free hit. The ball is placed at least 10 yards from the goal on the goal line. Only five defensive players are allowed behind the goal line and the rest must be past the centerline when contact is made.

10. Violations that prevent a score will result in a penalty stroke. One offensive player will challenge the goalie from seven yards out. Everyone else is beyond the 25-yard line.

11. When the defense intentionally hits the ball over the goal line, a penalty stroke will be awarded.

12. The entire ball must cross the goal line in order for it to score one point.

13. Scoring is not allowed from beyond the semi-circle.

14. After a team has scored, play is started again at center field.

15. A player may only score two goals in a row.

16. The defense will make all of the calls when there are no referees.

17. The team that is ahead after a given amount of time is the winner.

Student Tasks:

1. Pass to a teammate who then scores.

2. Be a goalie and do not let the other team score.

3. Dribble the ball around a defender and regain control.

4. Take the ball away from three different opponents.

Variations:

1. Form three teams and play a round robin. Each team would sit out one game.

2. Use two balls.

3. Change the ball to an eight-inch diameter vinyl-covered foam ball or softball-sized wiffle ball.

4. Divide each team into an attacking and defending group, in which neither may cross the centerline.

Illustration of a Field Hockey Layout

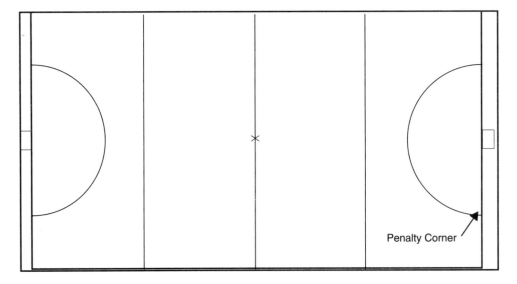

Penalty Corner

SUM IT FIELD HOCKEY

Objectives:

- Hit the ball into the opponent's goal.
- Score more goals than the opposition.
- Finish with the best overall record.

Essentials:

- Large field (100 yards by 60 yards)
- Field cones to mark the side lines, 10-yard strike zone, and goals
- Marked striking box 10 yards from the goal line
- Field hockey sticks
- Pinnies or flags
- Vinyl-covered Nerf™ ball (8-inch diameter)
- Shin guards

Terminology:

1. High Stick   Holding or swinging the blade above the knees
2. Slashing   Hitting with the stick
3. Hooking   Placing the stick between feet or legs
4. Body checking   Slamming into an opponent to gain an advantage

How to Play:

1. The rules of field hockey apply with a few exceptions.
2. Split a larger field into three smaller ones and play three games simultaneously (diagonally).
3. The field cones (goals) are placed five yards apart.
4. Divide into six teams composed of six players each.
5. Remember that a player may not shield or obstruct the ball by using the body. All participants have an equal opportunity to gain control of the ball during the dribble or pass.
6. Violations outside the strike box will result in a free or indirect hit from the point of the infraction.
7. Violations inside the 10-yard line or strike box will result in a penalty corner free hit. The ball is placed at the corner of the goal line. Only two defensive players are allowed behind the goal line and the rest must be past the center line when contact is made.
8. Violations that prevent a score will result in a penalty stroke. One offensive player will challenge the goalie from seven yards out. Everyone else is beyond the midfield markers.

9. Intentionally hitting the ball over the goal line, at any time by the defense, will result in a penalty stroke.

10. The entire ball must cross the goal line and travel below the goalie's waist in order to score.

11. Scoring is not allowed beyond the 10-yard strike box.

12. A player may not score two goals in a row.

13. Play a round-robin format with each game lasting from five to seven minutes.

14. The team that scores the most points during the day is the winner.

Student Tasks:

1. Pass to a teammate who then scores.

2. Be a goalie and do not let the other team score.

3. Dribble the ball around a defender and regain control.

4. Take the ball away from three different opponents.

Variations:

1. The team that allows the fewest scores during the day is the winner.

2. The team with the best record wins the tournament.

Diagram of a Sum It Field Hockey Field with Team Rotations

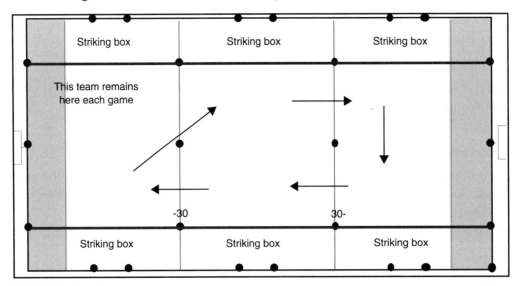

ATTACK ZONE

Objectives:

- ◆ Score more goals than the opposition does in a prescribed amount of time.
- ◆ Control the puck out of the attack zone.
- ◆ Hit the puck into the opponent's goal while on offense.

Essentials:

- ◆ Open floor or gymnasium
- ◆ Hockey sticks
- ◆ Soft rubber puck
- ◆ Face masks
- ◆ Shin protectors (optional)

- ◆ Goal
- ◆ Stopwatch (for penalties)
- ◆ Floor dividers (4 X 4's work well)
- ◆ Floor tape to mark the attack zone (optional)

Safety:

1. The goalies should wear protective face masks.
2. Do not allow the goalie to drop to her/his knees.
3. Never allow the stick blade to be brought higher than the knees.
4. Remove any player who is constantly being unsafe and allow that person to referee.

How to Play:

1. The rules of floor hockey apply with a few exceptions.
2. The game is played on half of a floor with one goal. Two different games can be played simultaneously (diagonally) also (use floor dividers).
3. Set up an attack zone with floor tape or use an existing line (see diagram below).
4. Start the game with a center bully in the attack zone. Whichever team hits the puck out of the attack zone immediately goes on the offensive.
5. Whenever the defensive team gains possession of the puck, they must get the puck into the attack zone and control it before going on the assault. If unsuccessful at this task, they will remain on defense.
6. Since only one player may be in the goalie box, opposing goalies must be ready to switch with each new defensive possession.
7. Play for a given amount of time to determine the winner.

Student Tasks:

1. While on defense, drag the puck into the attack zone and start the offense by passing it out.
2. Pass the puck into the attack zone to a teammate.
3. Prevent the defense from getting the puck to the attack zone.

Variations:

1. Use two goals and place them in the far corners. Goalies are always present.

2. Create two triangular attack zones in the near corners of the court.

3. Divide the gymnasium floor into four separate floors.

Illustration of a Court Layout for Attack Zone Hockey

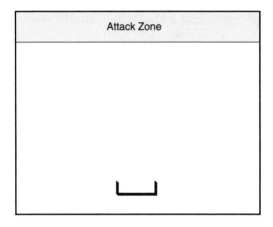

BARRIER BOUNCE

Objectives:

◆ Score more goals than the opposition can in a predetermined amount of time.

◆ Successfully negotiate the obstacles on the floor.

Essentials:

◆ Large open floor
◆ Hockey sticks
◆ Soft rubber puck
◆ Face masks

◆ Shin protectors (optional)
◆ 2 goals
◆ Stopwatch (for penalty box)
◆ 5 used car tires

Safety:

1. The goalies should wear protective face masks.

2. Do not allow the goalie to drop to her or his knees.

3. Never allow the stick blade to be brought higher than the knees.

4. Remove any player who is constantly being unsafe and allow that person to referee.

How to Play:

1. The basic rules of floor hockey apply to this game.

2. Create teams composed of four to six players each.

3. Place several used tires on the floor at strategic locations.

4. Participants may use the tires to pass against or as a defensive shield.

5. All players must travel around the tires. It is illegal to step over top of them, especially to gain an advantage.

6. Play for a predetermined number of minutes to determine a winner.

Student Tasks:

1. Pass to a teammate using a tire.

2. Pass to a player who then scores.

3. Be a goalie and prevent the opposition from scoring.

Variations:

1. Use a vinyl-covered (8-inch diameter) foam ball.

2. Add tumbling mats that are standing on end. Anytime a mat is knocked over by a player, the opposition will score an additional point.

Examples of Tire Locations used in Barrier Bounce

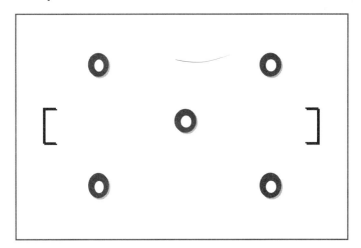

BOTTLENECK

Objectives:

◆ Score more goals than the opposition does in a prescribed amount of time.

◆ Knock over as many pins as possible with one shot.

Essentials:

- Large open floor
- Hockey sticks
- Soft rubber puck
- Face masks

- Shin protectors (optional)
- Stopwatch (for penalty box)
- 6 plastic bowling pins or large plastic soda containers

Safety:

1. The goalies should wear protective face masks.
2. Do not allow the goalie to drop to her/his knees.
3. Never allow the stick blade to be brought higher than the knees.
4. Remove any player who is constantly being unsafe and allow that person to referee.

How to Play:

1. With a few exceptions, the rules of floor hockey apply to this game.
2. Where the goal would normally be located, place three pins in a triangle about 12 inches apart (see illustration below).
3. The pins may be knocked down from any direction by the opposition.
4. The goalie must continually move around the pins in order to prevent them from being knocked over. If the goalie accidentally knocks one or more pins over while playing defense, the opposition is awarded one point, and a face off ensues near the goal.
5. Each pin knocked down by the puck is worth one point. (Three points could be scored at any one time.)
6. After the puck has toppled any or all of the pins, play is stopped. The pins are reset, and the scored-upon team begins play at center court.
7. Play for a predetermined amount of time to decide the winner.

Student Tasks:

1. Knock over a pin.
2. Upset all three pins with one shot.
3. The goalie allows her/his team to win by five or more points.

Variations:

1. When the puck knocks down all three pins, award five points.
2. Remove the floor cones, set up the pins like at a bowling alley, and allow one or two goalies to protect them. Award extra points for a strike.
3. Use a vinyl-covered foam ball.

Depiction of the Pin Placement in Bottleneck

BROOM BALL

Objectives:

- ◆ Score more points than the opposition does.
- ◆ Hit the ball into a goal.
- ◆ Develop teamwork.

Essentials:

- ◆ Large open area or gymnasium
- ◆ 12 long-handled brooms
- ◆ Vinyl-covered foam ball (11-inch diameter)
- ◆ 2 goals
- ◆ Stopwatch for timing penalties

How to Play:

1. The rules of floor hockey apply to this game.
2. Divide into equal teams and begin play for a predetermined amount of time.
3. Several times during the contest an alert whistle is blown to stop play. Each participant must begin balancing the broom on a finger or in the palm until the next whistle signals the resumption of play (10 seconds).
4. A player whose broom falls to the floor during the time out goes to the penalty box for 30 seconds.
5. A player may not score two goals in a row.
6. Highest score at the end of the game wins.

Student Tasks:

1. Never drop the broom.

2. Pass the ball for an assist.

3. Take the ball away from two different opponents.

Variations:

1. Give the opposition one point for each broom that falls to the floor.

2. Require that a player must remain stationary during the balancing act.

3. Allow players to run around and upset another's broom while balancing their own.

4. On the alert whistle, a player must exchange brooms with another teammate before resuming play.

FIVE TEAM

Objectives:

◆ Score more goals than the opposition does.

◆ Develop teamwork.

Essentials:

◆ Large open floor   ◆ Stopwatch

◆ Hockey sticks   ◆ Floor dividers (4 × 4s work well)

◆ 4 goals   ◆ Face masks for goalies

◆ 2 soft rubber pucks   ◆ Shin protectors (optional)

Terminology:

1. Hat Trick   Score three goals in a game

2. Center bully   Tap sticks together three times

3.	High Stick	Holding or swinging the blade above the knees
4.	Slashing	Hitting with the stick
5.	Hooking	Placing the stick between feet or legs
6.	Body checking	Slamming into an opponent to gain an advantage
7.	Lofting	Intentionally hitting the puck into the air

Safety:

1. The goalies should wear protective face masks.

2. Do not allow the goalie to drop to her or his knees.

3. Never allow the stick blade to be brought higher than the knees.

4. Remove any player that is constantly being unsafe and allow that person to referee.

How to Play:

1. Divide the floor in half and play two games simultaneously (diagonally).

2. Make five equal teams. Play a round-robin tournament with each team getting one rest session (see illustration below).

3. Start the game with a center bully at middle court. Both teams must be on sides.

4. The goalie must remain standing at all times. Goalies will use only their feet or stick to deflect a puck. They may only step on the puck within one step of the goal, in order to stop play. A face-off will transpire about 15 feet away at a 45-degree angle.

5. A spread handgrip must be maintained on the stick when shooting or passing.

6. Grabbing an airborne puck is legal as long as it is returned directly to the floor without an advantage.

7. A player may intentionally use the feet to control the puck but must use the stick to score a goal.

8. It is illegal to high stick, slash, body check, hook, or intentionally loft the puck. Violators will be sent to the penalty box for 30 seconds. Each time the same person returns to the penalty box thereafter, the time doubles.

9. The entire puck must cross the line in order for it to score.

10. Scoring is not allowed beyond half court.

11. After a team has scored, play is started at center court as in soccer.

12. A player may only score **two** goals in a row.

13. Defense makes the calls when there are no referees. (Arguing is not allowed.)

14. The team with the best record wins the Stanley Cup.

Student Tasks:

1. Pass to a teammate who then scores.

2. Be a goalie and do not let the other team score.

3. Pass the puck around a defender and regain control.

Variations:

1. Use the "Mix 'n' Match" 11-team format and play for several days. For the last day, have the Stanley Cup Championship. Each group will alternate playing two or three timed periods.

2. Turn both nets around and place them at center court about 10 feet apart.

Illustration of Five Team Floor Hockey

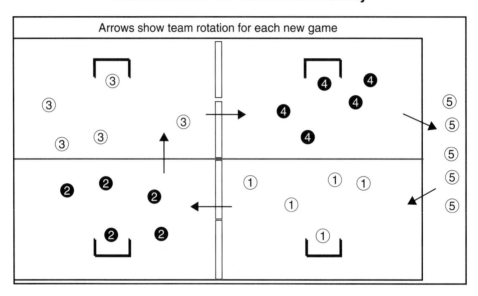

FLOOR HOCKEY GOLF

Objectives:

◆ Finish a course with the fewest strokes.

◆ Understand the basic rules and terms of golf.

◆ Develop hand-and-eye coordination.

Essentials:

◆ Gymnasium or large play area

◆ Hockey sticks

◆ Numbered hockey pucks

◆ Several pins (bowling pins, coffee cans, field cones etc.)

◆ Obstacles (tires, hula hoops, tumbling mats, football blocking pads, lumber, etc.)

◆ Scorecards and pencils (see the section on "Golf" for score sheets)

Terminology:

1. Bogey   Strokes taken over the par

2. Par   Average number of strokes needed make the pin

3. Birdie   One under par

4. Eagle   Two under par

5. Hole In One   Made a pin with the first shot

6. Pin   Object that the puck hits or goes into

7. Away   Player farthest from the pin

8. Lie   Where the puck stops and rests

9. Putt   Any short shot to the pin

How to Play:

1. The rules and etiquette of golf apply to this game.
2. Set up a 9 or 18 pin course by placing various obstacles on the floor.
3. Send a group of four players to each pin. Participants may share the same stick.
4. Take turns, as in golf, to make each pin.
5. Remove and replace any puck that impedes another player's shot.
6. Record the number of strokes taken at each pin.
7. Move to the next pin after all players have finished.
8. The player who uses the lowest number of strokes to complete the course, wins.

Student Tasks:

1. Win a game by three or more strokes.
2. Shoot a lower score than your opponent on a predetermined hole.
3. Shoot a hole in one.

Variations:

1. Allow the class to design the course layout.
2. Make teams and combine the scores.
3. Make teams and after both players have shot, pick the best lie.
4. Use one ball per team, and alternate players each stroke.

Illustration of a Floor Hockey Golf Course Layout

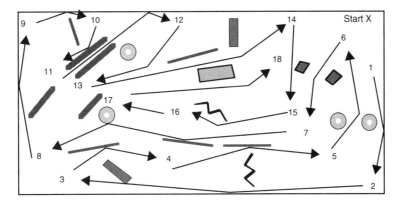

NO CURB

Objectives:

- ◆ Score more goals than the opposition does.
- ◆ Place the puck into the goal.
- ◆ Perform controlled and exacting stick movements to keep the puck in play.

Essentials:

- ◆ Open floor or gymnasium
- ◆ 8 hockey sticks
- ◆ Soft rubber puck
- ◆ 2 face masks
- ◆ Shin protectors
- ◆ 2 goals
- ◆ Stopwatch (for penalties)

Safety:

1. The goalies should wear protective face masks.
2. Do not allow the goalie to drop to her or his knees.
3. Never allow the stick blade to be brought higher than the knees.
4. Remove any player that is constantly being unsafe and allow that person to referee.

How to Play:

1. The rules of floor hockey apply to this game with a few changes.
2. The game is played with the boundaries located four to six feet within the walls.
3. The goals are placed at approximately quarter court on both ends.
4. Make two teams with each team lining up around the perimeter of its own half. These players can help retrieve errant shots or passes but are not allowed to participate in the action.
5. Four players from each team enter the court and play for two minutes. Every two minutes, four more players enter and the ones on the court will exit and proceed to the end of the line.
6. The rules for soccer apply to the puck when it is hit out of bounds or over the end line.
7. Players may not score from beyond the opposite goalie box.
8. Play for a predetermined amount of time to determine the winners.

Student Tasks:

1. Assist in a score.
2. Drag or pass the puck by one or more defenders while maintaining control.

3. Be a goalie.

4. Cause a shutout.

Variations:

1. Use a vinyl-covered (8-inch diameter) ball.

2. Play this game on an outdoor field.

3. Create four teams and join two different teams with each new contest. After the three games have been played, the best record determines the winners.

4. Allow players who are out-of-bounds to use their feet to stop and immediately kick the puck back into play.

Illustration of a No Curb Hockey Floor Layout and Team Rotation

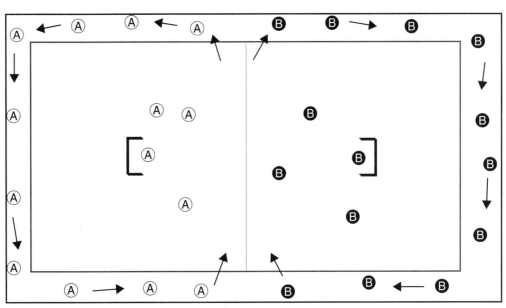

DISC FORT KNOX

Objectives:

- ◆ Score more points than the opposition does.
- ◆ Capture an opponent's guarded gold.
- ◆ Prevent the team's gold from being looted.
- ◆ Return frozen players back into play.

Essentials:

- ◆ Field or gymnasium
- ◆ 4 different colored discs
- ◆ Pinnies or flags
- ◆ Boundary cones

How to Play:

1. Divide the playing area into four equal sections. Place a hula hoop (vault) in the far corner of each zone. Place the disc (gold bar) inside each hula hoop.

2. Divide the class into four equal teams.

3. Teams may enter the opposing territories and attempt to steal that disc. If successful, a player will try and return it to her or his own vault by running over an inner boundary line or by throwing it to a teammate located in the same zone, who then runs it over.

4. Players may not throw the disc over any inner or outer boundary line. (Remember that the disc must be carried across.)

5. A player may possess more than one disc at a time.

6. If an offensive player is tagged (below the shoulders) with one hand or drops a thrown disc in an opponent's territory, that player must immediately squat down and remain frozen. Players may be unfrozen when a teammate leapfrogs over them.

7. A player who is tagged with one hand while in possession of a disc is frozen and must give it up. The disc is then collected and returned to the vault.

8. Any defender of Fort Knox must be 10 feet away from the vault (hula hoop) boundary.

9. When both bars of gold have been taken outside of a team's area, that team is eliminated.

10. Safe areas are a team's own side of the field or the other team's Fort Knox. Only one foot needs to be over the line to be safe. Also, there is no time limit once inside a safe zone.

11. First team to eliminate all of the other teams receives one point.

12. To start the next game, all teams will rotate one field clockwise (takes away wind or sun advantage).

13. The team with the most points at the end of the period is declared the winner.

FLYING DISC

Student Tasks:

1. Retrieve two or more gold bars.
2. Tag a person that is in possession of the gold.
3. Defrost a frozen runner.
4. Catch a thrown disc.
5. Intercept a thrown disc.

Variations:

1. Each player will wear one or two flags as in flag football. When a flag is pulled, the player is frozen.
2. Use four discs.
3. If player A tags player B in team C's territory, B is frozen and must relinquish the disc to A.
4. Allow only partners to thaw each other. If both players are frozen, then they are retired from play.
5. Tagged runners must stand with straddled legs. To be unfrozen, players must have another player crawl under their legs.
6. Be the first team to score a given number of points.

Diagram of a Disc Fort Knox Field Layout

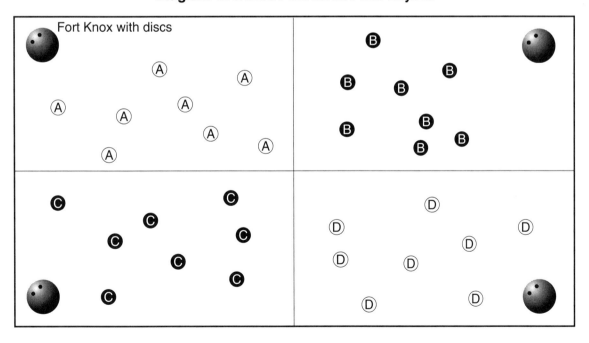

DISC GOLF II

Objectives:

◆ Cover the course in the least amount of throws.

◆ Know the basic rules and terms of golf.

◆ Develop throwing accuracy and catching skills.

Essentials:

◆ Large outdoor area

◆ Discs

◆ Course maps

◆ Pencils

◆ Score sheets (see "Golf" for copies)

◆ Field cones (pins)

Terminology:

1. Bogey — Over par
2. Par — Average
3. Birdie — One under par
4. Eagle — Two under par
5. Hole In One — Made in one throw
6. Fore — Protect your head
7. Pin — Hole or object that is to be made or hit
8. Away — Player farthest from the hole
9. Lie — Where the disc lands and stops
10. Putt — Any short toss to the pin
11. Mulligan — Extra throw that does not cost a stroke

How to Play:

1. Divide into pairs and challenge another couple.
2. Use a "shotgun start" by sending flights to different pins.
3. Start by throwing the disc to your partner from behind each pin.
4. The disc must be successfully caught each time.
5. Each missed catch will add an extra stroke to the team score. When dropped, the disc is returned to the same thrower and the toss is then repeated from the same location.
6. Any unplayable lie can be relocated with a one-stroke penalty.
7. Alternate successful throws and catches while working toward the next pin.
8. The disc can be thrown in any manner.

© 2001 Parker Publishing Company

9. The pair with the lowest score on the previous hole leads off. In case of a tie, go back one, two, or three holes if necessary.

10. The player farthest from the hole will always toss first.

11. A player may not step past the lie of the previous hit when attempting the next launch.

12. Follow through (steps) is not allowed within 30 feet of the pin.

13. In order for the pin to be made, the partner must have one foot in contact with the cone when the disc is caught.

14. The team that covers the course with the least number of strokes is the winner.

Student Tasks:

1. Make a hole in one.
2. Make ten catches in a row.
3. Make a certain number of birdies during a round.
4. Come from behind and win a match.

Variations:

1. When the disc is dropped or not caught, the next throw is from where it comes to rest. One penalty point is still given.
2. Play the course in reverse order: 18, 17, 16, etc.
3. Play mixed doubles.
4. Allow two chances with the first throw.
5. All participants must throw with the off arm.

FOUR-WAY ULTIMATE

Objectives:

♦ Score seven points before the opposition does.
♦ Develop teamwork and cooperation.

Essentials:

♦ Field or gymnasium
♦ 3 flying discs
♦ Pinnies or flags
♦ Boundary cones

How to Play:

1. The basic rules of Ultimate Disc pertain to this game with a few modifications.
2. Divide the playing area into four equal sections. Mark a scoring zone in the far corner of each.

3. Divide the class into four equal teams with six to eight players on each.

4. Each team may enter any territory and attempt to score a point by catching a disc in the opposition's scoring zone.

5. Play is continuous, even after a score.

6. If the disc is dropped, thrown out-of-bounds, or scored, the team that owns the square will take possession and put the disc back into play.

7. Trailing teams may unite and gang up against the leading team.

8. A player may possess more than one disc at a time.

9. The disc may be thrown in any manner.

10. The disc may not be handed from one player to another.

11. Players may not take steps once they are in possession. However, momentum must be taken into consideration when a player catches the disc and takes a step or two while trying to stop.

12. A player with possession may use one foot as a pivot.

13. The thrower may not push the defensive person to gain an advantage.

14. The player may not catch her/his own thrown disc.

15. The thrower will have 10 seconds of possession time.

16. A point is scored if the disc is caught while both feet are in the end zone.

17. Only one defensive person may guard the player that has possession of the disc and must be at least one step away.

18. The disc may not be forcefully taken or knocked away from the offense. (Play the disc, not the player with the disc.)

19. First team to score seven points wins.

Student Tasks:

1. Catch a disc in any scoring zone.
2. Intercept a thrown disc.
3. Prevent a score.
4. Assist in a score.
5. Catch four passes during a contest.

Variations:

1. The player with the disc may not be guarded.

2. When a thrown disc does not make contact with another player and lands on the playing surface, the first player to it gets possession.

3. Use two discs or more discs. After any score, play is stopped. Teams will regroup in their own territory before resuming play. The team that scored does not receive a disc to start play.

Illustration of a Four-Way Ultimate Field Layout

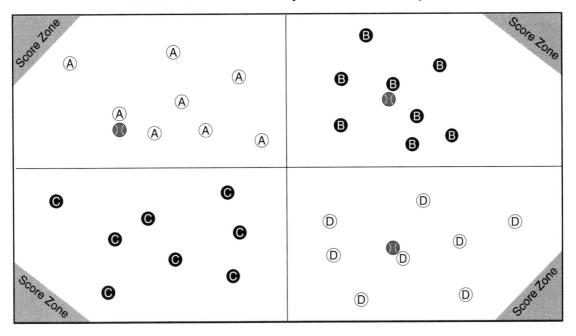

ULTIMATE II

Objectives:

◆ Catch the disc inside the end zone.

◆ Throw the disc to a teammate in the end zone.

Essentials:

◆ Field

◆ Pinnies or flags

◆ 1 disc for each game

How to Play:

1. Form teams composed of five to six players each.

2. Divide a standard football field into several smaller fields and play diagonally.

3. A throw-off will occur at the start of a game. After a goal is scored, both teams will switch ends.

4. Start with A on the goal line and B behind the centerline.

5. The A team throws it to the B team.

6. No player from A team may touch the disc while it is in the air before a player from B has.

7. If B team catches it they may start immediately at that point.

8. When B team attempts to catch the disc but drops it, A team takes possession at that point.

9. If B team lets it hit the field, they take it at that spot.

10. If the disc goes out of bounds, B can choose to take it at that spot or have A throw it again.

11. When the throw goes into the end zone, B will take it on the goal line.

12. Offense:

    a. Will attempt to throw and catch the disc in the end zone for a score.

    b. May toss the disc in any manner.

    c. The disc may not be handed from one player to another.

    d. Players may not take steps once they are in possession. However, momentum must be taken into consideration when a player catches the disc and takes a step or two while trying to stop.

    e. A player with possession may use one foot as a pivot.

    f. If the disc is dropped or thrown out-of-bounds, the defensive team will take possession at that point.

    g. The thrower may not catch the disc unless a defender deflected it first.

    h. The thrower may possess the disc for only 10 seconds.

    i. A point is scored if the disc is caught while both feet are in the end zone.

13. Defense:

    a. Will not guard the player that has possession of the disc.

    b. May count out loud to let the offense know the time of possession.

    c. A defensive player who deflects the disk to the ground still gains possession.

14. When playing coed, a girl and a boy must be involved in each scoring drive.

15. When a thrown disc does not make contact with any player before landing on the playing surface, the first player (from either team) to touch it gets control.

16. The team that is ahead after a predetermined amount of time is the winner.

Student Tasks:

1. Throw a number of completed passes.

2. Deflect a throw.

3. Directly prevent a score.

4. Assist in a score.

Variations:

1. If the disc is dropped or touched by the defense while trying to catch it, the offense will maintain possession. If this were to occur in the offensive end zone, then the offense would take possession one yard out.

2. Use the Mix 'n' Match format and play for several days.

3. Form four teams, join two different teams for each game and play a round-robin tournament.

Illustration of Ultimate II

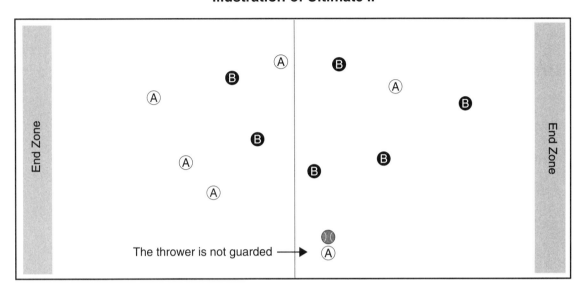

The thrower is not guarded

ARENA FOOTBALL

Objectives:

◆ Score more points than the opposition.

◆ Run or pass the ball over the goal line.

Essentials:

◆ Gymnasium basketball court

◆ Foam football

◆ Football flags

◆ 8 floor cones

Terminology:

1. Holding — Grabbing on to a defensive player
2. Flag guarding — Using the hands or arms to shield the flags
3. Lateral — Pitching the ball backwards
4. Line of scrimmage — Location of the ball each play
5. Safety — Downing the opposition in their own end zone

Safety:

1. Make sure there is plenty of room at each end of the court.

2. Unnecessary roughness should not be tolerated and will result in an automatic first down and/or penalty.

3. The ball is immediately down on any fumble and the point of contact becomes the line of scrimmage. (This prevents players from diving on top of each other in order to gain possession.)

How to Play:

1. All of the rules of football apply to this game with a few modifications.

2. Choose teams with five to six players each.

3. Using the floor cones, divide the basketball court into four equal sections (see diagram below).

4. Kick Off:

   a. The ball is held in place on the end line. The kicker is allowed only one step prior to kicking the ball.

   b. The ball must cross the far quarter line before it is returnable.

   c. If the ball is kicked out-of-bounds, the receiving team may elect to take another kick or take it parallel to where it went out.

   d. If the ball goes over the goal line without being touched, it may be run out or taken on the quarter line.

   e. The receiving team must line up behind its own quarter line.

5. Offense:

   a. Must be on side and motionless prior to any kickoff or hike.

   b. Any player may catch a pass.

   c. Forward passes are allowed behind the line of scrimmage.

   d. Incomplete passes will be returned to the original line of scrimmage with loss of a down.

   e. Laterals are allowed at anytime.

   f. Thirty seconds are given between the down, huddle, and resumption of the next play.

   g. Teams have three attempts to get to half court and then an additional three downs to score.

   h. The opposition may be blocked with the arms folded (moving screen). There is a one-zone penalty for holding.

   i. Must have flags available on the hips and cannot flag guard when running. One flag needs to be pulled for a runner to be down.

   j. A ball carrier will be down if the knee or body touches the floor.

   k. The ball must be hiked between the legs and from the floor.

   l. Players must rotate one position clockwise every play.

   m. Teams will switch ends after a touchdown.

   n. A player may score only two touchdowns in a row.

6. Defense:

   a. Must be on side prior to the offense hiking the ball and can move around freely prior to the hike.

   b. Can cross the line of scrimmage as soon as the ball is hiked.

   c. Cannot intentionally hit the ball from the hands of a runner.

   d. Will referee and call any violations. The call is never wrong.

7. Scoring:

   a. Touchdown = 6

   b. Extra point = 2 (run only)

   c. Safety = 2

   d. Field Goal = 3 (kicking the ball against the backboard or making the ball go directly over the top of it)

8. Play for a predetermined amount of time or to a given number of points to determine the winner.

Student Tasks:

1. Pull a given number of flags.

2. Complete a given number of passes.

3. Make a given number of interceptions.

4. Catch two passes.

5. Pass for a touchdown.

6. Kick a field goal.

Variations:

1. A team has four downs (attempts) in which to score.

2. Make four teams and play a round-robin tournament format on side-by-side basketball courts.

3. Use the Simple Mix 'n' Match format and play several games.

Example of an Arena Football Formation

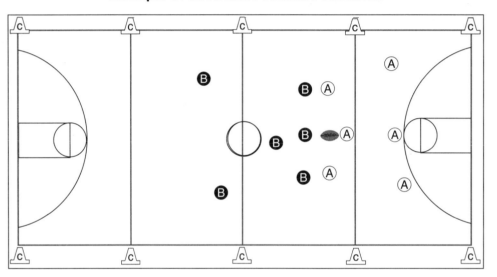

ARENA FOOTBALL ULTIMATE

Objectives:

◆ Score more points than the opposition does.

◆ Run or pass the ball over the goal line.

◆ Create teamwork and cooperation.

Essentials:

◆ Gymnasium basketball court

◆ Foam football

◆ Football flags

◆ 8 floor cones

Safety:

1. Make sure there is plenty of room at each end of the court for the end zone.

2. Unnecessary roughness should not be tolerated and will result in an automatic
   first down and/or a penalty.

3. The ball is down on any fumble and the point of contact becomes the line of scrimmage.

How to Play:

1. Each team will be composed of five or six players.

2. Using the floor cones, divide the basketball court into four equal sections (see diagram below).

3. General rules:

    a. The ball goes to the other team on all fumbles (except the kick off) and incomplete passes. Possession is taken where the ball first contacted the floor.

    b. If the defense deflects the ball to the floor, the offense will retain possession at the point of contact with loss of down. If it were fourth down, it would be repeated.

    c. If a ball falls incomplete in the end zone, the defensive team begins play on the near quarter line.

4. Starting the game:

    a. The ball is held in place on the end line. The kicker is allowed one step prior to kicking the ball.

    b. The ball must cross the far quarter line before it is returnable.

    c. If the ball is kicked out-of-bounds or against the far wall, the receiving team may elect to allow another kick, or take it where it went out.

    d. If the ball hits the far wall or goes over the goal line without being touched, it may be run out or taken on the quarter line.

    e. The defense must line up behind its own quarter line.

    f. When the ball is fumbled on the kick off, first down begins at the point of contact.

    g. Forward passing (as in keep away) is allowed after possession has been established.

5. Offense:

    a. Must be on side and motionless prior to any kickoff or hike.

    b. Can move past the line of scrimmage as soon as the ball is hiked.

    c. May never huddle.

    d. Have three tries (downs) to score.

    e. May block on the defense with the arms folded (moving screen).

    f. Can spin while running with the ball.

    g. Must have flags available on the hips and cannot flag-guard when running. Only one flag needs to be pulled to be down.

    h. The runner is down when the knee or body touches the floor.

    i. May pitch, lateral, or pass the ball any number of times and in any direction (keep away).

    j. Can hike the ball in any manner from the floor.

   k. Must have a new player be quarterback each down.

   l. The quarterback may run immediately after receiving the hike.

   m. Teams will switch ends after each touchdown.

   n. A player may score only two touchdowns in a row.

6. Defense:

   a. Must be on side prior to the offense hiking the ball and may move around freely prior to the hike.

   b. Is allowed to cross the line of scrimmage as soon as the quarterback touches the ball.

   c. Cannot intentionally hit the ball from the hands of a runner.

   d. Will referee and call out any violation. (The call is never wrong.)

7. Scoring:

   a. Touchdown = 7 points

   b. Safety = 2 points

   c. Field Goal = 5 (kicking the ball against the basketball backboard or going directly over the top of it)

8. Play for a predetermined amount of time to determine the winner.

Student Tasks:

1. Pull a given number of flags.

2. Complete a given number of passes.

3. Intercept a pass.

4. Pass for a touchdown.

5. Kick a field goal.

6. Have each member of a team score a T.D. during a tournament.

Variations:

1. Change the type of ball used.

2. Make four teams and play a round-robin tournament format on side-by-side basketball courts.

3. Use the Simple Mix 'n' Match format and play several games.

Illustration of an Arena Football Ultimate Kick-Off

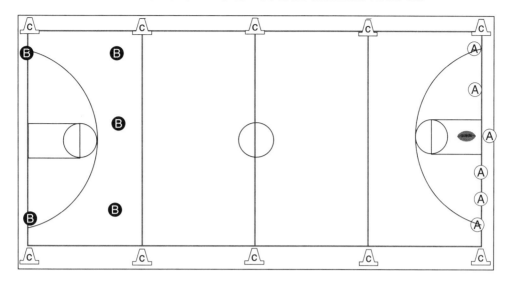

FOOTBALL HOOPS

Objectives:

- ◆ Score more points than the opposition.
- ◆ Dribble or bounce-pass the ball over the goal line.
- ◆ Shoot the ball into a basket.

Essentials:

- ◆ Gymnasium basketball court
- ◆ Basketball
- ◆ Football flags

Safety:

1. Make sure there is plenty of room at each end of the court for the end zone.
2. Unnecessary roughness should not be tolerated and will result in an automatic first down.

How to Play:

1. Divide into two equal teams. Issue contrasting colored flags to each team.
2. Send five players from each team to the court. The remainder of the team will line up along the opposite sidelines.
3. Rotate in six new players every three minutes.
4. Determine which team will initiate play by performing rock, paper, and scissors.

5. To start play, each team lines up on opposite end lines. One team has the ball and begins to advance it down the court either in the basketball mode (passing) or football mode (dribbling).

6. If the flag is pulled, the first play from the line of scrimmage is from a football formation.

7. Football mode:

   a. The ball must be dribbled.

   b. Double dribbling is illegal.

   c. If a player's flag is pulled while dribbling or in possession of the ball, she/he is down.

   d. The ball must be dribbled across the baseline in order to score a touchdown.

8. Basketball mode:

   a. Dribbling is not allowed.

   b. The ball must be passed in the air from player to player in order to score a basket.

   c. If the ball is fumbled or illegally dribbled, the defense takes over at the spot where the ball came into contact with the floor or where the ball left the court if it went out-of-bounds. (The next play is initiated from a football formation.)

9. To begin play after a score, the offensive team lines up on the three-point arc and the quarterback stands on the goal line. The quarterback passes or dribbles the ball to initiate play. The defense will line up on or behind half court and may advance as soon as the quarterback moves.

10. Offense:

    a. Can not go from one mode to another.

    b. Must be on side prior to the snap and motionless.

    c. The quarterback will determine the mode (basketball / football) with a dribble or pass from the hike, but may not shoot the ball at the basket directly from the hike.

    d. Can move across the scrimmage line as soon as the ball is hiked.

    e. Huddles are not allowed.

    f. Receive three chances (downs) to score.

    g. May block (set screens) on the defense with the arms folded.

    h. Must have flags available on the hips and cannot flag guard when dribbling or in possession of the ball. Only one flag needs to be pulled.

    i. Must hike the ball as in football.

    j. Everyone must be quarterback before a player may be it twice.

    k. Rebounds that hit the floor must be played in the football mode.

    l. Rebounds that are grabbed while in the air can be played either by dribbling, passing, or shooting.

    m. Defensive fouls will be called by the offense and will result in down over, or if the fouled player was shooting, she/he may elect to shoot two free throws.

    n. A player may only score five points in a row.

11. Loss of down:

    a. Dribbling out-of-bounds.

    b. Flag pulled while dribbling or holding the ball.

    c. Traveling (steps) while in the basketball mode.

12. Loss of possession:

    a. Any jump ball.

    b. Double dribbling.

    c. All incomplete passes or deflected passes by the defense.

    d. Failure to score in three downs.

    e. Dribbling while in the basketball phase.

    f. Shooting a ball at the basket that misses the rim and backboard then hits the floor.

13. Defense:

    a. Must be on side prior to the offense hiking the ball.

    b. Can cross the line of scrimmage after the quarterback has received the ball.

    c. May choose to intercept a pass or pull the flag of the person dribbling the ball.

    d. Will referee and call any violations. The call is never wrong.

14. Scoring:

    a. Touchdown   3 points

    b. Safety   2 points

    c. Basket   2 or 3 (depending on location)

    d. Free throw   1 point

15. Play for a predetermined amount of time to determine the winner.

Student Tasks:

1. Pull a given number of flags.

2. Complete a given number of passes.

3. Make a given number of interceptions.

4. Pass for a given number of touchdowns.

5. Kick a field goal.

6. Have each member of a team score a T.D. during the daily games.

Variations:

1. While in the football mode, allow bounce passes from player to player.

2. Make four teams and play a round-robin tournament format on side-by-side basketball courts.

3. Use a different type of ball (such as a football).

4. Use the "Mix 'n' Match" format and play several games daily.

Illustration of a Football Hoops Formation to Start Play

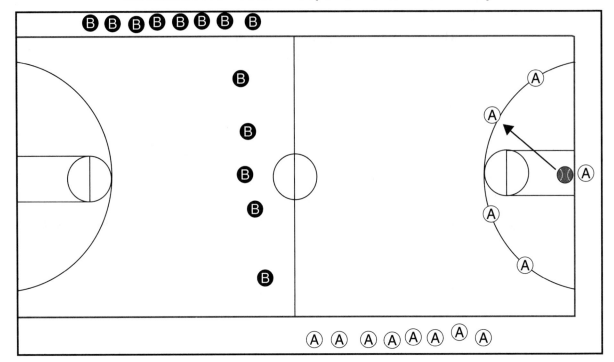

BEST BALL

Objectives:

- Finish a course with the fewest strokes possible.
- Improve and lower a score by sharing the better ball lie each stroke.
- Allow golfers to take a chance when one ball is already in good position.
- Learn from a partner's mistake.

Essentials:

- Outdoor area or field
- Golf clubs (can be shared)
- Small wiffle balls (numbered)
- Carpet squares (or something similar) for teeing off
- Several pins (hula hoops, coffee cans, or field cones)
- Pencils
- Scorecards (located at the end of this section)

How to Play:

1. The rules of golf apply to this game.
2. Design a 9- or 18-hole course.
3. Form teams of two players each. Each flight should have at least two teams.
4. Distribute a bag of clubs, scorecard, pencil, carpet, and balls to each group.
5. Send each flight to a different pin (shotgun start).
6. Everyone in the flight will hit from the same starting point. Each team will pick their best-positioned ball. All teammates will hit their next shot from this location. Continue this system with each pin.
7. Lowest team score wins.

Student Tasks:

1. Hit an eagle.
2. Make a certain number of birdies during a round.
3. Come from behind and win the match.
4. Use your ball position twice during any hole.

Variations:

1. Play mixed doubles.
2. Make teams consisting of three players.
3. Allow students to putt with a real golf ball.
4. Play the course in reverse.

Example of the Second Stroke Choice in Best Ball

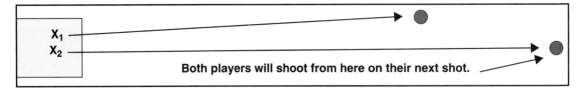

Both players will shoot from here on their next shot.

DRIVING RANGE

Objectives:

◆ Learn basic techniques of using a golf club.

◆ Practice swinging the club properly for distance and accuracy.

Essentials:

◆ Large outdoor field (football field works because of the yard lines)

◆ Golf clubs and irons (a few left-handed, too)

◆ Plenty of small numbered wiffle balls

◆ Carpet squares or something similar for teeing off (prevents divots)

◆ Field cones for distance markers

Safety:

1. Create plenty of space around players for swinging the clubs and irons. Use both ends of a field when more room is needed.

2. Never allow retrieval of the balls while others are still hitting.

How to Play:

1. Explain safety issues involved with golf and demonstrate the basics of the stance, grip, and swing, and then disperse the class to the driving range.

2. Each student will have one of the various drivers or irons, carpet square (for teeing off), and 10 wiffle balls.

3. Once everyone has finished hitting, the clubs are placed on the carpet and the students are sent to the field to gather up 10 wiffle balls each.

4. Upon returning to the carpet, all participants will rotate one position clockwise. This allows for practice with a different driver or iron. Repeat this process.

Student Tasks:

1. Make three balls land within five yards of each other.

2. Successfully hit five balls in a row.

3. Make five of the ten balls stop within five yards of a distance cone or line.

Variations:

1. Create pairs in which one stands behind the hitter and verbally assists with instructional tips. After shagging the balls, both switch roles.

2. One person hits a ball. The next golfer attempts to see how close she or he can place a ball to the first one. Switch and repeat scenario. Winner is determined by being the closest, four out of seven times.

Example of a Driving Range using Both Ends

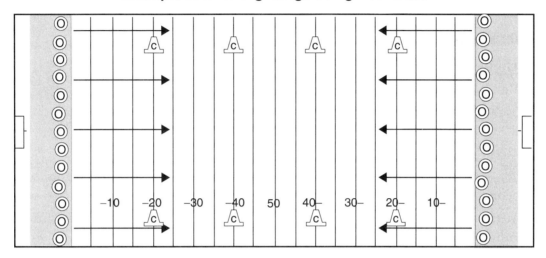

HIT A WINNER

Objectives:

◆ Hit the ball closer to an object than the others in the group did.

◆ Improve accuracy when hitting a ball.

Essentials:

◆ Large field

◆ Plenty of numbered wiffle balls

◆ Golf clubs

◆ Various types of objects (tires, cones, hula hoops, etc.)

◆ Measuring tape (track and field type)

How to Play:

1. Scatter several objects around the field.

2. Break into groups with two to four golfers in each.

3. Call out a designated target.

4. Each student will get two attempts to hit a ball closest to the target. Rotate until everyone in the group has finished.

5. Next, send everyone out to determine the winner.

6. Closest ball receives one point, next acquires two, and so forth.

7. Pick out a new pin and repeat the above process.

8. When a predetermined number of targets have been completed, tally the scores to determine the winner.

9. Lowest score in each group is the winner.

Student Tasks:

1. Hit the closest ball to the target twice.

2. Be first or second on two consecutive pins.

3. Make direct contact with a pin (hole in one).

Variations:

1. Alter the scoring so that closest ball acquires two points and the second closest scores one point.

2. Within a group of four, make two mini teams that will compete against each other. Use the scoring method mentioned in #1. A mini team could score all three points.

Example of a Field Layout for Hit a Winner

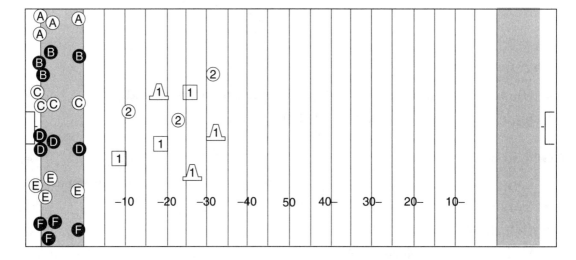

INDOOR PUTT PUTT

Objectives:

- Finish a course with the fewest strokes.
- Gain an understanding of the basic rules and terms of golf.
- Develop hand-and-eye coordination.

Essentials:

- Gymnasium or large indoor area
- Several putters
- Golf size wiffle balls with a different number written on each
- Several pins (bowling pins, coffee cans, field cones, etc.)
- Obstacles (tires, hula hoops, tumbling mats, football blocking pads, lumber, etc.)
- Pencils
- Scorecards (found at the end of this section)

Terminology:

1.	Bogey	Strokes taken over the par
2.	Par	Average number of strokes needed make the pin
3.	Birdie	1 under par
4.	Eagle	2 under par
5.	Hole in One	Make a pin with the first shot
6.	Pin	Object that the puck hits or goes into
7.	Away	Player farthest from the pin
8.	Lie	Location at which the puck stops
9.	Putt	Any short shot to the pin

How to Play:

1. The rules and etiquette of golf apply to this game.
2. Set up a 9-hole or 18-hole course by placing various obstacles and pins on the floor.
3. Send a group of four players to each pin. Participants may share putters.
4. Take turns, as in golf, to make each pin.
5. Remove and replace any ball that impedes another's shot.
6. Record the number of strokes taken by each player at each pin.
7. Move to the next pin after everyone has finished.
8. The player that used the fewest number of strokes wins.

Student Tasks:

1. Win a game by three or more strokes.

2. Shoot a lower score than your opponent on a predetermined hole.

3. Shoot a hole in one.

Variations:

1. Allow the class to design the course layout.

2. Make teams and after both players have shot, pick the best lie.

3. Make teams and combine the scores.

4. Use one ball per team, and alternate players each stroke.

Illustration of an Indoor Putt Putt Course Layout

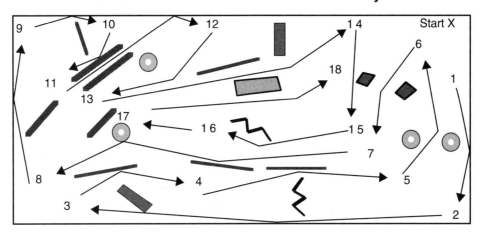

LONE RANGER

Objectives:

◆ Accumulate the most points.

◆ Hit a ball for distance and accuracy.

◆ Prevent hitting the ball so that it hooks or slices.

Essentials:

◆ Large field
◆ Golf clubs
◆ Carpet pads
◆ Plenty of wiffle balls
◆ Several field cones

Terminology:

1. Hook — A ball is whacked to the left side of a right-handed player

2. Slice — A ball is smacked to the right side of a right-handed player

GOLF

How to Play:

1. Set up the field with six stations. Place a driver at three of the locations and a #2 iron at the other three.

2. Send equal numbers of participants to each station.

3. Each player will hit two numbered balls down the line of cones.

4. The distance and accuracy is determined by walking in a line perpendicular to the row of cones. Count the number of steps taken to the ball. Walk back toward the tee this same number of steps. Place the ball at this point (see example below).

5. The person's ball that is the farthest from the tee is the winner and will receive two points. Second place receives one.

6. Rotate the groups through all six stations.

7. The player with the highest score after completing all six stations is the winner.

Student Tasks:

1. Score points at two different stations.

2. Finish in the top ten.

3. Hit a ball that rests less than a yard from a cone.

Variations:

1. Award points to the top four finishers in each line (four, three, two, and one).

2. Shoot only for distance. Use track and field measuring tapes.

Example for Measuring Distance and Accuracy

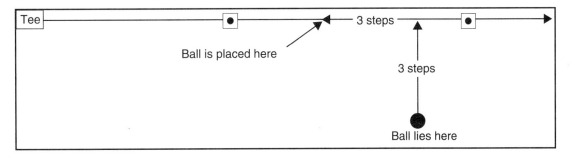

Depiction of a Long Ball Distance and Accuracy Field Layout

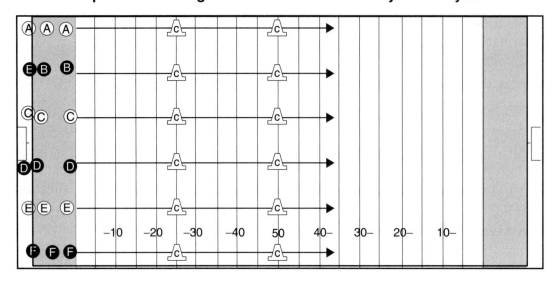

POINTERS

Objectives:

◆ Win a hole by making the pin with the fewest number of strokes.

◆ Collect the most points during a match.

◆ Learn from the mistakes made by the opposition.

Essentials:

◆ Outdoor area or field

◆ Golf clubs (can be shared)

◆ Numbered small wiffle balls

◆ Carpet squares (or something similar) for teeing off

◆ Several pins (hula hoops, coffee cans, or field cones)

◆ Pencils

◆ Scorecards (found at the end of this section)

Point values for each hole:

◆ First hole   10 points

◆ Second and third   5 points

◆ Fourth through eighth   7 points

◆ Ninth   20 points

◆ Tenth   10 points

◆ Eleventh and twelfth   5 points

◆ Thirteenth through seventeenth   7 points

◆ Eighteenth   20 points

© 2001 Parker Publishing Company

How to Play:

1. This game is a modified version of the "Skins Game" played by the professionals.

2. Allow students to create flights composed of four golfers each.

3. After receiving the equipment, shotgun start each flight from a different hole.

4. A player who makes any hole with fewer strokes than the others do, will collect the points assigned to that hole.

5. When any two players tie for the lowest score, the points are carried over to the next hole. Everyone in the flight will have a chance to win the accumulative total on the next hole. Repeat this procedure until there is a distinct winner. (Example: Ties on #1, #2, and #3. Player "A" wins #4 and earns 27 points.)

6. When two players tie, and the other two have no way of winning the hole, there is no need for the last two to shoot or putt. (This helps to accelerate the game.)

7. Holes #5, #10, and #15 will be best-ball holes. The closest player to the hole on the first shot will automatically win two bonus points.

8. When the last hole is tied, play a sudden death round (tie or die).

9. The most points acquired (after nine holes) determine the winner.

Student Tasks:

1. Win back-to-back holes.

2. Tie the leader and prevent a collection of points on any two holes.

3. Win one of the bonus holes.

4. Win three or more holes.

Variations:

1. Play on an 18-hole course (may take two days).

2. On day two, combine similar money winners and continue.

3. Pick a partner and play best ball pointers.

WIFFLE BALL GOLF

Objectives:

◆ Finish a course with the fewest strokes.

◆ Understand the basic rules and terms of golf.

◆ Learn basic techniques, strategies, and skills of golf.

Essentials:

- Outdoor area or field
- Golf clubs (left-handed, too)
- Numbered small wiffle balls
- Carpet squares (or something similar) for teeing off
- Several pins (hula hoops, coffee cans, or field cones)
- Scorecards and pencils (found at the end of this section)

Terminology:

1. Bogey — Strokes taken over the par
2. Par — Average number of strokes needed make the pin
3. Birdie — 1 under par
4. Eagle — 2 under par
5. Hole in One — Make a pin with the first shot
6. Fore — Protect your head
7. Pin — Object that the ball hits or goes into
8. Away — Player farthest from the pin
9. Lie — Where the ball stops and rests
10. Putt — Any short shot to the pin

How to Play:

1. Design a 9-hole or 18-hole course.
2. Form flights with pairs or teams. Distribute a bag of clubs, scorecard, pencil, carpet, and numbered wiffle balls to each group.
3. To prevent divots (removed turf), all drives and iron shots must be hit from the carpet.
4. Use a "shotgun start."
5. Missing the ball is counted as a stroke.
6. Making distracting noises or motions when other players are about to hit the ball is prohibited.
7. The players that had the lowest scores on the previous hole will determine the hitting order. In case of a tie, revert back to the previous pin.
8. During play, the player who is farthest from the hole (away) will hit first.
9. Any unplayable lie can be relocated with a one-stroke penalty.
10. Lowest score of the contest wins.

Student Tasks:

1. Hit an eagle.
2. Make a certain number of birdies during a round.

© 2001 Parker Publishing Company

3. Come from behind and win the match.

4. Place a star by any hole on the scorecard and win it.

Variations:

1. Allow students to putt with a real golf ball.

2. Play the course in reverse order.

3. Play mixed doubles.

Golf (9-Hole) Scorecards
(Copy and Distribute)

Hole #	1	2	3	4	5	6	7	8	9	Total
Name ▼ Par ▶										

Hole #	1	2	3	4	5	6	7	8	9	Total
Name ▼ Par ▶										

Hole #	1	2	3	4	5	6	7	8	9	Total
Name ▼ Par ▶										

Hole #	1	2	3	4	5	6	7	8	9	Total
Name ▼ Par ▶										

Hole #	1	2	3	4	5	6	7	8	9	Total
Name ▼ Par ▶										

GOLF

Golf (18-Hole) Scorecards
(Copy and Distribute)

Hole	1	2	3	4	5	6	7	8	9	10	11	12	13	14	15	16	17	18	Total
Boys Par																			
Girls Par																			
Name																			

Course Map

Hole	1	2	3	4	5	6	7	8	9	10	11	12	13	14	15	16	17	18	Total
Boys Par																			
Girls Par																			
Name																			

Course Map

Pointers (18-Hole) Scorecards
(Copy and Distribute)

	Hole	1	2	3	4	5	6	7	8	9	10	11	12	13	14	15	16	17	18	Total
	Par																			
	Points	10	5	5	7	7	7	7	7	20	10	5	5	7	7	7	7	7	20	
Name																				

Course Map

	Hole	1	2	3	4	5	6	7	8	9	10	11	12	13	14	15	16	17	18	Total
	Par																			
	Points	10	5	5	7	7	7	7	7	20	10	5	5	7	7	7	7	7	20	
Name																				

Course Map

COUNT ALL

Objectives:

- ◆ Score more points than the opposition does.
- ◆ Develop hand-and-eye coordination.

Essentials:

- ◆ Large open area
- ◆ Horseshoe pit/s
- ◆ 4 shoes per pit

Terminology:

1. Ringer	A shoe that encircles the stake far enough so that both heel calks can be touched with a straight edge, and still permit a clearance of the stake
2. Inning	Two players pitch two shoes each

Pitching rotations:

1. *Cancellation:* A person who scored in the preceding inning will throw first in the following inning. When neither player is successful, the thrower who pitched second during the previous inning will initiate the next inning.

2. *Alternating pitch:* Each participant receives an equal number of first pitches. Various methods include:

   a. Player A shall pitch first from one end and B will initiate play from the other.

   b. Player A will throw first in innings 1, 4, 5, 8, 9, 12, and 13 and so forth.

How to Play:

1. The rules of horseshoes apply to this game with a few exceptions.
2. Two players compete against each other from the same end.
3. The first contestant pitches both shoes, followed by the opponent.
4. Combatants will alternate pitching first (leading off) each inning.
5. Each ringer thrown will score three points.
6. Any shoe that remains within six inches of the stake, regardless of the opponent's shoes, will receive one point.
7. Whichever player accumulates the most points after completing 24 innings (48 shoes) is the winner.
8. Ties are decided by pitching an extra inning.

Student Tasks:

1. Score with both shoes.
2. Pitch two ringers in a row.
3. Score in three consecutive innings.
4. Come from behind and win the game.

Variations:

1. Reduce the pitching distance.
2. Any horseshoe leaning against the stake will be worth two points.
3. Decrease the number of innings for a complete game.
4. Players pitch and remain at opposite ends (speeds up the game).
5. Play two games at one pit.
6. Form teams of two players and challenge another group.
7. Create a tournament format.

Example of Scoring for Count All

HORSESHOES

Sample Scorecard for Count All
(Copy and Distribute)

2001 Parker Publishing Company

	(A)	(B)
1		
2		
3		
4		
5		
6		
7		
8		
9		
10		
11		
12		
13		
14		
15		
16		
17		
18		
19		
20		
21		
22		
23		
24		
25		
Total		

	(A)	(B)
1		
2		
3		
4		
5		
6		
7		
8		
9		
10		
11		
12		
13		
14		
15		
16		
17		
18		
19		
20		
21		
22		
23		
24		
25		
Total		

	(A)	(B)
1		
2		
3		
4		
5		
6		
7		
8		
9		
10		
11		
12		
13		
14		
15		
16		
17		
18		
19		
20		
21		
22		
23		
24		
25		
Total		

ON COMMON GROUND

Objectives:

- ◆ Score 21 points before the opposition does.
- ◆ Develop hand-and-eye coordination.

Essentials:

- ◆ Large open area
- ◆ 1 stake
- ◆ 4 shoes per pit

Terminology:

1. Ringer   A shoe that encircles the stake far enough so that both heel calks can be touched with a straight edge, and still permit a clearance of the stake

2. Inning   Two players pitch two shoes each

How to Play:

1. The rules of horseshoes apply to this game with a few exceptions.
2. Place one stake in the ground.
3. Two players compete against each other.
4. While standing even with the stake, either participant tosses one horseshoe in any direction and to any distance desired. Both players will now proceed to where the horseshoe rests and pitch back toward the stake, using this spot as a common pitch line during the first inning.
5. The player that established the common pitch line will lead off.
6. After the points have been determined (if any), the other player now repeats the above procedure. This procedure allows for the combatants to alternate establishing an unfamiliar common pitch line each inning.
7. Scoring is the same as in regular horseshoes.
8. Ties are decided by pitching an extra inning.
9. The first player to score 21 points wins.

Student Tasks:

1. Score with both shoes.
2. Pitch two ringers in a row.
3. Score in three consecutive innings.
4. Come from behind, after being down by six or more points, and win.

Variations:

1. The common pitch line must be at least 15 feet away.

2. Any horseshoe leaning against the stake will be worth two points.

3. Form teams of two players and challenge another group.

4. Create a tournament format.

Illustration of Pitch Lines for On Common Ground

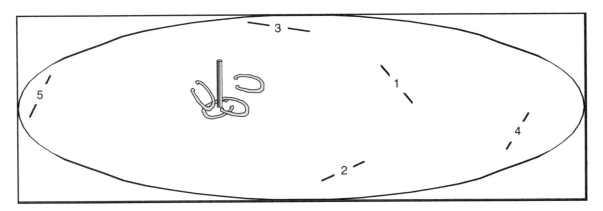

THREE HANDED

Objectives:

- ◆ Score 21 points before either opponent does.
- ◆ Develop hand and eye coordination.

Essentials:

- ◆ Large open area
- ◆ Horseshoe pit
- ◆ 3 pairs of horseshoes

Terminology:

1. Ringer	A shoe that encircles the stake far enough so that both heel calks can be touched with a straight edge, and still permit a clearance of the stake
2. Inning	Three players pitch two shoes each

How to Play:

1. The rules of horseshoes apply to this game.

2. Three players compete against each other from the same end.

3. The first contestant pitches both shoes, followed by the second, and finally the third player.

4. If two players score a ringer in an inning and the third does not, the third player's shoes are nullified.

5. Rotate the pitching order each inning.

6. The first player to score 21 points is the winner.

Student Tasks:

1. Score with both shoes during an inning.

2. Pitch a ringer after the competition has thrown one.

3. Score in three consecutive innings.

4. Come from behind and win the game.

Variations:

1. Decrease the number of points needed to win the contest.

2. Allow only a given number of throws per game.

3. Decrease the pitching distance.

4. Highest scorer of the previous inning starts the next.

5. Any horseshoe leaning against the stake is worth two points.

6. Create a nine-player tournament format (see below).

Sample of a Nine-Player Bracket for Three Handed Horseshoes

Group (A)		Group (D)
1) _____	1st place (A) _____	
2) _____	1st place (B) _____	
3) _____	1st place (C) _____	
Group (B)		**Group (E)**
1) _____	2nd place (A) _____	
2) _____	2nd place (B) _____	
3) _____	2nd place (C) _____	
Group (C)		**Group (F)**
1) _____	3rd place (A) _____	
2) _____	3rd place (B) _____	
3) _____	3rd place (C) _____	

Winner of (D) _____ 1st Place Champion

Winner of (E) _____ Second Place

Winner of (F) _____ Third Place

ABOUT KORFBALL

Objectives:

- Score more points than the opposition does.
- Develop passing and movement combinations to allow for a shot.
- Develop teamwork and cooperation.
- Eliminate the height advantage of tall players.

Essentials:

- Basketball court
- 2 baskets on poles (see illustration below)
- Basketball
- Pinnies or flags

How to Play:

1. This game is similar to basketball with several modifications.
2. Use half of a regular basketball floor with a korfball basket positioned in the middle of the free throw circle. When possible move the regular basketball backboards out of the way.
3. Divide into teams consisting of four players (two girls and two boys).
4. Two boys and two girls from each team start the game on offense, while the other two males and females from each team start by playing defense.
5. Offense:
   a. All players are limited to a half-court at all times, playing either defense or offense.
   b. Players change half-courts and roles as soon as two goals have been scored.
   c. The ball can only be passed.
   d. Dribbling with the ball is not allowed.
   e. The ball may be held for a maximum of five seconds.
   f. If fouls occur, the ball will be started at the point of contact.
   g. Players are allowed one step prior to shooting the ball.
   h. A participant may not attempt a shot when an opponent is playing defense between her or him and the basket.
6. Defense:
   a. Players may only guard opponents of the same gender.
   b. "Defended" means that the defender is between the basket and the person with the ball, within an arm's length away, and is trying to block or steal the ball. This restricts the advantages of taller players since players are not allowed to shoot a jump shot over an opponent when properly defended.
   c. The defense will call all violations and are never wrong.

7. One point is awarded for each basket.

8. A team that is ahead after a predetermined amount of time wins.

Student Tasks:

1. Grab three rebounds.

2. Come from four baskets down and win.

3. Steal the ball three times.

Variations:

1. Send the boys and girls to opposite sides of the court.

2. Allow free throws (from 10 feet away) when a player is fouled in the act of shooting.

3. Use basketball scoring and set a perimeter of cones for the three-point arc.

4. Add more players to each team.

5. First team to make a given number of baskets wins.

Illustration of a Korfball Basketball Net

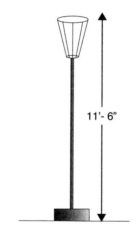

11'- 6"

Example of Player Positioning and Court Layout for Korfball

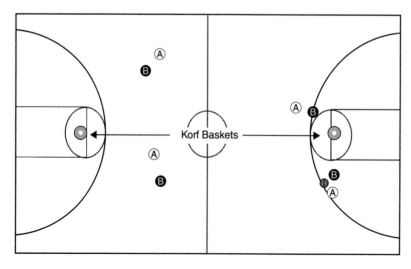

Korf Baskets

HALF QUICK KORFBALL

Objectives:

- ◆ Score three baskets first.
- ◆ Prevent the opposition from scoring.
- ◆ Develop passing and movement combinations to allow a shot opportunity.
- ◆ Develop teamwork and cooperation.
- ◆ Eliminate the height advantage of tall players.
- ◆ Allow a larger number of participants to compete.

Essentials:

- ◆ Basketball court
- ◆ 4 baskets on poles (see illustration below)
- ◆ Basketball
- ◆ Pinnies or flags

How to Play:

1. The rules of korfball apply to this game with a few modifications.
2. Use half of a regular basketball floor with the korfball basket positioned in the middle of the free throw circle. (Optional: Raise the regular basketball backboards when possible.)
3. Divide into several teams consisting of two players (one girl and one boy).
4. For the offensive and defensive rules, see "About Korfball."
5. The first team to score three baskets will stay and take on a new set of challengers.

Student Tasks:

1. Grab three rebounds.
2. Come from two baskets down and win.
3. Steal the ball three times.
4. Win three games during the event.
5. Win three contests in a row.

Variations:

1. Play three against three or four against four.
2. Rotations will occur every three minutes. The winners will stay. Both teams must leave in the event of a tie.
3. Raise the ante by requiring that five or more baskets be made before establishing a winner.

Illustration of a Half Quick Korfball Floor Layout

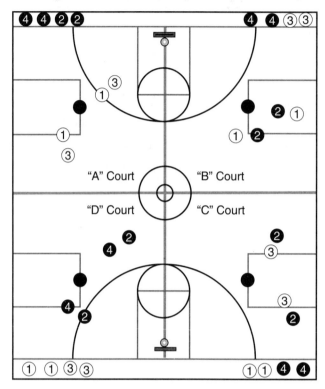

HOLLAND CLIMB

Objectives:

- Score three baskets first.
- Win three games in a row while in Holland.
- Prevent the opposition from scoring.
- Develop passing and movement combinations to allow a shot opportunity.

- Eliminate the height advantage of tall players.
- Allow a larger number of participants to compete.

Essentials:

- Basketball court
- 4 baskets on poles (see illustration below)

- Basketball
- Pinnies or flags

KORFBALL

How to Play:

1. The rules of korfball apply to this game with a few modifications.

2. Use half of two parallel basketball floors with the korfball basket positioned in the middle of each free throw circle. (Optional: Raise the regular basketball backboards when possible.)

3. Divide into several teams consisting of two players (one girl and one boy).

4. Start by dispersing eight different teams to the four courts.

5. Each team will attempt to win the game and move one court clockwise. The losing team will stay and take on a new challenger.

6. Once a team has arrived at the "Holland" court, it will attempt to win three successive games. Any team that loses a game, or wins three, will start over at court A.

7. When any team wins three in a row, the "Holland" court becomes vacant because the winners and losers had to leave. To solve this problem, stop the action and move all teams that are leading at the moment, ahead one court. Any team waiting in between the courts will then enter and challenge.

8. For the offensive and defensive rules, see "About Korfball."

9. The team that wins the most games at the "Holland" court becomes overall winners.

Student Tasks:

1. Win three contests in a row.

2. Win three games during the event.

3. Grab three missed shots.

4. Steal the ball twice.

5. Force an offensive turnover.

Variations:

1. Play three against three or four against four.

2. Rotations will occur every four minutes. The team that is ahead will move up. In the event of a tie, the game of rock, paper, or scissors is enacted to decide which team moves up.

3. Raise the ante by requiring that five or more baskets be made before establishing a winner.

Example of Holland Climb Winning Team Rotations

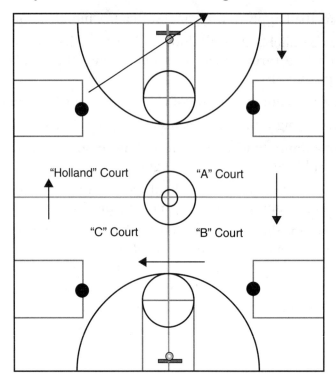

"Holland" Court   "A" Court

"C" Court   "B" Court

KORFBALL UNLIMITED

Objectives:

◆ Score more points than the opposition does.

◆ Prevent the opposition from scoring.

◆ Develop teamwork and cooperation.

Essentials:

◆ Basketball court

◆ Basketball

◆ 2 baskets on poles (see illustration below)

◆ Pinnies or flags

How to Play:

1. Rules from korfball and basketball apply to this game with a few modifications.

2. Use half of a regular basketball floor with the korfball basket positioned in the middle of the free throw circle. (Raise the regular basketball backboards when possible.)

3. Divide into teams consisting of four players (two girls and two boys).

© 2001 Parker Publishing Company

4. Two boys and two girls from each team start the game on offense, while the other two males and females from each team start by playing defense.

5. Offense:

    a. All players are limited to a half-court at all times, playing either in defense or offense.

    b. After two goals have been scored, players change half-courts and roles.

    c. The shooter is not allowed to enter the free throw circle either during or after any shot attempt.

    d. The ball can be dribbled for no longer than five seconds at a time.

    e. The ball may be held for a maximum of five seconds.

    f. If a foul occurs, the ball will be started at the point of contact.

    g. Players are allowed one step when shooting the ball.

    h. Players may attempt a shot of any type when an opponent defends them.

6. Defense:

    a. Defenders may guard opponents of either gender.

    b. The defense will call all violations and are never wrong.

7. One point is awarded for each basket.

8. A team that is ahead after a predetermined amount of time wins.

Student Tasks:

1. Grab three rebounds.

2. Come from four baskets down and win.

3. Steal the ball three times.

4. Block a shot.

Variations:

1. The offense is not allowed to shoot the ball from anywhere inside the key and circle.

2. The shooter is not allowed to shoot the ball from inside the three-point arc.

3. Send all of the boys to one half of the court and all of the girls to the other.

4. Allow for free throws from 10 feet away when a player is fouled in the act of shooting. Made baskets are now worth two points and free throws equal one point.

5. Add more players to each team.

6. Switch roles after three made baskets. The three baskets may not be made by the same player.

7. The first team to make a given number of baskets is the winner.

Illustration of Korfball Unlimited

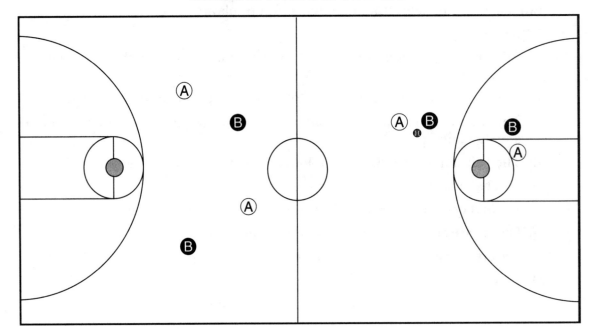

ABOUT LACROSSE

Objectives:

- ◆ Score more points than the opposition does.
- ◆ Develop teamwork and cooperation.

Essentials:

- ◆ Large field (football or soccer field will qualify)
- ◆ 1 ball (optional: tennis ball)
- ◆ 1 lacrosse stick for each player
- ◆ 1 softball face mask and chest protector for each goalie

- ◆ Field cones for boundaries and goals (a two-piece tumbling mat, folded and set on end, may be used for the goal)

How to Play:

1. The rules of both men's and women's lacrosse have been modified to create this game.
2. Divide a large field into two or more smaller fields.
3. The goals can be improvised by placing two field cones six feet apart.
4. Create teams comprised of six players each.
5. Players from each team must assume the positions of attack (#1–#2), mid-field (#3), defense (#4–#5), and goalie (#6). The two attackers attempt to score. The mid-fielder can roam anywhere. The two defenders play back and assist the goalie.
6. A face-off is used to initiate play when starting a game and after each score. The other players must go to their specific areas on each side of the midline (see illustration below).
7. To start play, the center mid-fielders (#3s) start the face-off at the "X" from a squatting position. The ball is placed on the field between the backsides of their sticks. The other middle position players (#2s and #4s) may release as soon as the ball is moved. All of the other players must remain stationary until either team gains control, the ball goes past the attack area, or the ball goes out-of-bounds.
8. Each team must keep at least two players (including goalie) on its defensive half of the field and two on its offensive half; otherwise they are offside. The mid-fielders may move around the entire field.
9. A player with possession of the ball in the basket of the stick may run with it or pass it to another teammate.
10. If the ball or a player in possession of the ball goes over a sideline or end line, the opposing team assumes control. If the ball goes out-of-bounds after an unsuccessful shot at the goal, the player nearest to the ball is awarded possession.

11. Body checking is illegal at all times.

12. Stick checking is permissible if an opponent is in possession of the ball. Only the basket of stick may be bumped or poked at.

13. Only the goalie is allowed in the crease area, and may not return to the crease with the ball.

14. The goalie is the only player that may use a hand to deflect a ball from scoring. When not in the crease, the goalie must follow the field rules.

15. The goalie has four seconds in which to put the ball back into play when in the crease.

16. One point is awarded for throwing (kicking is illegal) the ball into the goal or between the cones and below the goalie's shoulders when two field cones are used.

17. Goals cannot be scored from beyond the middle of the field.

18. The perpetrator of a personal foul will receive one minute in the penalty box. A player will receive two minutes for a second foul, and so on. The ball will automatically go to the fouled team.

19. Types of personal fouls:

    a. Cross checking: Using the handle of the stick to impede another player.

    b. Body checking: Checking or blocking any opponent.

    c. Slashing/tripping: Hitting the opponent's body with the stick.

    d. Unnecessary roughness: Use of excessive force or violence.

    e. Unsportsmanlike conduct: Arguing, cursing, taunting, etc.

20. The perpetrator of a technical foul will receive 30 seconds in the penalty box. The opposition will also receive the ball.

21. Types of technical fouls:

    a. Holding: Impeding the movement of an opponent or opponent's stick.

    b. Illegal procedure: Being off sides or in the crease.

    c. Interference: Preventing free movement of a player without the ball.

    d. Pushing: Shoving a player or running into a player.

    e. Illegal screen: An offensive player cannot impede the path of a defensive player.

    f. Delay of game: Trapping or keeping the ball out of play.

Student Tasks:

1. Be a goalie.

2. Cause a shutout.

3. Play each one of the various field positions.

4. Assist in a score.

5. Pass to three different teammates.

6. Dislodge the ball from an opponent's basket.

Variations:

1. Do not allow any contact, bumping, or hitting during play.

2. Use the entire football or soccer field. Increase the number of players on each team to 10. Each team must keep at least four players (including goalie) on its defensive half of the field and three on its offensive half; otherwise, they are offside. The three mid-fielders may move around the entire field (see illustration of 10-player positioning below).

3. After a player scores two points, she or he must become a defender.

4. Allow all of the players to go anywhere during play.

Illustration of a Lacrosse Round-Robin Field Layout

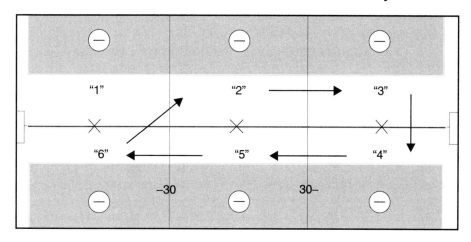

Diagram of a Large Lacrosse Single Field Layout

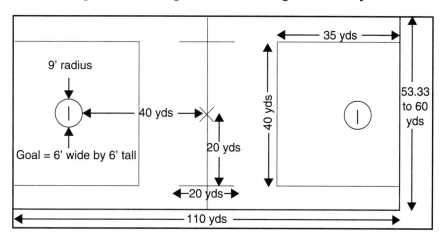

Illustration of Six-Player Positioning for Lacrosse

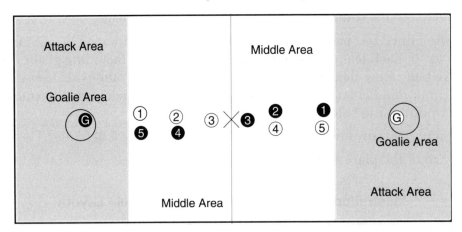

Illustration of 10-Player Positioning for Lacrosse

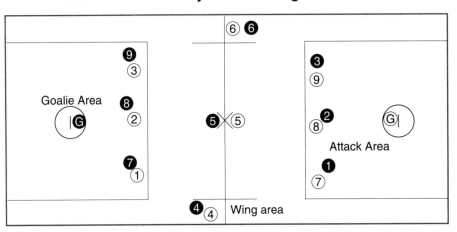

BLACK MAIL

© 2001 Parker Publishing Company

Objectives:

- ◆ Score 50 points before the opposing team does.
- ◆ Get rid of the balls located on the team's court.

Essentials:

- ◆ Open area (free of obstacles) that can be darkened quickly (wrestling area or mat room)
- ◆ 10 vinyl-covered foam balls
- ◆ 3 floor cones
- ◆ Scoreboard or pencil and paper

How to Play:

1. Place the floor cones across the court to designate the midline.
2. Divide the class into two equal teams. Send each team to opposite sides with five balls each. Players should be spaced evenly throughout the entire playing area.
3. Players must remain crouched or seated while on the floor. Locomotion is only allowed from a four-point stance such as crawling, bear walking, or crab walking.
4. The instructor will extinguish the lights. The blackout period will last for 30 to 60 seconds. (The lights may be briefly flashed on and off during this time.)
5. Teams do not want to have any of the balls on their half of the floor when the lights are eventually left on.
6. Each time the lights are turned on, all players must instantly freeze. Failure to do so will result in being eliminated for one blackout period.
7. All balls must be rolled underhand for safety reasons. Any player caught tossing or throwing a ball overhand will be removed from the contest.
8. One point is awarded for each ball on the other team's side.
9. At the conclusion of each blackout period, tally the scores, turn the lights back off, and repeat the procedure.
10. The first team to score 50 points wins.

Student Tasks:

1. Find and toss three balls during the contest.
2. Get rid of at least one ball during each blackout period.
3. Come from behind in the score and win.
4. Score three points or fewer at the end of any blackout period.

Variations:

1. Use table tennis balls on a hard-surfaced floor.

2. Create a "penalty ball" by writing a tiny #3 on it. If this ball is on a team's side when the blackout period ends, they will be penalized three points instead of one.

3. Insert several penalty balls with different point values ranging from two to four.

4. Make four teams; play a round-robin tournament by combining two new teams each game. The team with the best overall record is the champion.

5. Make four teams and divide the room into four sections. Play to 30 points.

Example of Black Mail Using a Penalty Ball

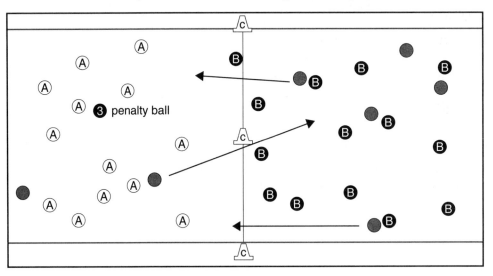

CAPTAIN PEG LEG

Objectives:

◆ Properly perform all of the orders given by the "Captain."

◆ Never be sentenced to go to the brig.

◆ Develop listening and memory skills.

Essentials:

◆ Large open area

◆ List of orders

Safety:

1. Students should try to slow down when running toward a wall.

2. Students must find an open space when arriving at a wall so they do not injure another player.

3. This game can cause rapid fatigue if rest commands are not used occasionally.

How to Play:

1. Explain that the students are shipmates of a pirate vessel and that the instructor is the "Captain." The floor is the deck of the ship. Prior to beginning the game, the class will need to know two reference points, where the bow is, and what direction is North.

2. The crew must always obey the orders of the "Captain" or they will be considered insubordinate and be sent directly to the brig.

3. Rapidly cover all of the commands so that the crew has only a short time to memorize each one.

4. Disperse the students around the floor, or "deck."

5. All students must continually walk around while on the deck.

6. Standing around with a partner or in a group is prohibited.

7. At random intervals, the captain (teacher) will call out a command, being sure not to repeat it.

8. Each shipmate must perform whatever is commanded, or risk being sent to the "brig." It is away from the main action. Once in the brig, each shipmate must perform a specific task (hard labor) such as 10 push-ups or sit-ups.

9. Elect or assign one person to be the "Brig Master," whose job is to make sure everyone does hard labor and returns properly.

10. Crew members will immediately report to the brig for one of the following:

    a. Not following or obeying an order.

    b. Performing a task improperly.

    c. Finishing last.

    d. Having the wrong number of players in a group.

    e. Being left out of a group.

11. No one may leave the brig until there are five players present.

12. Continue the commands for a specific amount of time. Any student that did not go to the brig will be promoted.

Student Tasks:

1. Never wind up in the brig.

2. Be one of the last five members that go to the brig.

3. Be in the top 20% that went to the brig the fewest times.

4. Be the Brig Master.

Variations:

1. Do not give the entire list of orders on the first day. Each time the game is played, add a few new commands.

2. Each time a player returns to the brig, the hard labor activity doubles.

3. When the crew is at "All hands on deck" or "Morning muster," play "Captain Says" (same as "Simon Says"). If a shipmate does something without the instructor first saying "Captain says," that shipmate will report to the brig.

Explanation of Captain Black Orders

1. *Abandon ship (2):* Sit facing each other, hold hands, and lean back and forth as if rowing a lifeboat.

2. *All hands on deck (All):* Stand at attention in a single line while saluting with the right arm.

3. *Back to the ship (All):* Get to the Captain's right side.

4. *Biting Spiders (All):* Walk around on the hands and feet with the rear toward the floor. Attempt to pull other spiders to the floor. Do not grab clothing.

5. *Bow, stern, port, starboard (All):* Touch any open space on that wall.

6. *Button down the hatch (All):* Sit on the deck in a "V" seat. The hands and feet extend upward so that only the rear is touching the floor.

7. *Cannonball on deck (All):* Lie down, form a ball and slowly roll around.

8. *Captain Says:* Played just like "Simon Says" during "Morning muster" or "All hands on deck."

9. *Clear the deck (All):* Drop to the deck then cover the head with the arms and hands.

10. *Crabs on deck (3):* Stand back to back. Bend over, reach between the legs and grab the hands of shipmates B and C. Walk around without letting go.

11. *Crow's nest (2):* Extend the arms and touch hands above the heads while alternating jumps so that A and B are not on the floor at the same time.

12. *Dead cockroach (All):* Lie on the back motionless with feet and arms fully extended skyward.

13. *Drop anchor (3):* Three shipmates stand with backs touching, lock elbows, and squat slightly while slowly rotating counterclockwise.

14. *Fish net (All):* Lie down and touch the hand or foot of another sailor.

15. *Go to the island (All):* Get to the Captain's left side.

16. *Hula dancers (3):* Form a triangle with A, B, and C and face in the same direction. B and C must mimic the movements of A.

17. *Iceberg (All):* Instantly remain motionless in any position.

18. *Jellyfish (All):* Lie on the stomach while methodically moving the feet and arms in the air.

19. *Keel Hauling (3):* Sailor A lies down on back; Sailors B and C grab A's hands and feet, lift and gently swing her/him about four inches above the deck.

20. *Leeward, windward (All):* Squat down next to the corresponding wall.

21. *Load the cannon (3):* Three sailors line up facing the same direction, and stand with legs spread apart. The last person crawls through, then stands in front. Repeat the process.

22. *Lower the aft mast (2):* Stand facing each other. Make fists and alternately stack one fist on the bottom of another. The top fist will continually be placed on the bottom of the stack as all hands are raised.

23. *Mate overboard (2):* A on hands and knees (freeboard), B with foot on back of A and scanning the horizon with the hand held over the eyes.

24. *Mend the sail (4):* Line up and last person continuously zigzags to the lead. Repeat the process.

25. *Morning muster (All):* Rows of five students. Must be motionless while standing at parade rest.

26. *North, East, South, West (All):* Touch an open space on that wall.

27. *Northwest, Northeast, Southwest, Southeast (All):* Find a partner, hook elbows, then run to that corner.

28. *Party time two/three/four (2-3-4):* Get a partner, hook elbows and do a jig.

29. *Prepare to be boarded (2):* Extend one arm and pretend to sword fight an opponent moving four slide steps forward and four slide steps back.

30. *Pump the bilge (2):* Face partner, grab hands, and alternate right and left feet on the deck at the same time.

31. *Raise the anchor (4):* Get back to back, lock elbows, squat slightly and slowly rotate clockwise.

32. *Raise the mainsail (3):* Stand together facing inward. Make fists and alternately stack one fist on top of another. The bottom fist will continually be placed on top of the stack as all hands are lowered.

33. *Reveille (All):* Lie down on the deck on your back as if sleeping. On a signal, stand up as fast as possible.

34. *Rough seas (All):* Go to a line on the deck, spin five circles. Now walk the line without stepping off of it.

35. *Row the raft three/four (3-4):* Sit in a circle. The arms paddle while everyone sings "Row, row, row your boat." No one may sing in unison.

36. *Run for cover (All):* Touch any wall.

37. *Seasick sailor (2):* A lies on side (freeboard), B crawls up to A, leans over her/him, and makes seasick sounds.

38. *Shark (4):* Sit with backs touching, hands and arms straight out and splashing the water.

39. *Sick Turtle (All):* Lie on either side and slowly raise and lower the top arm and leg.

40. *Swab the deck (2):* A in push-up position, B holds the feet of A off of the floor. Do not collapse or fall.

41. *Taps (4):* Lie side-by-side about three feet apart with head to feet, feet to head and snore loudly.

42. *To the galley (3):* Sit with the left hands joined and with the free hand pretend to be eating and drinking.

43. *Tsunami (4):* Form a line and continuously leapfrog over the others.

44. *Typhoon (5):* Form a circle, hold hands, and rapidly rotate in a circle.

45. *Walk the plank (All):* Place one hand over the eyes, extend the other arm and constantly walk around without touching anyone or anything.

Captain's Hand List of Orders

Abandon ship (2)

All hands on deck (All)

Back to the ship (All)

Biting Spiders (All)

Bow, stern, port, starboard (All)

Button down the hatch (3)

Cannonball on deck (All)

Clear the deck (All)

Crabs on deck (3)

Crows nest (2)

Dead cockroach (All)

Drop anchor (3)

Fish net (All)

Go to the island (All)

Hula dancers (3)

Iceberg (All)

Jellyfish (All)

Keel Hauling (3)

Leeward, windward (All)

Load the cannon (3)

Lower the aft mast (2)

Mate overboard (2)

Mend the sail (4)

Morning muster (All)

North, East, South, West (All)

NW, NE, SW, SE (All)

Party time (2-3-4)

Prepare to be boarded (2)

Pump the bilge (2)

Raise the anchor (4)

Raise the mainsail (3)

Reveille (All)

Rough seas (All)

Row the raft (3-4)

Run for cover (All)

Seasick sailor (2)

Sharks (4)

Sick Turtle (All)

Swab the deck (2)

Taps (4)

To the galley (3)

Tsunami (4)

Typhoon (5)

Walk the plank (All)

© 2001 Parker Publishing Company

FLAG TAG

Objectives:

◆ Capture as many flags as possible during a given amount of time.

◆ Prevent the opposition from taking a flag.

Essentials:

- ◆ Large open area with boundaries
- ◆ 2 football flags for every player
- ◆ 4 floor cones to mark boundaries
- ◆ Stopwatch

How to Play:

1. Pair up with another student.
2. Each student will tuck in her/his shirt and place one flag on each hip, then disperse throughout the playing area.
3. On the whistle, everyone tries to grab as many flags as possible from the other participants while staying within the boundaries.
4. Any player that loses both flags is eliminated and must go to the sideline.
5. A player may help her or his partner re-enter by giving up one extra flag.
6. Flags may not be taken from another player's hand.
7. If a person has a flag taken but has one or more in hand, she or he must immediate replace the lost flag.
8. Both flags may simultaneously be removed from anyone.
9. Flag guarding is allowed so long as the flag is not held.
10. After three minutes, stop the game. The partners who acquired the most flags are the champions.

Student Tasks:

1. Acquire five or more flags.
2. Never be sidelined.
3. Get your partner back into the game.

Variations:

1. Shrink the size of the floor after several people are out.
2. Pit everyone against everyone.
3. Form teams composed of three or four players.
4. Make two teams by dividing the class in half.

Illustration of Flag Tag

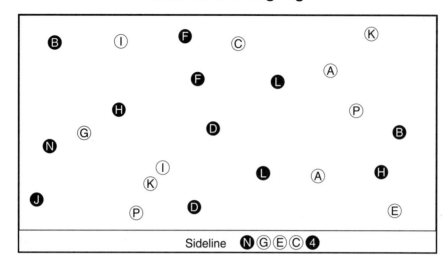

FOUR-WAY FORT KNOX

Objectives:

- Score more points than the opposition does
- Capture an opponent's guarded gold.

- Prevent the team's gold from being looted.
- Return frozen players back into play.

Essentials:

- Field or gymnasium
- 8 football flags
- 4 hula hoops

- Pinnies or flags
- Boundary cones

How to Play:

1. Divide the playing area into four equal sections. Place a hula hoop (vault) in the far corner of each zone. Place the two football flags (gold bars) inside each hula hoop.

2. Divide the class into four equal teams and distribute the colored flags or pinnies.

3. Participants may enter any territory and attempt to steal the gold and return it to their own vault.

4. A player may only possess one bar at a time.

5. An offensive player who is tagged in another territory must immediately squat down and become frozen. The player may be unfrozen by a teammate leapfrogging over her or his head.

6. A player who is tagged while in possession of a bar of gold is frozen and must give it up. The person who tagged the runner will collect the gold and return it to her or his vault.

7. Any defender of Fort Knox must be at least 10 feet away from it.

8. When both bars of gold have been taken outside of a team's area, that team is eliminated.

9. Safe areas are a team's own side of the field or the other team's Fort Knox. Only one foot needs to be over the line to be safe. Also, a player has no time limit once inside a safe zone.

10. First team to eliminate all of the other teams receives one point.

11. All of the football flags are returned and a new game is started.

12. The team with the most points at the end of the period is declared the winner.

Student Tasks:

1. Retrieve two or more gold bars.

2. Tag a person who is in possession of the gold.

3. Defrost a frozen runner.

Variations:

1. Add more flags.

2. Tagged runners must stand with straddled legs. To be unfrozen, the runner must have another player crawl through the legs.

3. Players within a team will pair up. Only the partners can unthaw each other. If both players are frozen, they are retired from play.

4. If player A tags player B in team C's territory, B is frozen and must relinquish the flag to A.

5. Be the first team to score a given number of points.

Illustration of a Four-Way Fort Knox Field Layout

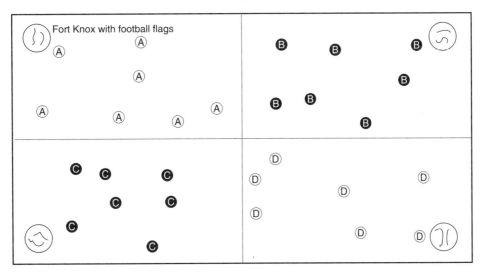

IT TAKES A THIEF

Objectives:

- ◆ Be the first player to tag all of the thieves.
- ◆ Steal an object without being caught.
- ◆ Prevent an object from being snatched.

Essentials:

- ◆ Large open area
- ◆ 1 object for each group (beanbag, sock, shuttlecock, etc.)

How to Play:

1. Divide into groups composed of six players.
2. Each group selects one player to be in the middle (miser). The miser stands guard over the treasure.
3. Everyone else (thieves) forms a circle around the miser and endeavors to gain possession of the booty without being tagged first.
4. If the miser touches a thief before he or she steals the stash, the thief is eliminated until the kitty is either taken or all of the thieves have been caught.
5. Any thief who is successful becomes the miser and initiates a new game.
6. The first player to tag all of the thieves is the winner.

Student Tasks:

1. Grab the moneybag three times.
2. As a miser, tag three or more players during any game.
3. Win a game after being behind by two or more points.

Variations:

1. The first player to snag the booty five times is the winner.
2. Once a participant is eliminated, she or he cannot get back into the action. Play continues until everyone has been eliminated. The last person left is the winner.
3. Place two misers and two moneybags in the middle.
4. Allow the winners of several groups to compete in a match.

Example of It Takes a Thief

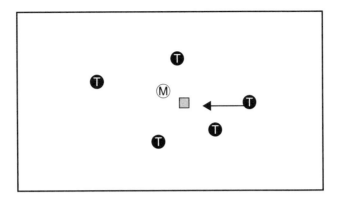

ROLL CALL SCRAMBLE

Objectives:

- ◆ Score 11 points first.
- ◆ Be the first team to find all of its corresponding numbered balls.
- ◆ Participate in a cardiovascular activity.

Essentials:

- ◆ Large open indoor area
- ◆ One tennis ball for each student (each ball is numbered)
- ◆ Floor cones with team numbers taped to them
- ◆ Score sheet and pencil

How to Play:

1. Assign each student a roll call number (if numbers have not been assigned already).

2. From a box, each student will retrieve the ball that has her or his corresponding roll call number. (This eliminates extra balls from absentee students.) After removing any extra balls, the active balls are returned to the box.

3. Divide into teams composed of three players each.

4. Each team is assigned a team number and will line up behind the matching cone located at one end of the floor.

5. The instructor will disperse the balls toward the opposite wall.

6. When the whistle sounds, each team will try to retrieve their numbered balls as fast as possible and return to the team cone.

7. Talking is not allowed during the hunt.

8. A player may only pick up one ball at a time.

9. If a player picks up a ball that does not have the right roll call number, the player may roll it in any direction. (Throwing is not allowed for safety reasons.)

10. Teammates will not announce or retrieve a teammate's ball.

11. As soon as the first team has found all of its items and is sitting behind its team cone, a signal is given to stop play. Everyone must freeze until directed to return to the cones. Players are not allowed to pick up a ball while returning.

12. The first team back receives three points.

13. All other teams will acquire one point for each ball retrieved.

14. Collect all of the balls and repeat the process.

15. The first team to amass 11 points wins.

Student Tasks:

1. Be the first player back.

2. Be one of the first ten to return.

3. Come from behind and win the contest.

Variations:

1. Vary the size of the teams.

2. Assign three different numbers that will represent each team. (Example, 1-2-3, 4-5-6, 7-8-9, etc.)

3. Use table tennis balls. Allow a participant to throw the ball when it does not have the necessary roll call number.

4. A player may find a teammate's ball and toss it to her or him.

© 2001 Parker Publishing Company

Diagram of the Roll Call Scramble Setup

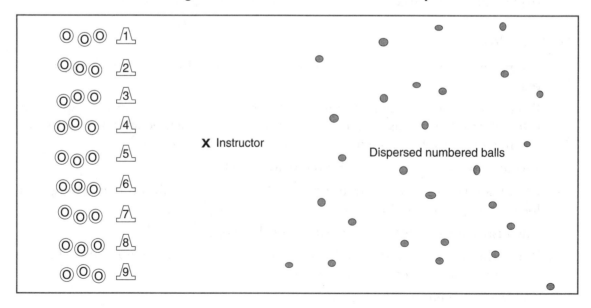

SQUASH EM

Objectives:

- ◆ Score 11 points before the opposition does.
- ◆ Have the best record after playing each opponent.
- ◆ Touch an opponent with the ball.
- ◆ Avoid being tagged with a ball.

Essentials:

- ◆ Large open area or gymnasium
- ◆ 2 vinyl-covered foam balls
- ◆ Pinnies or flag
- ◆ Boundary markers (when outside)

How to Play:

1. Divide into four equal teams and play a round-robin tournament format.
2. Two separate games will be played simultaneously at opposite ends of a basketball court.
3. Determine which teams will receive the ball by performing rock, paper, and scissors.
4. The ball is passed around from player to player in an attempt to tag an opponent (below the shoulders) with the ball. When successful, one team point is awarded.
5. The ball is never thrown at an opponent. It must be held when making the tag.
6. A player in possession of the ball may not dribble or take steps.
7. If the ball is dropped, thrown out-of-bounds, or intercepted, the other team will take control.
8. First team to score 11 points is the winner.
9. After the winner of each game has been established, rotate the teams and start a new contest.
10. The team with the best record, after playing each team once, is the champion.

Student Tasks:

1. Tag two or more opponents.
2. Avoid being tagged for an entire game.
3. Get three assists.
4. Intercept a pass.

Variations:

1. Use a different type of ball each game.
2. Play each game for a predetermined amount of time.
3. Divide into two teams and play one game.

Example of Squash Em

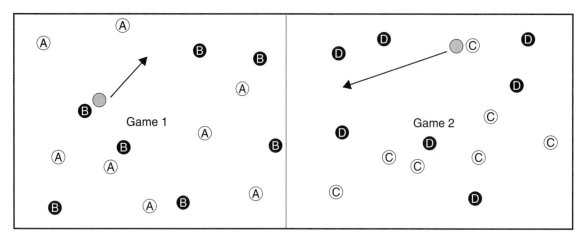

STAGECOACH

Objectives:

- Score more points than the opposition does.

- Accumulate more wins than the opposition does.

- Capture as many flags as possible.

- Promote cooperation and teamwork.

Essentials:

- Large playing area.

- 2 football flags for each driver.

- One jump rope for each team.

How to Play:

1. Form groups composed of five students each.

2. One person, the stagecoach driver, will place a flag (payroll) on each hip and grab on to one end of the jump rope with both hands. The other four members will form the team of horses. The horses will form two rows of two.

3. Each horse must continuously hold on to the rope with the inside hand.

4. Horses will attempt to steal the flags from the other drivers using the outside hands.

5. On the command "GO," the drivers will communicate with the team to either steal or defend the payroll. Once a stagecoach has lost its payroll (both flags), it is eliminated.

6. After three minutes, stop the game and tally the score (one point for each flag) to determine a winner.

7. Rotate drivers and play a new game.

8. The team that accumulates the most wins out of the five games is the overall winner.

Student Tasks:

1. Finish first or second.

2. Steal four or more payrolls.

Variations:

1. Have the horses in a single line.

2. Form groups of two players (pony express).

3. Cut down the dimensions of the playing area.

4. Form teams with two or more stagecoaches. Allow a stagecoach to give up a flag to an eliminated partner.

Illustration of Stagecoach

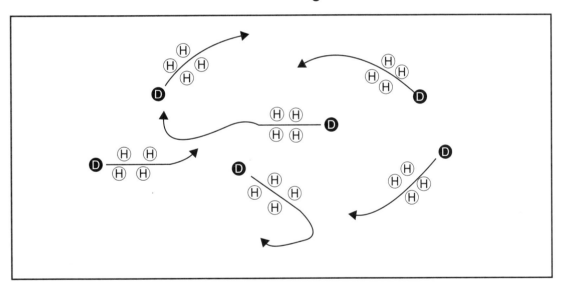

TIME LAPSE

Objectives:

◆ Determine when exactly one minute has passed.

◆ Develop focus and concentration.

◆ Develop the ability to estimate time.

Essentials:

- ◆ Open area
- ◆ Stopwatch

How to Play:

1. Everyone is to stand in a single file line facing the instructor.
2. Participants must close their eyes as both arms are held out directly in front and be as quiet as possible for one minute.
3. Each player will lower her or his arms after estimating that one minute has elapsed.
4. Eyes may be opened when the arms are dropped.
5. The player that is closest to one minute without going over is the winner.

Student Tasks:

1. Be the closest to one minute more than once.
2. Come within two seconds either under or over the required time.
3. Come within five seconds either under or over.

Variations:

1. Start in the up position of a push-up and slump at one minute.
2. Change the estimated amount of time.
3. Require that during the one minute, ten push-ups or ten crunches must be performed before dropping.

Illustration of Time Lapse

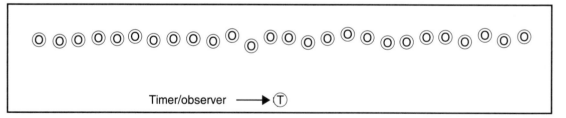

Timer/observer ⟶ Ⓣ

ZONE FOOSBALL

Objectives:

- ◆ Score seven points before the opponent does.
- ◆ Develop teamwork and cooperation.

© 2001 Parker Publishing Company

Essentials:

- Gymnasium or large room
- Indoor soccer ball or large vinyl-covered foam ball
- 22 floor cones or floor spots
- Pinnies
- Scoreboard

How to Play:

1. Set the floor layout as illustrated below. Floor spots may be used to divide the larger zones into smaller ones.
2. Divide into teams composed of 11 players each.
3. Players must stay within their zone at all times.
4. The ball may not be intentionally kicked into the air. It must stay low and in contact with the floor as much as possible.
5. A player can only touch the ball with the feet and legs.
6. One point is awarded when the ball hits the wall between the cones and below the goalie's waist.
7. The goalie must only use the feet and legs to deflect a shot.
8. Team members must rotate to a new position following a score or after a predetermined amount of time.
9. To restart play after a score, roll the ball in from the sideline at middle court.
10. First team to score seven points is the winner.

Student Tasks:

1. Be a goalie.
2. Block or deflect shots.
3. Create a shutout.
4. Complete three or more passes across a zone.
5. Make an assist.
6. Intercept a pass.

Variations:

1. Use two balls.
2. Allow for two goalies.
3. Play for a given amount of time.
4. Use the Mix 'n' Match format.

LARGE GROUP GAMES

Example of a Living Foosball II Floor Layout and Team Rotation

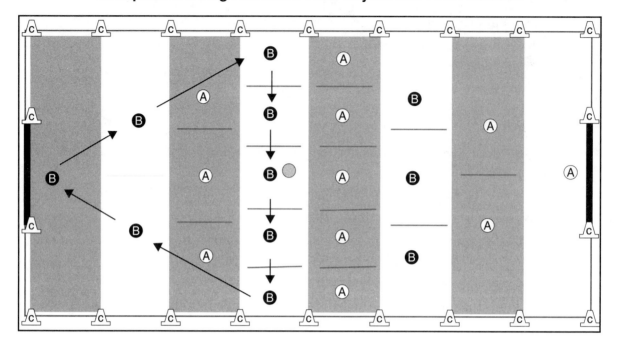

BACK TO BACK

Objectives:

- Perform more ball exchanges than the opposition does.
- Develop teamwork and cooperation.
- Enhance upper body strength and cardiovascular endurance.

Essentials:

- Open area
- 1 soft grip medicine ball (7–8 pounds)
- Stopwatch

How to Play:

1. Two players stand back to back with one medicine ball held in front of the initiator.
2. On a signal, the unit begins exchanging the ball in a circular rotation around their waists.
3. Stop the contest after 30 seconds have expired.
4. Each complete revolution is worth one point.
5. Any dropped ball will be cause for elimination.
6. The team with the most revolutions wins.

Student Tasks:

1. Finish as one of the top five groups in the class.
2. Never drop the ball.

Variations:

1. Allow three, four, or five in each group. (The entire group will face outward.)
2. Extend the time to one minute.
3. Exchange the ball 30 times in the shortest amount of time possible.
4. Switch the direction of the ball halfway through the timed session.
5. Require the ball to be passed from between the legs and then over the head each time.
6. Use a different type of ball.

Illustration of Two, Three, and Four Players in Back to Back

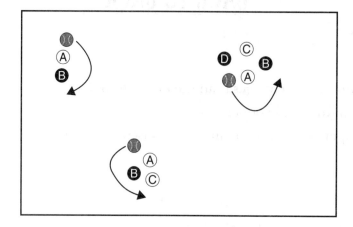

CAT AND MOUSE

Objectives:

- Pass and tag another ball in the least amount of time.
- Efficiently toss and catch a ball.
- Enhance upper body strength.
- Develop hand-and-eye coordination.

Essentials:

- Open area
- 2 soft grip medicine balls (7–8 pounds)
- Pennies
- Stopwatch

How to Play:

1. Divide into two teams with 12 or more players on each.
2. Form a large figure eight with all of the participants.
3. Teammates must have an opponent between them (see illustration below).
4. Players may not interfere with the opponent's ball or team members at anytime.
5. The mouse (first ball) leads off and is passed by team A from teammate to teammate around the course.
6. When the mouse has traveled a given distance, the cat (second ball) is started in the same direction by team B.
7. The cat will try to overtake (catch) the mouse in the shortest time possible.
8. The cat and mouse may either be passed over the top or in front of the opposition.
9. Skipping one or more players is forbidden.

10. As soon as the cat passes the mouse, stop the action and record the time.

11. If the cat cannot accomplish this feat in three minutes, switch the role of each team and play again.

12. The team with the shortest catch time is the winner.

Student Tasks:

1. Never drop the ball.

2. Be the player to pass the "cat" ball by the "mouse" ball.

3. Do not be caught during the allotted amount of time.

Variations:

1. Use two different types of balls.

2. During play, blow the whistle to immediately switch each team's role. The cat and mouse will now go in the reverse direction.

3. Form a circle or a square with the teams.

Example of the Cat and Mouse Figure Eight Team Positioning

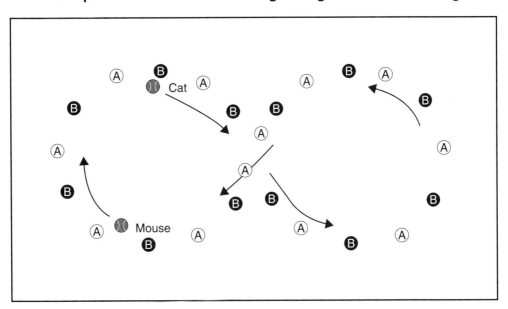

HOT POTATOES

Objectives:

◆ Win four out of seven matches.

◆ Overtake the opposition's ball.

◆ Develop passing and catching skills.

MEDICINE BALL

Essentials:

- ◆ Open area
- ◆ 2 soft grip medicine balls (each weighing 7–8 pounds)

How to Play:

1. Form two teams with an equal amount of players.

2. Team A will form a large single circle with each player standing about five feet apart and facing the middle.

3. Team B will form a similar circle three feet inside of Team A and facing outward.

4. Each team has a ball located at opposite sides of the circles. On the whistle the balls are simultaneously tossed in the same direction from teammate to teammate.

5. Players are not allowed to interfere with the opponent's ball.

6. If a bad pass is made or the medicine ball is dropped, it must be returned to the point of error before being replayed.

7. The first team to overtake the other team's ball is awarded a win.

8. Prior to the start of each new encounter, switch the location of each team circle and the direction in which the ball is tossed.

9. A team must win four out of seven matches to become champions.

Student Tasks:

1. Never make a bad pass.

2. Do not drop the ball.

3. Come from behind and win the contest.

Variations:

1. Win two out of three or three out of four.

2. Use two basketballs, volleyballs, footballs, etc.

3. Use two different types of balls such as a table tennis ball and a tennis ball.

4. Players may only use one hand when tossing and receiving.

5. Participants must throw with the right hand and catch with the left.

Illustration of Hot Potatoes

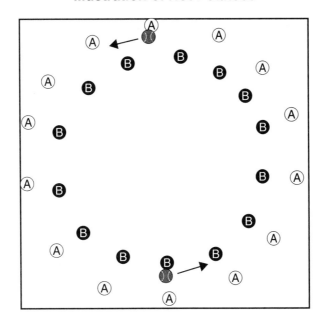

OVER AND UNDER

Objectives:

- ◆ Score more points than the opposition does.
- ◆ Pass a medicine ball down a line of players faster than the opposition does.

- ◆ Enhance upper body strength.
- ◆ Develop teamwork and cooperation.

Essentials:

- ◆ Open area
- ◆ 1 soft grip medicine ball for each team (7–8 pounds)
- ◆ Paper and pencil for scoring

How to Play:

1. Make three or four teams composed of six or more players each.

2. Each team will disperse in a straight line six feet apart and parallel to the others. All players will face in the same direction toward the front of the line.

3. On the signal, the first person in line (team leader) will toss the ball backward (over the head) to the next teammate in line. After receiving the ball, next person must hike it between the legs to the third. The third player tosses the ball over the head, and so forth down the line.

4. The last person in line, after catching the ball, will turn around and perform the same toss that was thrown to her or him so that each player will perform one under and one over the head pass during the contest.

5. Participants will turn around and get ready to receive the ball on its return path.

6. The ball is not allowed to touch the floor at any time.

7. Any pass that hits the floor or is not caught must be returned to the thrower for another attempt.

8. A direct hand-off between teammates is not allowed.

9. Scoring:

    a. First   4 points

    b. Second   2 points

    c. Third   1 point

10. After each down-and-back race, record the top three finishers.

11. To begin a new contest, move each player up one position and send the team leader to the end of the line.

12. After a given number of contests, the team with the highest score is declared champions.

Student Tasks:

1. Never drop the ball.

2. Never make a bad pass.

3. Come from behind and win the contest.

4. After dropping the ball, finish in the top three.

Variations:

1. Require that the ball must go down and back twice before finishing.

2. The first team to score a given number of points is the winner.

3. Close the distance and allow nothing but a hand-off.

4. The ball may be hiked from the floor.

5. Go for one minute. A team receives one point for every person who correctly catches and throws the ball. The team with the highest score is victorious.

6. Use any type of a ball.

Example of the Start in Over and Under

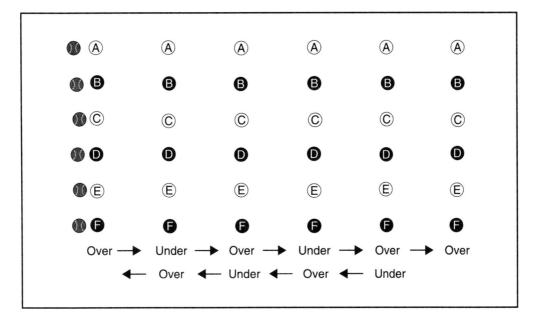

POPCORN POPPER

Objectives:

◆ Eliminate the opposition.

◆ Toss and catch a medicine ball.

◆ Enhance upper body strength and cardiovascular endurance.

Essentials:

◆ Open area

◆ 1 soft grip medicine ball (7–8 pounds)

◆ 4 floor cones

How to Play:

1. Place the four floor cones to form a square six feet wide.

2. Form a circular line with 10 to 12 players.

3. To begin the contest, a player standing in the square tosses the ball into the air then quickly moves forward. The next player in line moves into the box, catches the ball, and likewise casts the ball into the air. This process continues until there is an error.

4. The ball must elevate at least two feet above the thrower's head.

5. Participants are allowed to put spin on the ball during the toss.

6. A player is eliminated for:

   a. Making a bad toss (one that would have landed outside the square).

   b. Not catching a good toss.

7. Play continues until there are only two players left. They are co-champions.

Student Tasks:

1. Put two players out.

2. Wind up in the top five.

3. Put spin on the toss.

Variations:

1. Use a different type of ball.

2. Make teams composed of two players. When one teammate puts an opponent out, the other partner may re-enter if she or he is already out.

Illustration of the Popcorn Popper

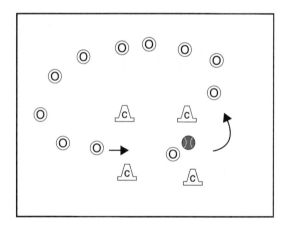

TWO-BALL LOB-IT*

Objectives:

◆ Do not drop the ball before the opposition does.

◆ Defeat four different participants in a row.

◆ Enhance upper body strength and cardiovascular endurance.

Created by Rayl Smith and Camila Thorndyke, 2000.

Essentials:

◆ Open area

◆ 2 soft grip medicine balls (each weighing 7–8 pounds)

How to Play:

1. Form a line with several players.

2. The first two individuals in line will possess a ball and stand approximately six to eight feet apart.

3. Both individuals will simultaneously pass and catch each other's medicine ball.

4. The toss:

   a. Must be within one step of the opponent.

   b. Must be at least thigh high (no throwing at the knees or feet).

   c. Spinning the ball during the release is allowed.

   d. May only be thrown with a six- to eight-foot high arc.

5. A player is eliminated and returns to the end of the line when:

   a. The received ball is not cleanly caught before hitting the floor.

   b. The player makes an unfair delivery.

   c. Two balls collide in the air and the opposition still catches the thrown ball.

6. Whenever both balls are caught or dropped, play continues.

7. Any player that defeats four adversaries in a row is crowned champion and also returns to the end of the line.

Student Tasks:

1. Eliminate a player within three tosses.

2. Catch eight or more passes in a row.

3. Defeat a past champion.

Variations:

1. Change the type of ball being used.

2. Use two different types of balls such as a tennis ball and a basketball.

3. Use three balls and three players by forming a triangle. All balls could be tossed either to the right, to the left; alternate directions each throw, or alternate directions after every two throws.

4. Players may only use one hand when tossing and receiving.

5. Participants must throw with the right hand and catch with the left.

Illustration of Two-Ball Lob-it

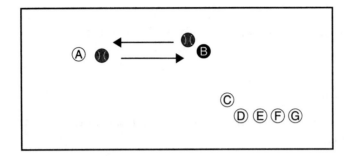

ABOUT ESCAPE FROM ALCATRAZ

Objectives:

- ◆ Complete an obstacle course without making an error.
- ◆ Learn by personal trial and error.
- ◆ Learn from the mistakes or successes made by others.

Essentials:

- ◆ Large space
- ◆ Obstacles and barriers (chairs, balls, ropes, tape, hula hoops, floor mats, rope climb, benches, chairs, stanchions, buckets, floor spots, bowling pins, etc.)

How to Play:

1. *Note:* Students prefer the obstacle course to be quite difficult and relish the challenge.
2. Set up the course in an area where it can be left for several days. If the course needs to be assembled every morning, assign groups of students to construct each station. This method takes very little time.
3. All prisoners will start at the cell house and try to negotiate each obstacle without making a mistake. The escapee advances each time an obstacle is successfully completed.
4. Any slip-up will alert the guards, who then capture the runaway. The apprehended player must start at the beginning after each mistake. (The honor system needs to be emphasized.)
5. The escape artists may help each other with verbal cues.
6. Any participant who is waiting in line is a guard and must inform the fugitive of any mistakes. An example might be that a hanging rope was slightly moved by the escapee's shirtsleeve. Any guard intentionally violating this rule will also be sent back to the beginning.
7. Reward any student who successfully completes the course and escapes from "The Rock."

List of Sample Stations:

1. *Blind fence walk:* Use a floor balance beam or 12-foot long 4″ X 4″ timber and walk the entire length either forward or backward without falling off.

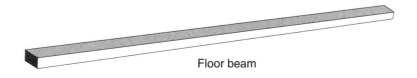

Floor beam

2. *Hornet nest:* Using a climbing rope, swing around a bucket (nest) without knocking it over and land on the small floor mat without falling off.

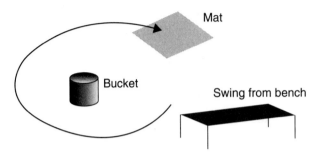

3. *Trap door:* Crawl under both chairs without dislodging the ball. The ball is placed in between the top legs.

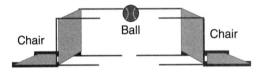

4. *Boulders and rocks:* Use floor spots and hop on either the right or left foot from rock to rock. Do not touch the floor.

5. *Raft row:* While standing in a large plastic bucket, grab the sides and hop to the floor mat. Do not fall over or knock down any bowling pins. Jump from the plastic bucket to the crash pad without touching the floor, and then return the raft (bucket).

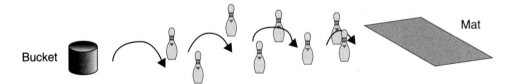

6. *Wall jump:* Jump from one mat to the next without knocking over or touching the upright mat in the middle. Floor cones can be placed on top of the folded mat to add height.

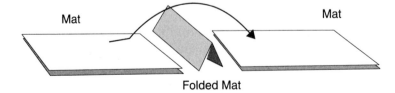

(4) (7. *Electric fence:* Go behind the mat and do not knock either sensor (wiffle ball) off of the ends.

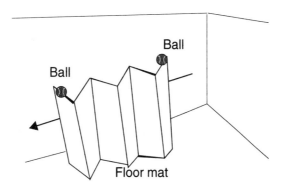

(5) (8. *Exit a window:* Step through a suspended hula hoop onto a tumbling mat without dislodging a wiffle ball. The hula hoop can also be attached to the back of a chair. (Tape is folded in such a way that the ball will rest on a flat spot.)

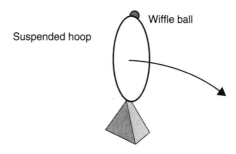

9. *Destroy a siren:* From 15 feet away and in three attempts, slide or toss the beanbags and topple two of the three bowling pins.

(6) (10. *High voltage:* Slide under and past the jump ropes without making them move. Do not disturb the bowling pin during the exit.

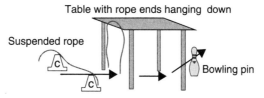

11. *Cross the sewer pipes:* Step over the first bench, slide under the second, and step between the chairs without moving any of the sensors (wiffle balls).

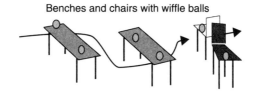

12. *Build a bridge:* Stack eight of the cups (small end to small end, big to big) and then walk around the stack one time before the top cup hits the floor (if it falls).

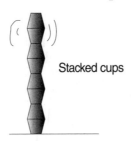

Stacked cups

13. *Short circuit:* While balancing the broom or pole on one finger, walk between the wall and a rope placed on the floor. The broom must remain on the finger while moving through the narrowing path without touching anything. (The rope can also be suspended on two poles about five feet above the floor.)

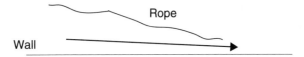

Rope

Wall

14. *Unlock the door:* From eight to ten feet away, toss a ball into a box within three attempts. If the second toss misses, the player may elect to go back three barriers and begin again. If the third attempt is missed, the thrower will start over at the beginning. The box should be slightly larger than the ball being used.

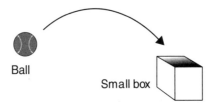

Ball

Small box

15. *Lock the door:* Toss the ring (can be a flying disc with the center cut out) over an inverted stool leg from six to eight feet away. Three chances will be given. A player will gain one extra life if she/he can make all three tosses. Extra lives may be used at anytime, but the student must start from the beginning of the missed barrier each time a life is utilized.

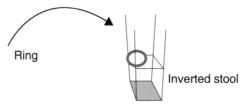

Ring

Inverted stool

16. *Steam tube:* Crawl on top of the football blocking bags and under the hula hoops without touching the floor. Go under the table and past the two hanging ropes (sensors) without touching them.

Table with hanging rope   Pads and hoops

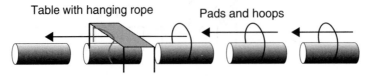

17. *Log roll:* While on the hands and knees, roll the bag sideways to the mat without touching the floor. Holding on and hopping with the bag is illegal.

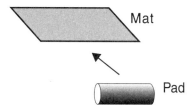

18. *Cover the camera lens:* Within six attempts, toss three playing cards into a hat from five feet away.

19. *Imitate a crab or be eaten:* While crawling face up on the hands and feet (crab walk), move through an area covered with wiffle balls (crabs) without disturbing any.

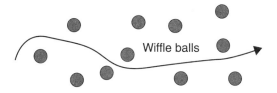

20. *Spoon dug tunnel:* Crawl or slide under the mats without making either mat collapse.

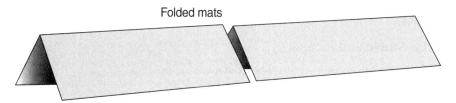

21. *Disable a motion detector:* Given only three chances, toss a beanbag and hit a small object that is suspended and swinging.

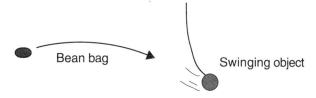

22. *Slime pit:* From the knees or buttocks, move a scooter board from point A to point B (10 feet) without touching the floor.

23. *Kill two mosquitoes:* Place two pennies on the back of the hand. Flip both coins into the air and catch them with the same hand before either penny hits the floor. The palm must always face down. (For extreme difficulty, add a third coin.)

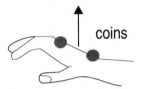

coins

24. *Razor wire:* Enter and exit through a given route without toppling the wiffle ball (alarm). (Tape is folded in such a way that the ball will rest on a flat spot.)

Hula hoops taped together and held up with a stanchion

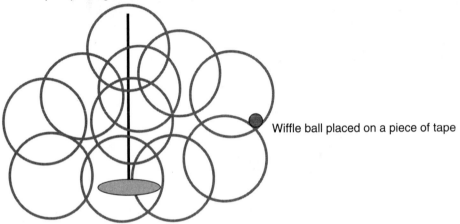

Wiffle ball placed on a piece of tape

Student Tasks:

1. Finish the course and escape.
2. Successfully complete six obstacles in row.
3. Never fail on the same obstacle twice.
4. Gain an extra life.

Variations:

1. Designate one barrier that if missed will force the escapee to go back three spots.
2. Designate stations that will provide extra lives if completed successfully. The bonus life can be used when needed.
3. Reverse the course in order to escape.
4. Allow some modifications for escapees that might be physically challenged. An example might be to slightly widen the space between two stanchions for larger participants to get through or after three unsuccessful attempts at an obstacle, allow an individual to move on.
5. Give an opportunity for students to create new obstacles or design a new course.
6. Go the farthest in the shortest amount of time. Each participant would need a watch with a second hand, or a stopwatch.

Illustration of Escape from Alcatraz Floor Layout

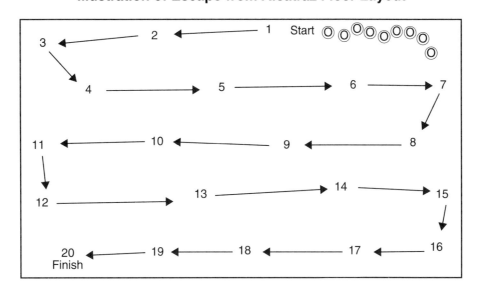

ALCATRAZ TEAM CHALLENGE

Objectives:

- ◆ Score more points than the opposition does.
- ◆ Complete the obstacle course without making an error.
- ◆ Learn from others' mistakes.

Essentials:

- ◆ Large space
- ◆ Obstacles and barriers (chairs, balls, ropes, tape, hula hoops, floor mats, rope climb, benches, chairs, stanchions, buckets, floor spots, bowling pins, etc.)

How to Play:

1. All of the rules of "Escape from Alcatraz" apply to this game with the following exceptions.
2. Build two smaller identical courses composed of four or five barriers each.
3. Create four equal teams and place them in a double-elimination tournament format (see below).
4. Each team will be on the course for only four minutes.
5. Two teams will start at the cell house and try to get past the required obstacles.
6. One team point is awarded for each team member that successfully navigates the course.

7. Players are never eliminated. Each time a player makes errors or finishes the course, the player returns to the starting line and proceeds again.

8. Continue this procedure until the tournament has a winner.

Student Tasks:

1. Never make an error during a match.

2. Make three or fewer mistakes during the entire tournament.

3. Come from the losing side and win.

4. Go undefeated in the tournament.

Variations:

1. Extend the competition time for each match.

2. Reverse the course in order to escape.

3. Allow students to create new obstacles or design duplicate courses.

Sample Double-Elimination Bracket for Alcatraz Team Challenge

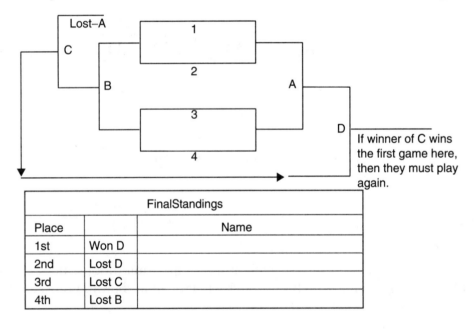

If winner of C wins the first game here, then they must play again.

FinalStandings		
Place		Name
1st	Won D	
2nd	Lost D	
3rd	Lost C	
4th	Lost B	

ALCATRAZ TEAM ESCAPE

Objectives:

♦ Score more points than the opposition does.

♦ Complete the obstacle course without making an error.

♦ Learn from others' mistakes.

Essentials:

- ◆ Large space
- ◆ Obstacles and barriers (chairs, balls, ropes, tape, hula hoops, floor mats, rope climb, benches, chairs, stanchions, buckets, floor spots, bowling pins, etc.)

How to Play:

1. All of the rules of "Escape from Alcatraz" apply to this game with the following exceptions.
2. Create five equal teams.
3. Each team will be on the course for only five minutes.
4. The first team will start at the cell house. One team point is awarded for each teammate that makes an obstacle. The points are recorded on the team's score sheet.
5. The team may not proceed to the next obstacle until everyone has attempted the prior one.
6. Any slip-up will alert the guards (waiting teams) who then capture the runaway. The apprehended player is eliminated.
7. The escape artists may help each other only with verbal cues.
8. After five minutes, or when everyone is caught, the next team begins. Continue this procedure until all of the teams have had a go at it.
9. The team with the highest score wins.

Student Tasks:

1. Come from behind and win.
2. Lose only two or less team members within the timed session.

Variations:

1. An earned extra life may bring back an eliminated teammate.
2. Reverse the course in order to escape.
3. Allow students to create new obstacles or design a course.

Sample Alcatraz Team Escape Score Sheet

Team 1		Team 2		Team 3		Team 4		Team 5	
Barrier	Score	Barrier	Score	Barrier	Score	Barrier	Score	Barrier	Score
1-->		1-->		1-->		1-->		1-->	
2-->		2-->		2-->		2-->		2-->	
3-->		3-->		3-->		3-->		3-->	
4-->		4-->		4-->		4-->		4-->	
5-->		5-->		5-->		5-->		5-->	
6-->		6-->		6-->		6-->		6-->	
7-->		7-->		7-->		7-->		7-->	
8-->		8-->		8-->		8-->		8-->	
9-->		9-->		9-->		9-->		9-->	
10-->		10-->		10-->		10-->		10-->	
11-->		11-->		11-->		11-->		11-->	
12-->		12-->		12-->		12-->		12-->	
13-->		13-->		13-->		13-->		13-->	
14-->		14-->		14-->		14-->		14-->	
15-->		15-->		15-->		15-->		15-->	
16-->		16-->		16-->		16-->		16-->	
17-->		17-->		17-->		17-->		17-->	
18-->		18-->		18-->		18-->		18-->	
19-->		19-->		19-->		19-->		19-->	
20-->		20-->		20-->		20-->		20-->	
Total->		Total->		Total->		Total->		Total->	

BLACK OUT

Objectives:

♦ Score fewer points than the opposition does.

♦ Successfully negotiate an obstacle course in the dark.

♦ Finish without disturbing or knocking over any equipment.

Essentials:

♦ Large open area that can be quickly darkened

♦ 40 obstacles that can be easily tipped over or moved (bowling pins, blocks of wood, balls that are touching, plastic soda containers, plastic cups, stack of bean bags, juggling batons, two playing cards on edge leaning against each other, relay batons, jump rope suspended (not attached) between two cones, etc.)

How to Play:

1. Divide into two equal teams.

2. Each team will set up 20 identical obstacles on half of the floor.

3. Designate one obstacle to be worth five penalty points if disturbed.

4. Teams will next switch sides and line up on the sideline. This prevents a team from making a simple course. Give each team a short period of time to study the course.

5. Next, turn off the lights and each member will attempt to cross to the other side and touch the wall without knocking down or moving any of the obstacles.

6. Teammates are not allowed to hang on to each other during the voyage.

7. Running is not allowed for safety reasons.

8. After a given amount time, turn the lights back on and count the number of barriers that have been disturbed.

9. Any player caught going over into another team's course will cause her or his team to be penalized 10 points.

10. Any player who has not traveled at least three-fourths of the course (when the lights are turned back on) will receive one penalty point.

11. One penalty point is given for each displaced obstruction.

12. Five penalty points are received if the designated stumbling block has been altered.

13. Redesign the course and continue the process a couple more times.

14. The team with the least number of points is declared the winner.

Student Tasks:

1. Set up a course in which the opponents knock over at least six objects.

2. Beat a team by five or more points.

3. Never knock down a barrier.

Variations:

1. Briefly flash the lights during the contest.

2. During the black out, play loud obnoxious music to interrupt student concentration.

3. Make four teams and combine two different teams with each new three-inning game.

4. Make four teams and create four narrow lanes with 10 obstacles on each. Each team starts with 20 points. The first team to lose all of its points terminates the contest. The team with the most points remaining is declared the champion.

5. Teammates pair up and lock arms during the midnight crossing.

Example of a Black Out Floor Plan

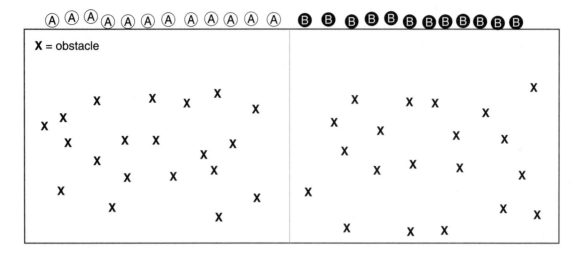

BLIND MICE

Objectives:

- Score fewer points than the opposition does.
- Successfully negotiate an obstacle course while visually impaired.

- Listen to the instructions.
- Give precise and correct information.

Essentials:

- Large open area
- 4 blindfolds
- 28 obstacles that can easily be tipped over or moved (bowling pins, blocks of wood, balls that are touching, plastic soda containers, plastic cups, stack of bean bags, juggling batons, two playing cards on edge leaning against each other, relay batons, jump rope suspended (not attached) between two cones, etc.)
- 9 floor cones to mark lanes

How to Play:

1. Divide into four equal teams. If any team has fewer members, someone must go twice so that each team performs an equal amount of attempts.
2. Each team will set seven identical barriers in a lane.
3. Next, rotate each team one lane to the left. This process is done to ensure that a team does not design an easy course.
4. Each team will now split and set half of its members to the opposite side of the obstacle course.

5. One player from each team goes to the middle and will be the escort for the person with the blindfold (blind mouse) by shouting directions and orders. The escort may not touch the mouse.

6. A blind rodent must make one complete circle around any one barrier before attempting to cross the finish line. The guide will go to the end of the line when the mouse has finished.

7. The mouse will shed the blindfold and give it to the next person in line. The mouse now becomes the mentor and verbally directs the new mouse back across the course.

8. Continue this process until everyone has been a mouse and a guide.

9. The guide must reset any barrier that is knocked over.

10. Any obstruction knocked over by the mouse gives that team a one-point penalty.

11. Any mouse that crosses over into another lane will receive a two-point penalty.

12. After each team has covered the course an equal amount of times, the team with the lowest score wins.

Student Tasks:

1. Instruct a mouse that never hits an obstruction.

2. As a mouse, never knock down a barrier.

3. As a team, finish as one of the top two.

Variations:

1. Use paper bags instead of blindfolds. The chin must be held against the chest to prevent peeking.

2. Require the mouse to circle two obstructions before finishing.

3. Require two blind mice to cross at the same time.

4. Require two blind mice to cross at the same time while locking arms.

5. Get rid of the navigator and have teammates from both sides of the lane do the shouting and guiding.

Diagram of a Blind Mice Layout

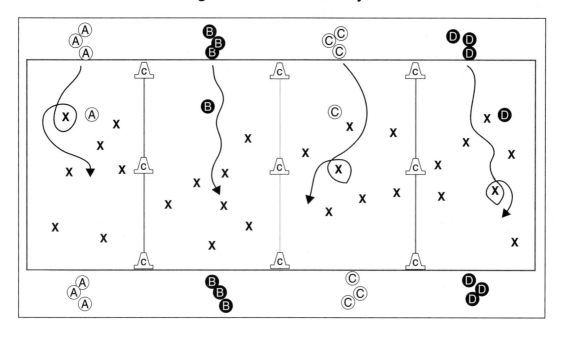

BUSY BODIES

Objectives:

◆ Finish the obstacle course ahead of the competition.

◆ Successfully accomplish each task.

◆ Finish the course without touching, disturbing, or displacing any teammate.

Essentials:

◆ Large open area

◆ 12 floor cones

◆ 6 stunt cards (2 matching sets)

◆ Stopwatch

How to Play:

1. Set up the cones with the stunt cards taped to them (see illustration below).

2. Divide into four teams with eight to ten players each.

3. Allow the teams to study the instructions on each task card for a couple of minutes.

4. After lining up on the sideline, the first six players will each stand near a different task cone and follow its instructions.

5. On the "Go" command, the first player on each team will quickly attempt to complete each duty in sequence. When finished, the player will assume a position at the last cone.

6. Any runner that makes a mistake or dislodges a teammate must repeat that assignment.

7. Once a runner has successfully completed an assignment and moved on, the teammate at that cone will move up one station toward the start line. This process is repeated until everyone has gone.

8. The second person may not proceed until the previous player has completed the course.

9. Example course task cards:

   a. Leap frog over this squatting person.

   b. Run around this person three times.

   c. Go through this person's legs without touching them.

   d. Hop back and forth over this person lying on the floor five times.

   e. Move backward under this person's outstretched arms while staying in between her or his hands and body.

   f. Crawl on the hands and knees around this crouching person two times and bark like a dog.

10. Record each team's final time and repeat the same contest.

11. The team with the fastest combined times is the winner.

Student Tasks:

1. Never make a mistake.

2. After making a mistake, redo the same skill without an error.

3. Come from behind after the first round and win.

4. Move up one place after the second round.

Variations:

1. Change the required skills during the second run.

2. Run the race three or four times and combine the times.

3. Create more stations over the course.

4. Add five seconds for each error.

5. Place objects on the floor instead of players.

6. Place objects and players on the course.

Illustration of a Busy Bodies Obstacle Course Layout

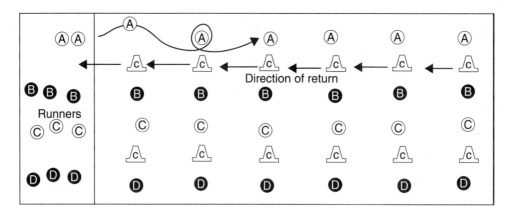

DODGE MAZE

Objectives:

◆ Score more runs than the opposition does.

◆ Successfully complete an obstacle course without getting hit.

◆ Throw a ball with accuracy.

Essentials:

◆ Gymnasium or large open room

◆ 12 to 15 vinyl-covered foam balls

◆ Floor cones to designate the throwing zone

◆ Abundant supply of protective barriers. These could be items like standing floor mats, chairs, football hand and field blocking pads, desks, volleyball or badminton net strung between supports, plastic cargo tarp, five-gallon paint buckets, plastic garbage cans with lids, wastebaskets, portable chalkboard, giant playground ball, and a section from a high jump pit.

How to Play:

1. Divide the class into two teams, throwers and runners.

2. Teams will have four minutes in which to have as many players as possible touch the "home base" cone.

3. One point is awarded for each successful touch.

4. Switch teams after the time has expired. Continue until a given number of innings have been completed.

5. Runners:

   a. Proceed one at a time through the course.

   b. May occupy the next barrier as soon as it has been vacated.

   c. Must touch the numbered cone at each barrier before proceeding.

   d. When the ball is thrown in the air and hits a runner (below the shoulders), she or he must return to the end of the line.

   e. Once the ball hits the floor, wall, or barrier, it is considered dead.

6. Throwers:

   a. Have to be inside the throwing zone when firing the ball.

   b. May throw or lob the ball in any manner in order to hit a runner.

   c. Must have five designated rovers that retrieve and toss back all dead balls.

   d. There must be five new rovers each inning.

   e. Rovers may not interfere with the travel of the runners.

7. Team with the highest score after a given number of innings wins.

Student Tasks:

1. Go halfway through the course before getting tagged.

2. Touch the finish cone.

3. Hit three different runners.

4. Defeat a team after being behind in the score.

Variations:

1. A team is finished after a given number of outs.

2. Runners are out if a ball touches them in any manner (the ball is poison).

3. Allow the students to design the course.

4. Make four teams. Play a two-inning game. At the conclusion, rearrange the teams and start a new game. Team with the best record wins. Game #1 = 1 + 2 vs. 3 + 4. Game #2 = 1 + 3 vs. 2 + 4. Game #3 = 1 + 4 vs. 2 + 3.

OBSTACLE COURSE

Illustration of a Dodge Maze Floor Layout

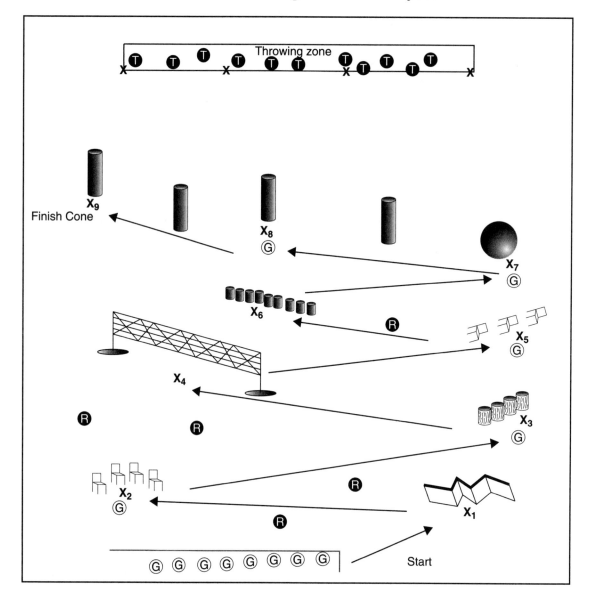

ABOUT RELAYS

Objectives:

- ◆ Develop teamwork and cooperation under pressure.
- ◆ Understand the different types of relay formats.

Essentials:

- ◆ Large open area
- ◆ Props (defined by the type of relay)

How to Play:

1. Create a safe environment by making sure the playing area is harmless and free from obstacles.
2. Discuss safety concerns when a relay requires special care.
3. Monitor fatigue in the participants.
4. Form several teams composed of four to six players each. By doing this, player movement is increased and idle time is reduced.
5. Deploy a variety of relays that invoke interest and excitement.
6. Use relays as a warm-up activity prior to a game.
7. Student input can create a new activity or improve upon an existing one.

Variations:

1. Shuttle	An object is carried over a course and relinquished to a teammate.	
2. Challenge	Move through a course in a prescribed manner.	
3. Alternate	Move an object from player to player by a designated method.	
4. Imitate	Perform a task through or around the entire unit.	

© 2001 Parker Publishing Company

Illustration of Variations for About Relays

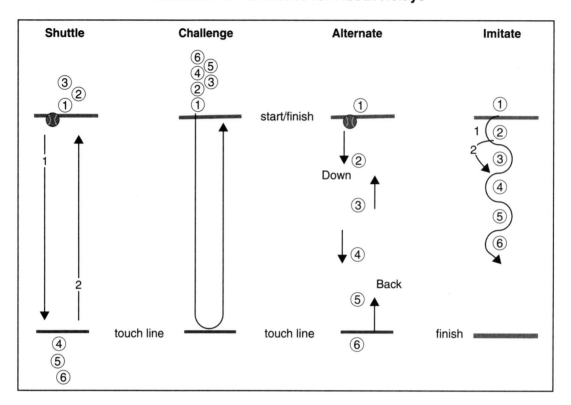

DORSAL 2 DORSAL

Objectives:

◆ Be the first group to finish.

◆ Develop teamwork and cooperation.

◆ Allow for competition in a challenge relay.

Essentials:

◆ Large open area

◆ Start/finish line

◆ Touch line

◆ Floor cones to mark line locations (optional)

How to Play:

1. Form several teams composed of six players each. (If any team has one less person, one of its players will have to fill in twice.)

2. Team members will pair up and stand back to back with the arms linked at the elbows.

3. The first player will always face toward the touch line (30 to 40 feet) when running down and back.

4. Each pair will go down and back once.

5. As soon as the first pair completes the circuit, the second, then third couples will repeat the process.

6. After finishing, players must sit down. (This requirement makes it easier to determine the winner.)

7. The first team to complete the course is the winner.

Student Tasks:

1. Make up ground on the opposition during any segment.

2. Come from behind on the last leg and win.

3. After assuming the lead, never relinquish it.

Variations:

1. Modify the distance of the touch line.

2. After waiting a turn, each pair must go for a second time.

3. Three people must link arms.

4. Execute the relay three times. Award points to the first (3), second (2), and third (1) place teams. The team with the most points wins.

5. Four players link arms to form a box. Each time back, one pair must drop off while a new one is added. The foursome must go down and back a total of three times (1-2-3-4, 3-4-5-6, and 1-2-5-6) in order to finish the contest.

Illustration of Dorsal 2 Dorsal

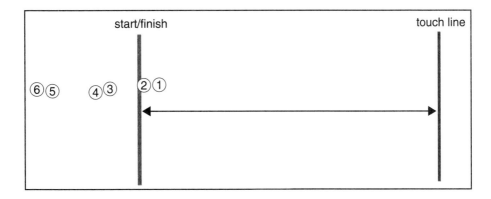

INDY 500

Objectives:

- ◆ Finish the course ahead of the competition.
- ◆ Develop teamwork and cooperation.
- ◆ Allow students to compete in a shuttle relay.

Essentials:

- ◆ Gymnasium
- ◆ Start and finish lines
- ◆ 1 scooter board for each team
- ◆ Floor cones to mark the inner boundary (volleyball court)

How to Play:

1. Divide into teams composed of six players each. (If any team has one less person, one participant will go twice.)
2. Drivers will bend over, grab the sides of the scooter board (racecar), and propel it around the racetrack for one lap. After crossing the finish line, each driver will relinquish the scooter board to the next driver.
3. Teams will be disqualified (black-flagged) for either displacing any floor cones or intentionally running into other drivers.
4. After finishing, drivers must sit down. This procedure also makes it easier to determine the winner and to see which teams are still participating. (Participants will probably want to sit anyway since this is quite an exhausting race.)
5. The first team to complete six laps around the oval will receive the checkered flag.

Student Tasks:

1. Make up ground on the opposition during any segment.
2. Pass two cars during a lap.
3. Come from behind on the last leg and win.
4. Move up two positions during the race.

Variations:

1. Modify the distance of the oval.
2. After waiting, each driver will go for a second time.
3. Execute the race three times. Award points to the first (3), second (2), and third (1) place teams. The team with the most points wins.
4. Remove the scooter boards. Each driver will either drag or carry an object around the course.

Illustration of Indy 500 Track Layout

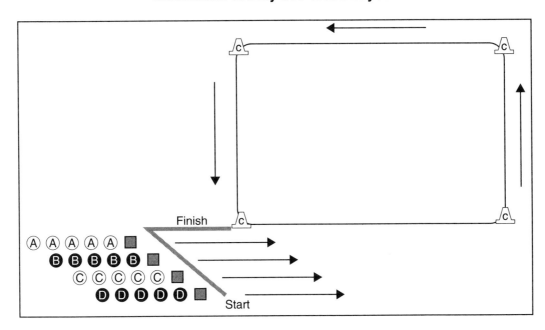

MACHINE GUN

Objectives:

◆ Be the first group to finish.

◆ Develop teamwork and cooperation.

◆ Allow students to perform in an alternation relay.

Essentials:

◆ Large open area

◆ 1 matching object per team (ball, bean bag, pillow, rubber chicken, water balloons, raw eggs, etc.)

◆ Floor cones to mark player locations (optional)

How to Play:

1. Form teams composed of six players each.

2. Team members will disperse in a straight line at equally spaced distances apart. (This distance can vary depending on the type of object being used.)

3. On the signal "START," the first person in line will pass the object to the next person in line. This second person passes it to the third and so on until the object travels down the entire line and returns back to the first person.

4. If an object is dropped along the way, it must be retrieved and passed from the spot of error.

5. Upon completion of the event, the entire team will sit down.

6. The first team to finish wins.

Student Tasks:

1. Make up ground on the opposition during a segment.

2. Come from behind and win.

3. Never drop the object.

Variations:

1. Require that the object must go down and back twice.

2. Use a basketball and require a different type of pass be thrown each session.

3. Use two objects that are started from opposite ends of the line.

4. Execute the relay three times. Participants must rotate one position toward the start line, with the starter going to the end for each new game. Award points to the first (3), second (2), and third (1) place teams. The team with the most points wins.

5. Arrange the players in a fan line (see below). Two balls can be used.

Example of a Straight Line for Machine Gun

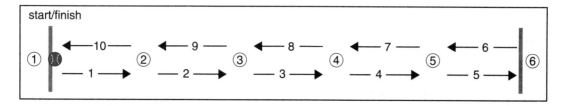

Example of a Fan Line for Machine Gun

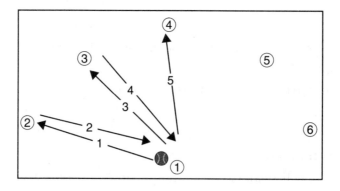

OBSTACLE COURSE RELAYS

Objectives:

◆ Be the first group to finish.

◆ Develop teamwork and cooperation.

◆ Allow students to compete in a challenge relay.

Essentials:

◆ Large open area

◆ Matching objects per team (tumbling mats, floor cones, chairs, boxes, ropes, hula hoops, etc.)

◆ Floor cones to mark lines (optional)

How to Play:

1. Form teams composed of six players each. (If any team has one less person, one player will have to go twice.)

2. Each team will line up in single file behind a common start/finish line.

3. On the signal "START," the first person in line will traverse the course and conquer a prescribed number of obstacles (two or three). Upon completion of the final hurdle, the runner will sprint back to the finish line and tag the next teammate, who will repeat the course.

4. Any obstacle that is displaced or moved must be set back up before the guilty party may return.

5. Upon completion of the event, the entire team will sit down.

6. The first team to finish wins.

Student Tasks:

1. Make up ground on the opposition during any segment.

2. Come from behind and win.

3. Never hit a barrier.

4. Create a new obstacle that can be implemented on the course.

Variations:

1. After resting, require that players must repeat the course for a second time.

2. Allow students to design a new layout with barriers.

3. Disqualify any team that disturbs an obstacle.

4. Make three members be obstacles. After a teammate passes, the student obstacle will move up one position toward the start line.

5. Include either a leapfrog (vault over), alternate (over one and under the next), or tunnel (under all) relay race.

6. Execute the relay three times. Modify the obstacles each time. Award points to the first (3), second (2), and third (1) place teams. The team with the highest total of points wins.

Illustration of an Obstacle Course Relay

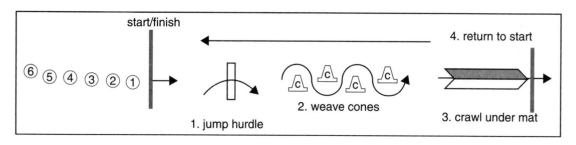

REAR 2 REAR

Objectives:

◆ Be the first group to finish.

◆ Develop teamwork and cooperation.

◆ Allow students to compete in a shuttle relay.

Essentials:

◆ Large open area

◆ Start/finish line

◆ Touch line

◆ Floor cones to mark line locations (optional)

◆ 2 large objects per team (basketballs, boxes, balloons, etc.)

How to Play:

1. Form several teams composed of six players each. (If any team has one less person, one player will have to go more than twice.)

2. Team members will pair up and stand back to back with the arms linked at the elbows.

3. Each beginning pair will possess two objects.

4. On the signal "START," each pair will travel to the touch line (30 feet from the start) and back before handing off the objects to the next pair.

5. If an object is dropped along the way, the pair must fetch it and return to the spot of error before proceeding on.

6. Each pair will go down and back twice.

7. Upon completion of the second opportunity, players must sit down.

8. The first team to complete the itinerary and cross the finish line wins.

Student Tasks:

1. Make up ground on the opposition during a segment.

2. Come from behind and win.

3. Never drop an object.

Variations:

1. Modify the distance of the touch line.

2. Three people must link arms and use three objects. Each group must complete the course three times.

3. Place the two objects in between the backs of each pair. The arms are not linked.

4. Perform a wheel barrow relay race. Partners will switch positions when reaching the touch line.

5. Execute the relay three times. Award points to the first (3), second (2), and third (1) place teams. The team with the most points wins.

Example of the Team Setup for Rear 2 Rear

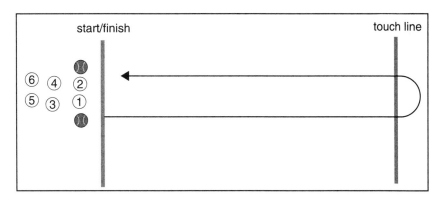

SIXTY-SIX THICK SHOE SOLES

Objectives:

◆ Be the first team to retrieve all of the shoes.

◆ Locate each pair of shoes as fast as possible.

Essentials:

◆ Open area

◆ 8 floor cones (boundary markers)

How to Play:

1. Divide the class into four equal teams.

2. Each player will go to the center, untie and remove her or his shoes, then toss the footwear into a common pile.

3. Each team is then sent to a different corner.

4. The pile is mixed up thoroughly.

5. On a signal, the first player in each line will sprint to the center pile, find her or his shoes, sit down, put them on, and scamper back to touch the hand of the next player in line. (For safety, the shoes must be tied before returning.)

6. Play continues until a team finishes first. They are "sole" winners.

Student Tasks:

1. Find the shoes on the first try.

2. Come from behind and win.

3. Do not finish last.

Variations:

1. Place all of the shoes in a plastic garbage can or large cardboard box. No shoe may be placed outside the container when players are scrounging around.

2. Shoes must be placed on the wrong feet when returning.

3. Each player must bring back a teammate's shoes. They do not have to wear them, though.

Illustration of Sixty-Six Thick Shoe Soles Floor Layout

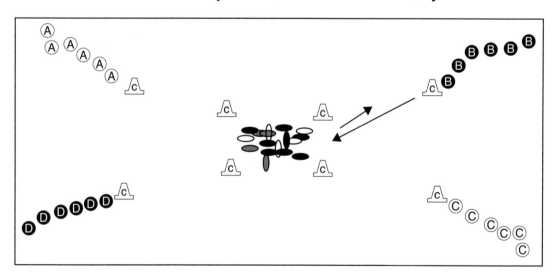

STUNT RELAYS

Objectives:

◆ Be the first group to finish.

◆ Develop teamwork and cooperation.

◆ Allow students to compete in a challenge relay.

Essentials:

◆ Large open area

◆ Cards to describe stunts (optional)

◆ Floor cones to mark lines and stunt stations (optional)

How to Play:

1. Form several teams composed of six players each. (If any team has one less person, one player will have to go twice.)

2. Each team will line up in single file behind a common start/finish line.

3. On the signal "START," the first person in line will traverse the course and perform a prescribed number of stunts (two or three). Upon completion of the final requirement, the runner will sprint back to the finish line and tag the next teammate who also will repeat the course.

4. Possible stunt stations:

   a. Place objects in a box, upright position, in stacks, pyramid, etc.

   b. Move with an item located between the legs, knees, ankles, on the shoulder, back of neck, or top of the head.

   c. Dribble some type of a ball in a given manner, over, under, around, or in between objects.

   d. Perform a specific number of physical movements such as push-ups, sit-ups, somersaults, cartwheels, getting up without use of the hands, etc.

   e. Move in a prescribed manner to the next station by skipping, sprinting, heel and toe walking, hops, backwards, jumping, walking on carpet squares or sheets of newspaper only, etc.

5. Upon completion of the event, the entire team will sit down.

6. The first team to finish is the winner.

Student Tasks:

1. Make up ground on the opposition during any segment.

2. Come from behind and win.

3. Invent a new stunt that can be used by the class.

Variations:

1. After resting, require that players must repeat the course for a second time.

2. Allow students to lay out the course and create new tasks.

3. Execute the relay three times. Modify the stunts each time. Award points to the first (3), second (2), and third (1) place teams. The team with the most points wins.

Illustration of a Stunts Relay

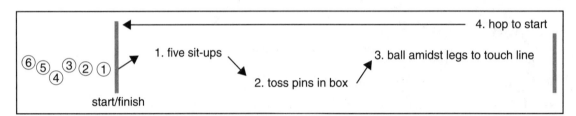

ABOUT SHUFFLEBOARD SINGLES

Objectives:

- ◆ Accumulate 50 points before the opposition does.
- ◆ Propel the discs onto the scoring diagram.
- ◆ Prevent an opponent from scoring.

Essentials:

- ◆ Indoor or outdoor area
- ◆ Shuffleboard layout (6 feet wide by 39 feet long, plus a 6-foot, 6-inch standing area at each end)
- ◆ Shuffleboard cues
- ◆ 4 red and 4 black discs
- ◆ Scoreboard or scorecards
- ◆ Pencils

Terminology:

1. Head of court — End of layout at which play starts
2. Foot of court — End of layout from which the discs are returned
3. Half Round — Completed play at one end of the court
4. A Round — Completed play at Head and Foot of court
5. Dead disc — Disc that is not in play
6. Live disc — Disc that is in play
7. Mounted disc — A disc is resting on top of another disc

How to Play:

1. The rules have been modified for shuffleboard singles.
2. Determine color by lagging one disc each. Being closest to the farthest dead line sets choice of color. If the second disc hits the first disc, choice goes to the opponent.
3. Red is always played from the right side of Head of court and the left side of Foot of court.
4. The game is started by red, then alternates back and forth with black. After all of the discs have been played, both participants walk to the opposite end to tally the score. Play is resumed with black leading off.
5. Discs are played from the "clear" from within the respective half of the 10-off area.
6. Players may not step on or over the baseline when shooting. The penalty is 10 off, offender's disc removed, and the opponent credited with any displaced discs.
7. If a played disc touches the front or back line: Penalty—5 off.

8. If a played disc touches the side line or triangle: Penalty—10 off, offender's disc removed, and the opponent credited with any discs that were displaced. All displaced discs shall be removed from the court. Any 10-off discs that the offender had on the court, that were displaced, will be removed before further play and also be deducted from the offender's score.

9. Hook shots are not allowed. Forward motion of the cue must be continuous, without hesitation: Penalty—10 off, offender's disc removed, and the opponent credited with any discs that were displaced.

10. A player, after shooting a disc, shall step to the rear of his or her portion of the shooting area and not disturb or interfere with the opponent who is executing a shot: Penalty—5 off.

11. A disc in motion may cross outside the diagonal line.

12. A disc that stops between the near baseline and the farthest dead line is immediately removed from play (dead disc).

13. A disc is played (live disc) when it is completely in the 7-area, but when the disc stops between the farthest dead line and the 7-area, it is removed before further play.

14. If a disc is touching the farthest dead line, it is in play.

15. Any disc that clearly leaves the court beyond the farthest baseline, or goes off the sides of the court, is dead.

16. A disc that rests less than 8 inches beyond the farthest baseline shall be removed.

17. Players shall not touch a live disc at any time: Penalty—10 off.

18. A disc or discs returning or remaining on the playing area of the court, after having struck any object outside the playing area, shall be removed before further play.

19. If a dead disc comes from another court and moves or displaces a live disc, that half-round shall be played over, with no score credited to either player.

20. The scoring diagram consists of one 10-point area, two 8-point areas, two 7-point areas, and one 10-off point area.

21. Score all discs on the diagram that are within the lines, but not touching a line. The separation triangle in 10-off area is not considered.

22. When a mounted disc occurs, each disc shall be judged separately according to scoring rules. This can happen when players use excessive force.

23. Play continues until all discs have been shot, even if game point has been earned.

24. If a tie score results at game point or over, one extra round is played.

25. First player to score 50 points is declared the winner.

Student Tasks:

1. Score with two of the discs during a half round.

2. Eliminate an opponent's scoring disc.

3. Block a scoring disc.

4. Land a disc onto the 10-area.

Variations:

1. Change the number of points needed to win.

2. Score all discs that remain on the playing surface.

3. Play a non-walking pairs game from opposite ends of the layout. Players do not have to walk from end to end each time.

4. A team must win two out of three games to win the match. The second game is initiated by black.

5. Create a round-robin tournament.

Example of a Scoring Layout and Disc Placement

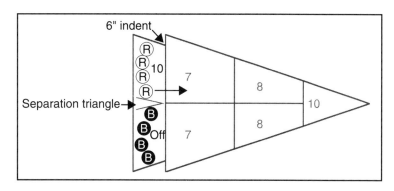

Diagram of a Regulation Outdoor Shuffleboard Layout

(Note: The separation triangle in the 10-off space is 3 inches wide at the base. The outline is 1/4-inch lines that have a space of 1/2-inch at the point and base from the 10-off lines.)

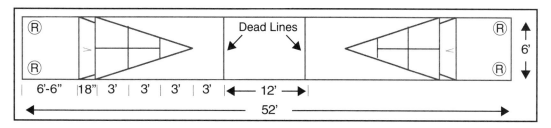

Diagram of a Reduced Indoor Shuffleboard Layout

(Note: When playing indoors and space is a problem, reduce the above court layout dimensions to 2/3 of the values shown below.)

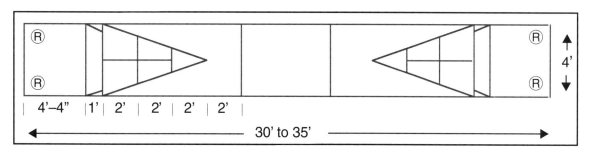

LAG 'N' TAG

Objectives:

- ◆ Accumulate 15 points before the opposition does.
- ◆ Propel the discs onto a scoring zone.
- ◆ Prevent an opponent from scoring.

Essentials:

- ◆ Indoor or outdoor area
- ◆ Shuffleboard layout
- ◆ Shuffleboard cues
- ◆ 4 red and 4 black discs
- ◆ Scoreboard or scorecards
- ◆ Pencils
- ◆ Floor

How to Play:

1. Determine lead off and color using rock, paper, and scissors.

2. Both players participate from the same end and alternate sliding discs toward the distant scoring zone. After all eight discs have been played, the competitors proceed to the opposite end to tally the score.

3. Discs are played from any location within the 3-point zone.

4. Players may not step on or over the 3-point zone when shooting.

5. Each player attempts to pass (lag) or dislodge (tag) the opponent's disc(s). Players may also endeavor to shield their own scoring disc(s).

6. The winner of the previous round shoots first.

7. Hook shots are allowed.

8. Any disc that stops in front of the second dead line, beyond the 3-point end line, or winds up more than halfway over either sideline is dead and will be immediately removed from play.

9. Scoring:

   a. Only the advanced or leading discs of the color farthest away from the shooting end will count toward the score. In other words, if red is the most distant disc, score the sum total of all red discs ahead of the leading black disc. Any red disc behind the leading black disc would be negated.

   b. Only one side scores in a round.

   c. Discs touching or in front of the 2-line, score 1 point.

   d. Discs between the 2-line and 3-line, or touching the 3-line, score 2 points.

   e. Discs between the 3-line and the end of the board, but not hanging over the far end, score 3 points.

   f. Discs beyond but still touching the far end line of the 3-zone are called hangers and score 4 points.

10. Play until all discs have been shot, even if game point has been earned.

11. First player to score 15 points is declared the winner.

12. If a tie score results at game point or over, one an extra round will be played.

Student Tasks:

1. Score three discs during any round.

2. Eliminate two or more of the opponent's discs during any round.

3. Knock two of the opponent's discs out of play with one shot.

4. Throw two 4-point discs during a game.

5. Come from behind and win a game.

Variations:

1. Use hockey pucks.

2. Use objects that will slide by releasing them as in bowling or curling.

3. Score all discs that remain on the playing surface.

4. Play doubles and score to 21.

Dimensions for a Lag 'n' Tag Layout

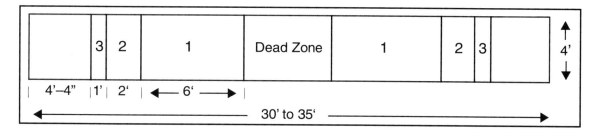

Example of Disc Point Values for Lag 'n' Tag

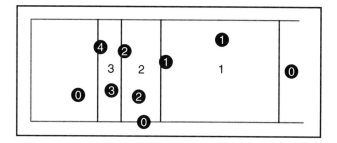

Sample of Scoring for Lag 'n' Tag

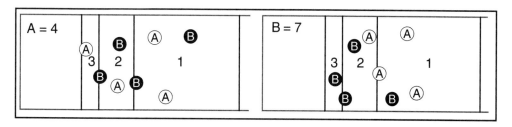

Example of a Converted Shuffleboard Layout for Lag 'n' Tag

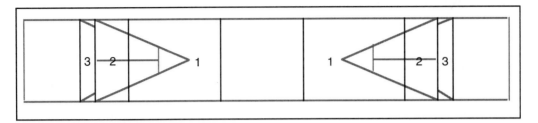

SHUFFLEBOARD DOUBLES

Objectives:

◆ Accumulate 75 points before the opposition does.

◆ Propel the discs onto the scoring diagram.

◆ Prevent an opponent from scoring.

Essentials:

◆ Indoor or outdoor area

◆ Shuffleboard layout (6 feet wide by 39 feet long, plus a 6-foot, 6-inch standing area at each end)

◆ Shuffleboard cues

◆ 4 red and 4 black discs

◆ Scoreboard or scorecards

◆ Pencils

Terminology:

1. Head of court   End of layout at which play starts

2. Foot of court   End of layout from which the discs are returned

3. Half Round   Completed play at one end of the court

4. A Round   Completed play at Head and Foot of court

5. Dead disc   Disc that is not in play

6. Live disc   Disc that is in play

7. Mounted disc   A disc is resting on top of another disc

How to Play:

1. The rules for shuffleboard singles apply to this game with a few exceptions.

2. Pick a partner and challenge another group.

3. Partners shall play the same color at both ends of the court.

4. The game is started by red. Red and black alternate back and forth. After all of the discs have been played at the head of court, play starts at the foot of court

with red leading and black following. Color lead does not change until both ends have been played (a round).

5. Players must remain seated when play is to their end of the court until all disc are shot: Penalty—5 off.

6. Any remarks or motions to the partner which indicate coaching are prohibited: Penalty—10 off.

7. If a tie score results at game point or over, two complete rounds shall be played. If the score is tied again, play continues as before.

8. First team to score 75 points is declared the winner.

Student Tasks:

1. Score with two of the discs during a half round.

2. Eliminate an opponent's scoring disc.

3. Block a scoring disc.

4. Land a disc onto the 10-area.

Variations:

1. Play to 100 points.

2. Score all discs that remain on the playing surface.

3. Use only two discs each.

4. Create a double-elimination tournament.

5. A team must win two out of three games to win the match. The second game is initiated by black. When a third game is needed, red starts.

Illustration of Shuffleboard Doubles

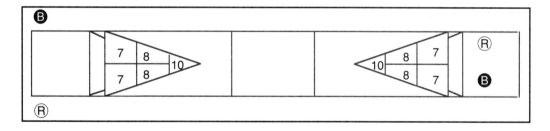

DEUCE SOCCER

Objectives:

♦ Score more points than the opposition does.

♦ Win by two points.

♦ Promote teamwork and cooperation.

Essentials:

♦ Tennis court

♦ Vinyl-covered foam ball
(11-inch diameter)

♦ Pinnies or flags

♦ Floor or masking tape

How to Play:

1. The rules of indoor soccer apply to this game.

2. Place two vertical tape strips on the net approximately 12 feet apart. Use the tape and mark a goalie box.

3. Make teams composed of seven players each.

4. Determine the starting possession with rock, paper, and scissors.

5. To begin the game or after any score, the ball is placed on the service line and kicked over the net.

6. Kicking the ball past the goalie and hitting the net in between the two pieces of tape scores a point.

7. The ball can be kicked over the net at any time by the court players.

8. Whenever the goalie catches the ball, it must be returned to the goalie's own court to initiate play.

9. Players are not allowed to jump over the net.

10. Heading is allowed with the foam ball.

11. Rough play is prohibited and penalty shots will be awarded.

12. The first team to score three points wins if they are ahead by two. In other words, if the score is 2 to 2, one team must score two points in a row to be victorious.

Student Tasks:

1. Dribble the ball from the defensive side to the offensive side.

2. Take control of a ball on the defensive side, and pass it over the net to a teammate on the offensive side.

3. Assist in a score.

4. While playing goalie, stop the ball from crossing the net from the opposite side.

Variations:

1. The team that is ahead after a predetermined time is the winner.

2. Use two goalies and the entire net as a goal.

3. Use three courts and play a round-robin tournament.

Illustration of a Ball being Kicked into Play for Tennis Court Soccer

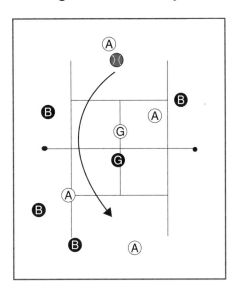

ELIMINATION SOCCER

Objectives:

◆ Possess the best team record.

◆ Eliminate the other three teams.

Essentials:

◆ Large floor or gymnasium

◆ Vinyl-covered foam ball (11-inch diameter)

◆ Pinnies or flags

◆ 4 large plastic soda bottles or bowling pins

◆ Floor tape to mark the goalie triangle and pin placement

How to Play:

1. Indoor soccer rules apply to this competition.

2. Mark a 12-foot wide goal line in each corner. Mark a spot three feet from each wall for the pin location.

3. Divide into four equal teams. Send each team to their respective areas with a ball.

4. Once the game begins, each team will attempt to knock over the other pins with any of the four soccer balls.

5. Players may go anywhere on the court except into the triangle areas.

6. Rough play such as slide tackling, tripping, or body checking is prohibited.

7. Heading is allowed with a foam ball.

8. Only the goalie is allowed to go into the goal triangle to retrieve a dead ball.

9. The goalie may be in possession of a ball for just three seconds before it must be rolled back into play.

10. When a team pin is knocked over, the entire squad is eliminated and sent to the goal area.

11. Play until three teams have been eliminated, then record the winner.

12. Rotate each team one court clockwise and begin a new contest.

13. The team with the best record, after several contests, wins.

Student Tasks:

1. Be a goalie.

2. Knock over a pin.

3. Take the ball away from an opponent.

4. Pass the ball to a teammate, who then knocks over a pin (assist).

Variations:

1. Change the scoring. The second team put out receives one point, the third team eliminated earns two points, and the winning team acquires three points.

2. Use more balls.

Illustration of Elimination Soccer Floor Layout

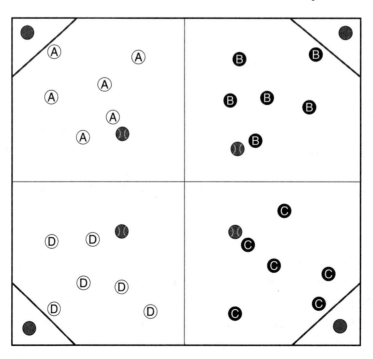

HULA SOCCER

Objectives:

- ◆ Do not acquire 10 points.
- ◆ Have the lowest score.
- ◆ Displace the other teams' pins.

Essentials:

- ◆ Large floor or gymnasium
- ◆ 4 vinyl-covered foam balls (11-inch diameter)
- ◆ Pinnies or flags
- ◆ 4 large plastic soda bottles or bowling pins
- ◆ 4 hula hoops

How to Play:

1. Indoor soccer rules apply to this game.
2. Secure a hula hoop (use tape) 20 feet from each corner wall and place a pin in the middle.
3. Divide into four equal teams. Send each team to an area with a ball.
4. Once the game begins, each team will attempt to knock over the other pins with any of the four soccer balls.
5. Players may go anywhere on the court.
6. Rough play such as slide tackling, tripping, or body checking is taboo.
7. Heading is allowed with the foam ball.
8. Only one player is allowed to guard the pin and must defend it from all angles.
9. The goalie may be in possession of a ball for just three seconds before rolling the ball back into play.
10. A team receives one point each time their pin is toppled.
11. If the pin has not been retrieved and reset within ten seconds, one additional point is assessed.
12. The game is over when any team reaches 10 points.
13. The winner has the lowest score.

Student Tasks:

1. Be a goalie.
2. Knock over a pin.
3. Take the ball away from another player.

Variations:

1. Place the hoops directly in the middle of each court.

2. Use more or fewer balls.

3. Allow two goalies to defend the pin.

Diagram of a Hula Soccer Floor Layout

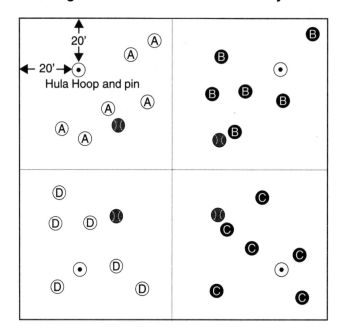

INDOOR BONUS BALL

Objectives:

◆ Score more goals than the rival does in a set amount of time.

◆ Acquire the best team record.

◆ Encourage teamwork.

Essentials:

◆ Large gym or indoor area

◆ Marked goal on each end of the wall (15 to 20 feet wide by 6 feet high)

◆ 2 vinyl-covered foam balls of different colors or markings (11-inch diameter)

◆ Pinnies or flags

◆ Scoreboard

How to Play:

1. Soccer rules apply to this game with a few exceptions.

2. Divide into four equal teams.

3. Play three games by combining two different teams each contest. The first game will involve A + B taking on C + D, the second incorporates A + C opposing B + D, and the third will consist of A + D against B + C.

4. Within each group, one team will be the offense and the other the defense. Neither team may cross the half-court line during play. At the midpoint of each game, teams will switch roles.

5. Designate which ball is the bonus ball. This ball is worth two points when scored.

6. The goalie will put any scored ball back into play by throwing or kicking it anywhere. Goalies may only be in possession of a ball for three seconds.

7. This is a nonstop action game since the ball is played off of the walls and the goalie returns all balls.

8. Wild kicks and blasting of the ball are not allowed at any time. It may only be dribbled, passed to a teammate, or kicked with finesse and control at the goalie.

9. Heading is allowed with a foam ball.

10. Participants may use their hands to protect the body from an oncoming ball.

11. Rough play, such as body checking, tripping, and slide tackling is prohibited. A direct kick at the goalie will be awarded.

12. The team with the best record, after all three games have been played, wins the event.

Student Tasks:

1. Be a goalie.

2. Block three shots on goal during the same game.

3. Create a shutout.

4. Assist a score.

5. Score both balls during a game.

Variations:

1. Play is stopped each time a goal is scored. Both balls are returned to center court.

2. Allow two goalies at each goal.

3. Play outdoors. Use the Mix 'n' Match format and play several short games.

Illustration of Multiple Choice Soccer

(A+B vs. C+D with A and D on defense)

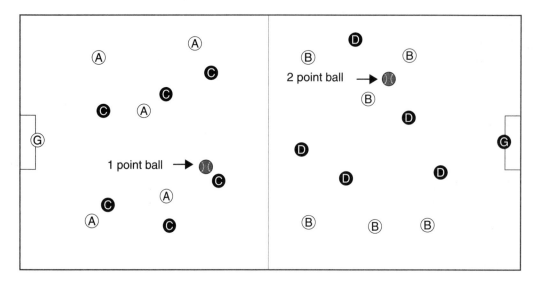

SHADOW SOCCER

Objectives:

- ◆ Score more points than the opposition does within the time period.
- ◆ Kick a ball through the goal.
- ◆ Develop cooperation with teammates.

Essentials:

- ◆ Field
- ◆ Field cones
- ◆ Soccer balls
- ◆ Pinnies or flags
- ◆ 20 pieces of rope (see diagram below)

How to Play:

1. The basic rules of soccer apply to this game.
2. Divide a standard football field or soccer field and play several games (diagonally).
3. Place the goal cones in the middle of each side about 15 feet apart (see below).
4. Form teams of eight to ten players. Players will pair up and acquire one piece of rope. They must hold on to the rope with one hand at all times.
5. Any pair that lets go of the rope will go to the sideline for a 30-second penalty.
6. The pair of goalies may only move one step away from the imaginary goal line.

7. Players may let go of the rope and use their hands to protect the face, chest, or groin.

8. Once the ball is in play, there are no offside calls. Companions are allowed to go anywhere on the field.

9. Swarming is not allowed. Only one pair from each team is allowed to compete for the ball.

10. The ball must be passed, dribbled, or control kicked through the goal. Wild or forceful kicking of the ball is prohibited.

11. The entire ball must go across a sideline or end line before it is out of play.

12. Players may score a goal through the cones from either direction.

13. Heading the ball or slide tackling is not permitted for safety reasons.

14. The ball may not be kicked away from either goalie once it has been trapped with the goalie's hands or feet.

15. Teammates must switch to a new partner after each score. Each team member must have paired up with everyone else before going back to her or his original partner.

16. A winner is declared after a given amount of time.

Student Tasks:

1. Block three shots on goal during the same game.
2. Create a shutout.
3. Assist a score.
4. Dribble around a defensive pair.
5. Steal the ball from an offensive pair.

Variations:

1. Require that both hands must remain on the rope at all times.
2. Combine any number of teams and use two or more balls at once.
3. Play with four goals, four teams, and two or more balls.
4. Play indoors and rotate small groups into the game every two minutes.
5. Use the **Mix 'n' Match** format and play several short timed games of only five to six minutes each.

Depiction of the Rope

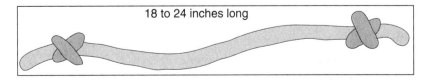

18 to 24 inches long

Diagram of a Shadow Soccer Field Layout

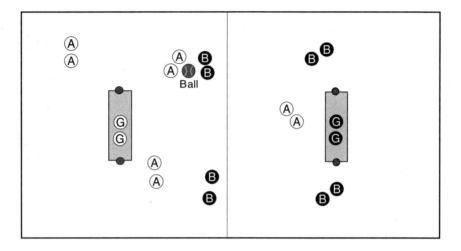

SIDELINE SOCCER

Objectives:

◆ Score more goals within a timed session than the opposition does.

◆ Develop teamwork.

Essentials:

◆ Field

◆ Soccer ball

◆ Pinnies or flags

◆ Soccer goals (may use 2 field cones)

How to Play:

1. The rules of soccer apply to this contest.

2. Make two equal teams.

3. Five players, including the goalie, will begin play.

4. A field player may kick the ball to a sideline teammate at any time.

5. Sideline participants:

   a. May move freely up and down the sidelines.

   b. Cannot score.

   c. Must kick the ball back to a field player.

   d. Cannot kick the ball to another sideline teammate.

6. Rotate five new players into the contest every three minutes.

7. Slide tackling, tripping, or body checking is prohibited.

8. Direct kicks are awarded for rough play or violations during any scoring attempt.

9. The team that is ahead, after a given amount of time, wins.

Student Tasks:

1. Be a goalie.

2. Pass the ball to a sideline player, get open, and receive the ball again.

3. Pass the ball from the sideline for an assist.

4. Prevent a ball from getting to the opponent's sideline player.

Variations:

1. Divide into four equal teams. Play three games by combining two different teams each contest (round robin).

2. Play the game indoors on a basketball court with vinyl-covered foam balls.

Diagram of Sideline Soccer

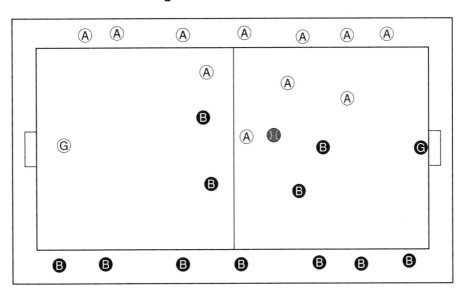

SOCCER GOLF

Objectives:

♦ Cover the course with the fewest kicks.

♦ Learn the basic rules and terms of golf.

♦ Develop control and accuracy when kicking a soccer ball.

Essentials:

- ◆ Outdoor field
- ◆ Ball for each student (soccer balls are not required)
- ◆ Course map, pencil, and score sheet per group (see "Golf" for forms)
- ◆ Several pins (i.e., posts, walls, poles, cones, and buckets)

Terminology:

1.	Bogey	Over par
2.	Par	Average
3.	Birdie	One under par
4.	Eagle	Two under par
5.	Hole In One	Made in one kick
6.	Fore	Protect your head
7.	Pin	Hole or object that is to made or hit
8.	Away	Player farthest from the hole
9.	Lie	Where the ball lands and stops
10.	Putt	Any short kick to the pin
11.	Mulligan	Extra kick that does not cost a stroke

How to Play:

1. The rules and etiquette of golf apply to this game.
2. Can be played by singles, pairs, or teams. Each group should use the same kind of kicking ball.
3. Use a "shotgun start" by sending players to different pins to begin the game.
4. Players will kick the ball and attempt to hit an object (pin) with the fewest number of kicks.
5. Do not make distracting noises or motions when other players are about to kick the ball.
6. During play, the kicker who had the lowest score on the previous hole determines the tee off. The lowest score will boot the ball first. If there was a tie, go back two or three holes, if necessary.
7. The player who is the farthest away from the hole will always kick first.
8. Any unplayable lie can be relocated with a one-stroke penalty.
9. Lowest score after completing the course is the winner.

Student Tasks:

1. Make a hole in one.
2. Make an eagle.
3. Win three or more holes.

4. Make a certain number of birdies during a round.

5. Come from behind and win a match.

Variations:

1. Make teams of two or three students. After everyone has kicked, determine the best lie. The entire team will kick from this point.

2. Play the course in the reverse.

3. Play mixed doubles.

4. The ball must be kicked with the alternate foot each time.

SPEED SOCCER

Objectives:

◆ Score three points before the opposition does.

◆ Win two out of three games.

◆ Promote teamwork and cooperation.

Essentials:

◆ Half of a tennis court

◆ Vinyl-covered foam ball (11-inch diameter)

◆ Pinnies or flags

◆ Floor or masking tape

How to Play:

1. The rules of indoor soccer apply to this game.

2. Use only one side of a tennis court. Tape a goal on the wall or fence approximately 12 feet wide by 4 feet high. Mark a goalie box the same width and five feet out.

3. Make teams composed of four players each.

4. Determine which team starts with possession (use the rock, paper, and scissors game).

5. The ball is placed at center net and indirectly kicked to a teammate.

6. Kicking or heading the ball and hitting the wall or fence (inside of the box) scores a point.

7. Any ball kicked off of the court, either into another one or over the fence, will result in a point for the opposition.

8. The ball must first be kicked against the center tennis net before any team can take the offense. For example, if defensive team B intercepts the ball but does not kick it against the net before team A reacquires it, team A is still on offense.

9. Only the defensive team is allowed to have a goalie in the goalie box. Goalies must be ready to switch instantly and the waiting goalie cannot be involved in play.

10. Whenever the goalie catches the ball, she or he must throw or kick the ball against the net. The goalie's team is now on offense.

11. Heading is allowed with a foam ball.

12. Penalty shots are awarded for rough play.

13. First team to score three points wins the game.

14. First team to win two out of three games wins the contest.

Student Tasks:

1. Prevent the defense from passing a controlled ball to the center net.

2. Pass the ball to the center net three times during a game.

3. While playing goalie, stop three scoring attempts.

4. Assist in a score.

5. Create a shutout.

Variations:

1. Play to four, five, or six points.

2. Allow the waiting goalie to play offense, too.

3. Determine the winner after a predetermined amount of time.

4. Use six half courts and play a round-robin tournament.

Illustration of Speed Soccer

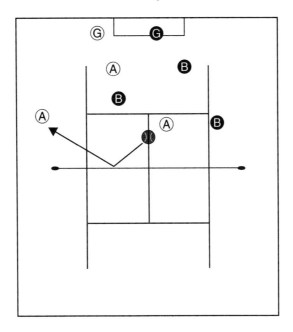

TENNIS COURT SOCCER

Objectives:

◆ Score more points than the opposition does.

◆ Promote teamwork and cooperation.

Essentials:

◆ Tennis court

◆ Vinyl-covered foam ball (11-inch diameter)

◆ Pinnies or flags

◆ Floor or masking tape

How to Play:

1. The rules of indoor soccer apply to this game.

2. Place two vertical tape strips on the end wall or fence approximately 12 feet apart. Tape the box about six feet out.

3. Make teams composed of seven players each.

4. Determine the starting offensive team with rock, paper, and scissors.

5. Not counting the goalie, only three players from each team are allowed on each side of the net.

6. All players will switch from offense to defense anytime two points have been scored. In other words, if the score is 1 to 1, switch.

7. The goalie always puts the ball into play by kicking or throwing it anywhere.

8. Kicking the ball and hitting the wall or fence below the extended arms of the goalie scores a point.

9. A point is awarded to the opposition for kicking the ball out of bounds.

10. The court players are not allowed to kick the ball over the net at any time.

11. Whenever the goalie catches the ball, it must be returned to the goalie's own court to initiate play.

12. Players are not allowed to jump over the net.

13. Heading is allowed with a foam ball.

14. Direct kicks are awarded for rough play or violations during any scoring attempt.

15. The team that is ahead after a predetermined amount of time wins.

Student Tasks:

1. Dribble the ball from one side to the other.
2. Assist in a score.
3. Be a goalie.
4. Win by three or more points.
5. Cause a shutout.

Variations:

1. Only allow two players plus the goalie to be on the defensive side.
2. Allow the ball to be kicked over the net during play.
3. Make larger teams and have several goalies defend the entire fence (see "Wall Soccer").
4. Use three courts and play a round-robin tournament.

Diagram of Tennis Court Soccer

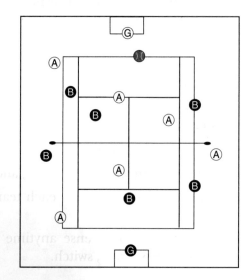

WALL SOCCER

Objectives:

- ◆ Score more goals than the competition.
- ◆ Obtain the best team record.
- ◆ Promote team play.

Essentials:

- ◆ Large indoor area or gymnasium
- ◆ Vinyl-covered foam ball (11-inch diameter)
- ◆ Pinnies or flags
- ◆ Scoreboard

How to Play:

1. Soccer policies apply to this game.

2. Create four teams.

3. Play three games by combining two different teams each contest. The first game will involve A + B battling C + D, the second focuses on A + C opposite B + D, and the third will match A + D against B + C.

4. Send the combined teams to opposite ends of the court.

5. Four players from each team will enter the playing arena and compete for two minutes. When time has expired, rotate four new individuals into play. The exiting team members will return to the end of the goalie line and defend the wall.

6. If and when the ball is kicked against either end wall below a given height, six feet for example, a point is scored.

7. The goalies will put the ball into play after a score or controlled possession.

8. Goalies are restricted from being more than six feet away from the wall at any time.

9. This is a nonstop action game since the ball is played off of the walls.

10. No wild kicks or blasting of the ball is allowed. It may only be dribbled, passed to a teammate, or kicked with finesse and control at the goal.

11. Heading is allowed with a foam ball.

12. Participants may use their hands to protect the body from an oncoming ball.

13. Rough play, such as body checking and slide tackling, is prohibited. A penalty shot will be given.

14. The team with the best record, after all three games have been played, wins the overall contest.

Student Tasks:

1. Block the ball from hitting the wall.
2. Do not allow the opposition to score.
3. Assist a score.
4. Dribble around a defensive player by passing the ball off of the wall.
5. Use the wall and pass the ball to a teammate.

Variations:

1. Each team sends five or six players to the floor.
2. Use two balls and send half of each team to compete.
3. Make two teams and play only one game.

Illustration of Wall Soccer Rotation

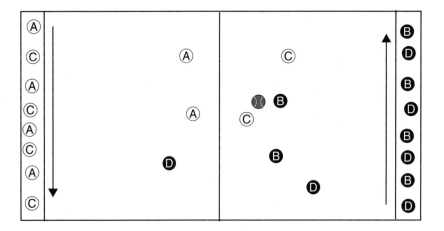

ZONE SOCCER

Objectives:

◆ Score more points than the opposition during a time period.
◆ Develop teamwork and cooperation.

Essentials:

◆ Football field
◆ 1 soccer ball
◆ 14 field cones (The cones may be placed on the sidelines but when moved to the hash marks, identification of the zones is easier.)
◆ Pinnies or flags

SOCCER

How to Play:

1. Soccer rules apply to this game with a few exceptions.
2. Divide into two equal teams.
3. Each team will send an equal number of players to each zone. If there are unequal numbers, then those players must locate to the middle zones.
4. Each competitor must stay within the zone during play.
5. The ball may not be kicked completely over top of an adjoining zone. A player in each zone must touch it as it is advanced in either direction.
6. The offense must constantly attempt to push the ball down the field in the direction of the goal. The ball may not be kicked backwards to a teammate in the preceding zone (opposite direction) for defensive purposes.
7. One point is awarded when the ball travels between the cones and below the goalie's head (unless soccer goals are used). However, the goal does not count if the goalie deflects the ball over the top of her or his head.
8. The goalie may attempt to stop or deflect a shot in any manner.
9. Once the goalie has custody of the ball, all play stops until the goalie initiates play.
10. Team members must rotate one zone in opposite directions following a score or after a predetermined amount of time.
11. After a score, the ball is initiated into play from the middle zone.
12. Play for a predetermined amount of time. The team that is ahead is victorious.

Student Tasks:

1. Be a goalie.
2. Successfully block two shot attempts.
3. Do not allow the opposition to score.
4. Complete three or more passes.
5. Make an assist.
6. Intercept a pass.

Variations:

1. Use two balls.
2. Play indoors and use the rules of "wall soccer."
3. Allow two goalies to defend each goal.
4. Change the size of the zones (see illustrations below).
5. Play until a team reaches a given number of scores.
6. Play three games by combining two different teams each contest. The first game will involve A + B taking on C + D, the second incorporates A + C opposing B + D, and the third will consist of A + D against B + C.
7. Use a round-robin format and play several short games on narrowed fields.

Illustration of Zone Soccer Field Layouts
(A: Full field - 15 yards)

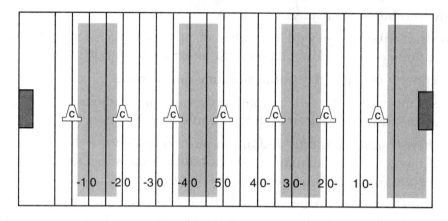

(B: Full field - 20 yards)

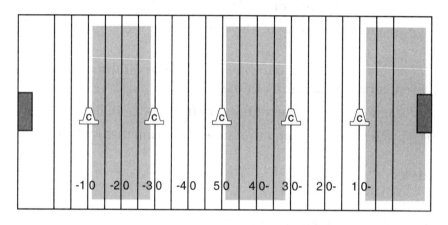

(C: Full field - 25 yards)

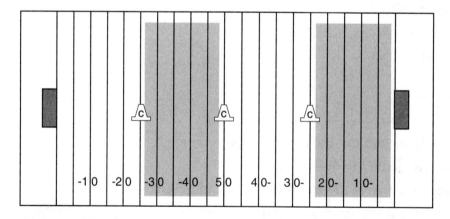

(D: Full Field, 25 yards - 20 yards - 15 yards)

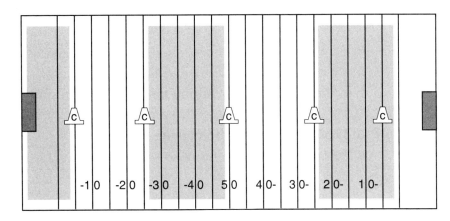

(E: Narrow football field - round robin)

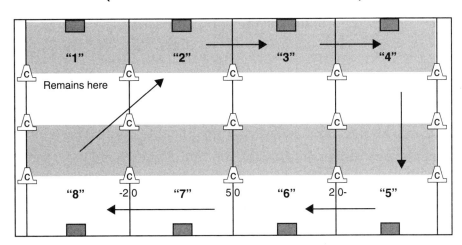

BASES ARE LOADED

Objectives:

- ◆ Score more runs than the opposition by hitting the ball and running around the bases safely.
- ◆ Create teamwork and cooperative decision-making.

Essentials:

- ◆ Field
- ◆ 4 bases, 1 bat, and 1 super-soft softball
- ◆ Face mask and chest protector
- ◆ Safety cone to mark the next batter's box if no backstops are present

Safety: (See "Modified Softball" for the complete list.)

How to Play:

1. The rules of "Modified Softball" will apply to this game.
2. Create teams with eight or nine players on each. Divide each team into two smaller teams. Mini teams must switch from infield to outfield each inning.
3. There may be one runner at first base, two runners at second base, and three runners at third base.
4. When a base contains the maximum number of runners and a base runner advances from a preceding base, at least one of the runners must advance to the next base.
5. When two or more runners advance on a force out, the lead runner is out when the base is tagged. However, the second runner must be tagged with the ball.

Student Tasks:

1. Get a single, double, triple, or home run.
2. Catch a fly ball.
3. Be involved in a double play.

Variations:

1. Allow three runners to occupy first base, two runners to remain on second base, and only one to inhabit third base.
2. The batting team is given five outs before being retired.

Illustration of Bases Are Loaded

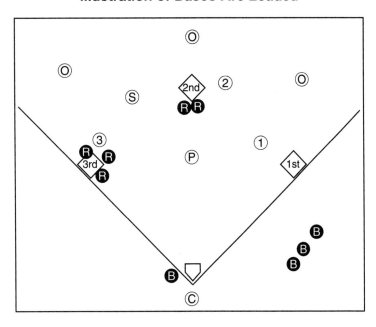

DOUBLE DIAMOND REVERSE*

Objectives:

◆ Score more runs than the opposition does.

◆ Hit the ball and run around a chosen base path.

◆ Promote creative strategy planning.

◆ Enhance quick decision-making.

Essentials:

◆ Field

◆ Set of softball bases placed 60 feet apart

◆ Set of softball bases placed at 90-foot intervals

◆ 1 bat and 1 super-soft softball

◆ Face mask and chest protector

◆ Safety cone to mark the next batter's box if no backstops are present

Safety:

1. Placing the 60-foot third base six feet inside the baseline, and the extra home plate 10 feet from the hitting home plate, will prevent collisions of runners traveling in opposite directions.

2. See "Modified Softball" for additional guidelines.

*Created by Ken Lumsden, 1999.

How to Play:

1. The rules of "Double Diamond" softball will be used for this game.

2. Divide into two teams composed of 10 to 12 players each.

3. The field layout: (see illustration below)

   a. Reverse the 60-foot 1st and 3rd bases.

   b. Use an extra home base for the 90-foot base path by placing it 10 feet to the left of the hitting home plate.

   c. Place the 60-foot 3rd base six feet inside the baseline.

4. Only one base runner is allowed to occupy a base.

5. Runners who elect to go around the shorter diamond must stay on this chosen path. One run will be awarded for scoring.

6. Runners who elect to go around the larger diamond will be given two runs. However, a runner may run from the 90-foot third base to the 60-foot first base, because it is open, and may continue around this inside diamond and score four runs for the team.

Student Tasks:

1. Score from both base paths during a game.

2. Score four points by running both diamonds in an inning.

3. Get a single, double, triple, or home run.

4. Catch a fly ball.

5. Be involved in a double play.

6. Tag a runner.

7. Never be put out during a game or during the day.

8. Assist in an out.

Variations:

1. Use a different ball.

2. Give the batting team five outs.

3. Allow runners to return to the same base they occupied when the last out was made during the previous inning.

4. Initiate a 10-run rule. A team may score only 10 runs per inning, unless it is behind by more than 10 runs. In that case, it can score as many runs as needed to go ahead by one run. This will prevent blowouts and keep the game much more interesting and enjoyable.

Illustration of Double Diamond Reverse

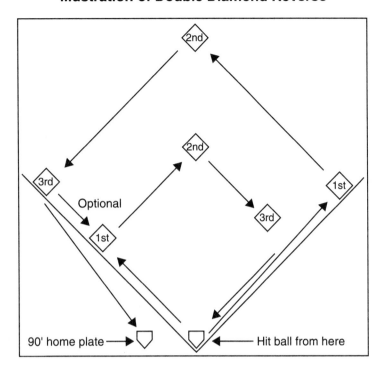

DOUBLE DIAMOND*

Objectives:

- ◆ Score more runs than the opposition makes.
- ◆ Hit the ball and run safely around a chosen base path.
- ◆ Enhance quick decision-making.

Essentials:

- ◆ Field
- ◆ 1 bat and super-soft softball
- ◆ Set of softball bases placed 60 feet apart
- ◆ 3 bases placed 90 feet away from each other

- ◆ Face mask and chest protector
- ◆ Safety cone to mark the next batter's box if no backstops are present

---

*Created by Ken Lumsden, 1999.

Safety: (See "Modified Softball" for the entire list.)

How to Play:

1. The rules of "Modified Softball" apply to this game.
2. Make teams composed of 10 to 12 players each.
3. Bunting is not allowed.
4. After successfully hitting the ball, a batter will attempt to make it safely to either first base. The first base runner must stay on that base path.
5. Any runner on first base must advance when the ball is hit, unless it is a caught fly ball.
6. If the ball is thrown to the 60-foot base before the runner arrives, the runner is out.
7. A runner on the 90-foot third base may pass a teammate that is on the 60-foot third base in order to score.
8. Defensive players may not interfere with the base runners.
9. When both base paths are loaded and the ball is hit and returned to the catcher before the third base runners can score, both runners are out (double play).
10. Scoring:
    a. Advancing safely around the 60-foot base path is worth one point.
    b. Two runs are scored for proceeding around the 90-foot base path.

Student Tasks:

1. Score from both base paths.
2. Get a single, double, triple, or home run.
3. Catch a fly ball.
4. Be involved in a double play.
5. Tag a runner.
6. Never be put out during a game or during the day.
7. Assist in an out.

Variations:

1. When both first bases are occupied and the ball is hit, allow the 60-foot first base runner to advance to the 90-foot first base.
2. Use a different type of ball.
3. Use a tennis ball and racket.
4. Allow runners to return to the same bases they occupied when the last out was made during the previous inning.
5. Initiate a 10-run rule.

Illustration of a Double Diamond Field

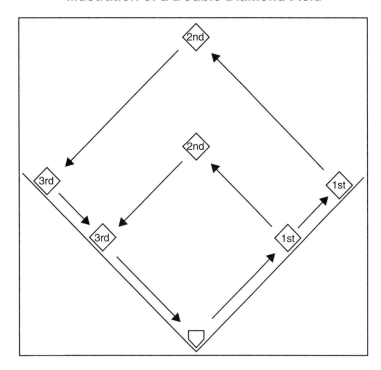

ENGLISH ROUNDERS

Objectives:

◆ Score more runs than the opposition.

◆ Do not allow the defense to capture the home box.

◆ Develop hitting, running, and throwing skills.

Essentials:

◆ Field

◆ 3 wooden dowels (1 inch X 6 feet)

◆ 1 Tennis ball

◆ Wooden dowel bat (1 inch in diameter by 18 inches in length)

◆ 4 field cones

Terminology:

1. Castle	Home box
2. Sanctuary	Bases
3. Striker	Batter
4. Feeder	Pitcher
5. Plugged	Hit with a thrown ball

6. Rounder   Homerun
7. Foray   Run

How to Play:

1. This is a modified version of official English Rounders.
2. Divide into teams with eight or nine players each.
3. The pitcher (feeder) will deliver the ball underhand.
4. The batter (striker) has an unlimited number of attempts in which to hit the ball.
5. The striker is out if the ball is caught in the air or on one bounce.
6. Once the ball makes contact with the stick, be it fair or foul, the batter begins running around the pole bases (sanctuaries) in a clockwise manner. The runner may travel anywhere outside of the bases and does not need to touch them.
7. When a runner grabs hold of a pole base, she or he is considered safe. A runner may only use a base one time. Once the hand is removed, that player must advance.
8. Base runners may be put out by being tagged or hit (plugged) with the ball.
9. Base runners may not lead off or steal a base. They may, however, advance as soon as the ball makes contact with the stick, no matter what the outcome is.
10. Any successful runner returning to the home box (castle) scores a run (foray) for the team. The runner will continue until being put out.
11. Any player stepping outside of the home box is automatically out.
12. If the last batter can hit back-to-back home runs (rounders), then the entire team is allowed to return.
13. The inning is over when the last batter is out, or is unable to return to the home box before the defense hits one of its four cones with the ball.

Student Tasks:

1. Run around the bases three times.
2. Throw and hit a runner.
3. Hit a home run.
4. Be the last person up.

Variations:

1. The inning is over after six, seven, or eight outs. Players that are put out return to the home box and continue hitting in order.
2. Lengthen the base paths to 50 or more feet.
3. Initiate a 10-run rule.

Illustration of an English Rounders Field Layout

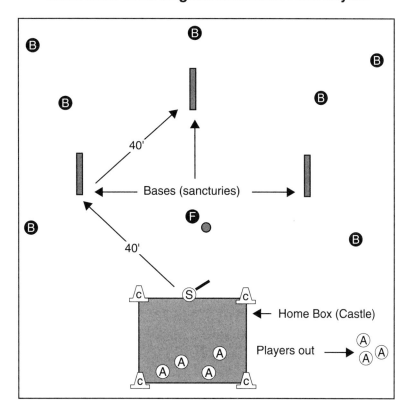

FIVE HUNDRED

Objectives:

◆ Field the ball and get to 500 points first.

◆ Develop hitting and catching skills.

Essentials:

◆ Open field

◆ 1 bat

◆ 1 softball (restricted flight)

How to Play:

1. Break into groups of five to seven players each.

2. Everyone goes to the outfield except the batter.

3. The batter tosses the ball into the air and hits it to the fielders.

4. Scoring:

    a. Fly ball   100 points

    b. One bounce   75 points

    c. Two bounces   50 points

    d. Grounder   25 points

5. Any player is given minus points for making an error when attempting to field the ball.

6. Once a player has touched the ball, no one else may receive credit for playing it.

7. The first person to receive 500 or more points will trade places with the batter and begin a new game.

Student Tasks:

1. Catch three fly balls.

2. Catch three one-bouncers.

3. Be the first person to bat twice.

Variations:

1. Change the type of ball.

2. Require a different number of points to become a hitter.

3. Eliminate the minus points rule.

Illustration of Five Hundred

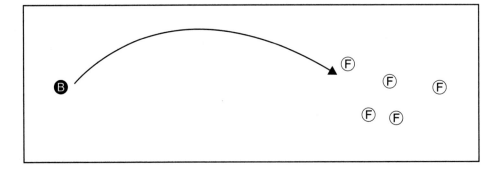

GRAB BAG*

Objectives:

◆ Score more runs than the opposition by hitting the ball and running around the bases safely.

◆ Score bonus runs by carrying the bonus object to home plate safely.

Essentials:

◆ Field

◆ 4 bases, 1 bat, and 1 super-soft softball

◆ Face mask and chest protector

◆ Safety cone to mark the next batter's box if no backstops are present

◆ Large open playing area or field

◆ Bonus object (anything cumbersome such as a football blocking dummy or a large cardboard box)

Safety: (See "Modified Softball" for the guidelines.)

How to Play:

1. The rules of slow-pitch softball will apply to this game.

2. Create teams composed of eight or nine players each.

3. Place the bonus object just outside of first base. Each time this object is carried over home plate, four additional points are awarded.

4. A runner who gets on first base safely may or may not elect to carry the object around the bases.

5. A player in possession of the object may drop it at any time and proceed around the bases. The object must remain at this spot until the next runner chooses to grab it.

6. The object can never travel in the reverse direction. It must be dropped if a player decides to return back to the previous base. (That runner may pick it up again on the return trip.)

7. If a player is thrown out while in possession of the bonus object, the object is placed at the runner's approximate location on the base path when the out was made.

8. A player who scores with the object will return it to first base.

9. The object will remain at its position on the base path when the third out is made. The new team at bat will attempt to bring the object home from there.

10. The team with the highest score, after a given number of completed innings, is the winner.

Created by Ken Lumsden, 2000.

Student Tasks:

1. Carry the bonus object from one base to another.
2. Score with the object.
3. Get a single, double, triple, or home run.
4. Assist in an out.
5. Catch a fly ball.
6. Be involved in a double play.

Variations:

1. A runner who drops the object may not grab it again while on base.
2. The batting team is given five outs before being retired.
3. Play the game indoors or outdoors using kickball rules. If the object is hit with the ball, the runner is also out.

Illustration of Grab Bag

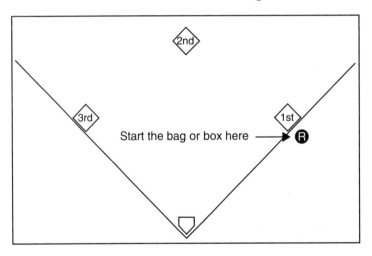

MODIFIED SOFTBALL

Objectives:

◆ Score more runs than the opposition by hitting the ball and running around the bases safely.
◆ Develop teamwork.

Essentials:

◆ Field
◆ 4 bases, 1 bat, and 1 super-soft softball

- ◆ Face mask and chest protector
- ◆ Safety cones to mark the next batter's box when no backstops are present.

Safety:

1. If there are no backstops, future batters are to be no closer than 25 feet to home plate. The batter is out if any teammate is within 25 feet of home plate when the ball is pitched. It is the responsibility of the pitcher and batter to keep the area clear.
2. The offense lines up on the first base side of the field.
3. The catcher should wear a face mask and chest protector.
4. The batter is out if the bat is thrown more than four lengths from home plate.
5. Batters must always grip the bat with both hands.
6. To reduce injuries to both runner and base person, sliding is not allowed.
7. The first base person is allowed to block or cover first base.

How to Play:

1. Create teams composed of seven to nine players each.
2. The batting team will provide its own pitcher.
3. The pitcher must not intentionally interfere with a hit ball. If this happens, the runner is out. If it is unintentional, redo the pitch.
4. A hitter will receive only three pitches in which to hit the ball fair.
5. Bunting is illegal.
6. Base runners cannot lead off before the ball is hit and must tag up on all caught fly balls.
7. Runners must touch each base when traveling around the base path.
8. A base runner will neither overrun second or third base nor run out of the baseline in order to avoid a tag.
9. A base runner who is off of a base and subsequently is hit with a batted ball is out.
10. All runners are given one extra base on any overthrown, out of play ball.
11. The offensive team is retired to the outfield after three outs.
12. Nobody may play the same defensive position two times in a row.
13. The defensive team cannot block a base runner or stand in the baseline when not in possession of the ball.
14. Runners must be tagged on all unforced plays.
15. All ties go to the runner.
16. The defense will act as umpires and make all the calls. They are never wrong.
17. In order to determine a winner, revert to the last completed inning.

Student Tasks:

1. Get on base safely.
2. Catch a fly ball.

3. Be involved in a double play.

4. Be a pitcher.

5. Have everyone on the team score a run during the game.

6. Trap a runner in between two bases (pickle) and then tag the runner out.

Variations:

1. Use the 10-run rule: The team is out after scoring 10 runs. Any team behind by more than 10 runs can score as many runs as needed to go ahead by one.

2. Use a 5-run rule instead of the 10-run rule. This speeds up the game and prevents a blowout.

3. Allow stranded runners to return to the same base the next inning.

4. The offensive team may provide a catcher but this catcher will not put runners out. The defense must send someone in to make an out at home.

5. Divide each team into two small teams that must switch from infield to outfield each inning.

6. Use a tournament format.

Illustration of Modified Softball

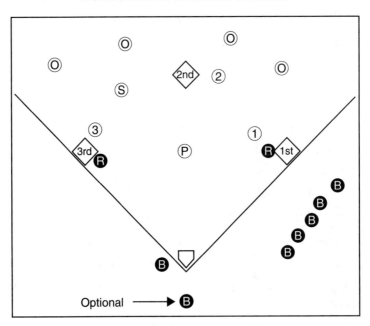

PONY EXPRESS*

Objectives:

◆ Score more runs than the opposition by hitting the ball and running around the bases safely.

◆ Score bonus runs by carrying the team's pennant back to home plate safely.

Essentials:

◆ Field

◆ 4 bases, 1 bat, and 1 super-soft softball

◆ Face mask and chest protector

◆ Safety cone to mark the next batter's box if no backstops are present

◆ 2 pennants (football flags, pinnies, etc., of contrasting colors)

Safety: (See "Modified Softball" for the rules.)

How to Play:

1. The rules of modified softball will be used for this game.

2. Create teams composed of eight or nine players each.

3. The first batter receives the team's flag. Each time this flag is carried over home plate, two additional points are awarded.

4. If a player in possession of the team flag is thrown out while running from first to second, the flag is placed at the runner's approximate location on the base path when the out was made. The next runner may or may not elect to pick it up while running the bases.

5. A player who scores with the bonus flag will give it to the next batter.

6. When the third out is made, the bonus flag will remain at its present position until the team is up again and can advance a runner to pick it up.

7. The team with the highest score, after a given number of completed innings, is the winner.

Student Tasks:

1. Score with the bonus flag.

2. Get a hit that scores the runner with the flag.

3. Put the runner with the flag out.

4. Catch a fly ball.

© 2001 Parker Publishing Company

*Created by Ken Lumsden, 2000.

Variations:

1. Provide three flags for each team. Each runner who makes an out must drop the flag and return to the end of the batting line. The next runner (without a flag) may pick it up.

2. The batting team is given five outs before being retired.

3. Use fewer players on a team.

4. Play the game indoors or outdoors using kickball rules.

5. Use the 10-run rule.

6. Make several teams and play a round-robin tournament.

Illustration of Pony Express

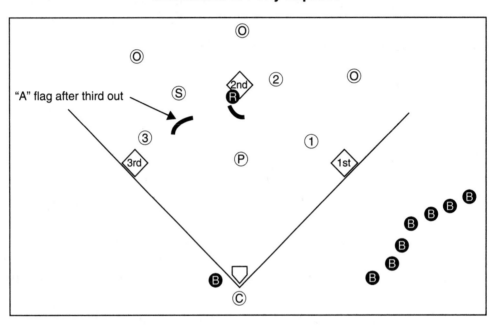

ROGUE'S GALLERY

Objective:

◆ Score more runs than the opposition by hitting the ball and running around the bases safely.

◆ Eliminate the entire batting team.

Essentials:

◆ Field

◆ 4 bases, 1 bat, and 1 super-soft softball

◆ Face mask and chest protector

◆ Safety cone to mark the next batter's box if no backstops are present

Safety: (See "Modified Softball" for a list of the rules.)

How to Play:

1. The rules of modified softball apply to this game.
2. Create teams composed of seven to ten players each.
3. The offensive team will provide a pitcher.
4. Every player on offense will bat once.
5. An inning is over after everyone has attempted to hit the ball.
6. A player has only two chances in which to hit the ball fair.
7. Any batter who hits a home run will promptly bat again.
8. If the last batter hits a single, one bonus hitter is allowed. A double is worth two extra batters, a triple equals three, and a home run receives four additional batters.
9. The team can choose who the bonus batter is so long as it is a new person each time.
10. A bonus batter is never considered a last batter. Whether that person scores, gets on base, or is put out, the inning is over after the last bonus batter is up.
11. There must be a new last batter every inning.
12. The defense must provide a catcher at all times.
13. To determine a winner after time expires, revert to the last complete inning.

Student Tasks:

1. Get on base safely.
2. Hit a home run.
3. Be a pitcher.
4. Participate in a double play.
5. Get a run batted in (RBI).
6. Have half of the team score a run during an inning.
7. Make sure everyone on the team scores a run during a game.

Variations:

1. Any number of runners may be on a given base (see below).
2. Use a kick ball. The runner is also out if hit below the waist with a thrown ball.
3. Divide each team into two small teams that must switch from infield to outfield each inning.
4. Use a tournament format.

Example of Rogue's Gallery with the Option of Extra Runners at Any Base

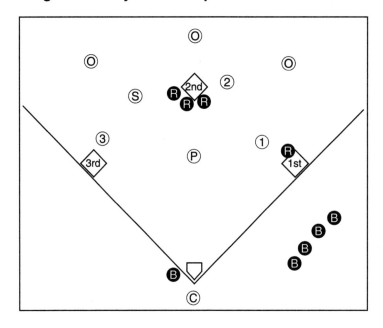

SOFTBALL GOLF

Objectives:

◆ Cover the course in the least amount of hits.

◆ Understand the basic rules and terms of golf.

◆ Develop hitting skills for accuracy and distance.

Essentials:

◆ Outdoor fields

◆ Softball and bat for each student (two players may share a bat)

◆ Course map, pencil, and score sheet (See "Golf" for copies)

◆ Pins (posts, walls, poles, cones, buckets, etc.)

Terminology:

1. Bogey   Number of shots taken over the par

2. Par   Average number of shots

3. Birdie   1 under par

4. Eagle   2 under par

5. Hole in One   Made a pin with the first shot

SOFTBALL

6. Fore — Protect your head
7. Pin — Object to be made or hit
8. Away — Player farthest from the pin
9. Lie — Position where the ball stops
10. Putt — A short shot to the pin

How to Play:

1. Design a 9-hole or 18-hole course.
2. Form flights with pairs or teams. Distribute one map, scorecard, and pencil to each group.
3. To begin the game, use a shotgun start by sending players to different pins.
4. The ball is tossed into the air prior to every swing. Missing the ball is counted as a stroke.
5. It is prohibited to make distracting noises or motions when other players are about to hit.
6. The players who had the lowest score on the previous hole will determine the lead off and hitting order. When necessary, go back two or more holes.
7. A player may not step past the lie of the previous hit when attempting the next swing.
8. During play, the player who is farthest from the hole (away) will bat first.
9. Any unplayable lie can be relocated with a one-stroke penalty.
10. Lowest score of the contest wins.

Student Tasks:

1. Make a hole in one.
2. Hit an eagle.
3. Make a certain number of birdies during a round.
4. Come from behind and win the match.
5. Choose one hole, prior to playing, and win it.

Variations:

1. Use one-inch wooden dowels and tennis balls.
2. Take away the bats and throw, toss, or roll softballs, hardballs, or even real golf balls. Alternate each throw with the right and left arm.
3. Make teams of two or three students. After everyone has hit, determine the best lie. The entire team will bat from this point.
4. Play the course in the reverse manner of 18, 17, 16, etc.
5. Play mixed doubles.

SOFTBALL SCORECARDS

Inning	1	2	3	4	5	6	7
X							
Y							
Outs							

Inning	1	2	3	4	5	6	7
X							
Y							
Outs							

Inning	1	2	3	4	5	6	7
X							
Y							
Outs							

Inning	1	2	3	4	5	6	7
X							
Y							
Outs							

Inning	1	2	3	4	5	6	7
X							
Y							
Outs							

Inning	1	2	3	4	5	6	7
X							
Y							
Outs							

Inning	1	2	3	4	5	6	7
X							
Y							
Outs							

Inning	1	2	3	4	5	6	7
X							
Y							
Outs							

STRAIGHTAWAY SOFTBALL

Objectives:

- ◆ Score more runs than the opposition.
- ◆ Throw the ball into the air and hit it.

Essentials:

- ◆ Field
- ◆ 4 bases, 1 bat, and 1 super-soft softball
- ◆ Face mask and chest protector
- ◆ Safety cone to mark the next batter's box if no backstops are present

Safety: (See "Modified Softball" for a complete listing.)

How to Play:

1. The rules of slow-pitch softball apply to this game.

2. Put together teams comprised of eight or nine players.

3. Set the bases in a straight line approximately 35 feet apart (see diagram below).

4. The batter:

   a. Tosses the ball into the air, hits it fair, then runs towards first base.

   b. Does not have to swing at every toss.

   c. Get three chances to hit the ball fair.

   d. Is not allowed to bunt the ball.

5. The base runner:

   a. May not overrun first or second base. After an overrun, the runner must continue on to the next base.

   b. Is not allowed to steal or lead off from any base.

   c. Scores a run when reaching third base. The runner then jogs around the outfield and returns to the batting line.

6. The fielders:

   a. Cannot play at the same base for two innings in a row.

   b. Do not have to tag runners because every base runner is a force out situation.

   c. Can cause an out by catching a fly, tagging a base, or tagging a runner who is advancing between bases.

7. The offensive team is retired to the outfield after three outs.

8. Play for a predetermined number of innings or for a given amount of time to determine a winner.

Student Tasks:

1. Throw two runners out during a game.
2. Catch a fly ball.
3. Hit a ball and make it to second base safely.
4. Never miss the ball when swinging at it.

Variations:

1. Place the bases 50 feet apart.
2. Vary the distance between bases. For example, place the first base 30 feet from home base, second is 40 feet from first, and third is set 50 feet from second.
3. Play the game indoors with a kickball. The ball can be pitched.
4. Initiate a 5- or 10-run rule.

Illustration of Straight Base Softball

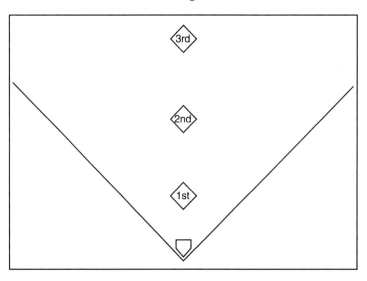

TENNI-S-OFTBALL*

Objectives:

◆ Score more runs than the opposition does.
◆ Hit the ball and run safely to each base, while jumping over hurdles.

---

*Created by Ken Lumsden, 1998.

SOFTBALL

Essentials:

- ◆ Field
- ◆ Set of bases
- ◆ Tennis racket
- ◆ Tennis ball
- ◆ 4 hurdles

Safety:

1. Jumping over a hurdle from the opposite direction is prohibited. When hit from the wrong direction, the front edge actually rises. This action may snare the foot and cause a fall.
2. See "Modified Softball" for additional safety rules.

How to Play:

1. The guidelines of modified softball will apply to this game.
2. Divide into teams composed of nine to ten players each.
3. One hurdle is placed directly on the baseline between all bases.
4. The offense will provide a pitcher who may deliver the ball either underhand or overhand.
5. Hitters may hold the racket with one or both hands.
6. The ball may be hit from the air or after one bounce.
7. A base runner:
   a. Must jump over each hurdle when advancing to the next base.
   b. May not use a hurdle as a shield from being tagged.
   c. Can return to the previous base, but must go around the hurdle. The hurdle must be jumped every time a runner advances to the next base. (This can become quite difficult when a player is caught in a "pickle.")
8. Play a predetermined number of innings or for a set amount of time to establish a winner. When time is used, revert back to the last completed inning.

Student Tasks:

1. Get a single, double, triple, or home run.
2. Assist in an out.
3. Catch a fly ball.
4. Be involved in a double play.

Variations:

1. Vary the height of each hurdle.
2. Divide each team into two smaller teams. The micro teams must switch from infield to outfield with each new inning.
3. The pitcher must throw overhand from within 10 feet of second base.

4. Make four small teams. Combine two new teams each game for a round-robin tournament.

Illustration of Field Layout for Tenni-S-oftball

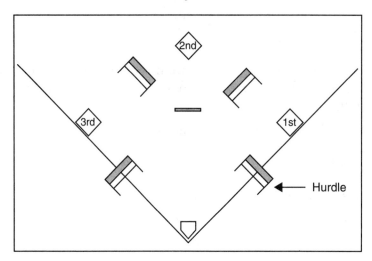

TRIPLE DIAMOND DELUXE*

Objectives:

◆ Score more runs than the opposition.

◆ Hit the ball and run safely around all of the base paths.

◆ Enhance quick decision-making.

Essentials:

◆ Field

◆ 1 bat and 1 super-soft softball

◆ Set of softball bases placed 45 feet apart

◆ 3 bases placed 60 feet apart

◆ 3 bases placed 75 feet apart

◆ Face mask and chest protector

◆ Safety cone to mark the next batter's box if no backstops are present

Safety:

1. Placing bases #3 and #4 six feet inside the baseline will prevent collisions by runners traveling in opposite directions.

2. See "Modified Softball" for the complete listing.

© 2001 Parker Publishing Company

*Created by Ken Lumsden, 1999.

SOFTBALL

How to Play:

1. The rules of "Modified Softball" apply to this game.

2. Set up the three diamonds as illustrated below. Remember to place base #3 and #4 six feet inside the baseline.

3. Create teams with 10 to 12 players each.

4. After hitting the ball, a runner will run toward base #1. A runner who reaches base #3 can either return to #10 for one point, or continue on to #4. If the entire gambit is completed, the runner's team will receive three points.

5. A runner left stranded on base when the third out was made, will return to the same location the next time her or his team is up to bat.

6. Any runner put out while running the bases will return to the batting line.

7. Play for a predetermined number of innings to determine a winner.

Student Tasks:

1. Score six or more runs during a game.

2. Score by running bases #1 through #10.

3. Catch a fly ball.

4. Be involved in a double play.

5. Tag a runner.

6. Never be put out during a game.

7. Assist in an out.

Variations:

1. Require five outs.

2. Runners may not go back to base the next time up.

3. Allow two or more runners to occupy the same base.

4. Use tennis ball.

5. Use a tennis ball and racket.

Illustration of a Triple Diamond Deluxe Field

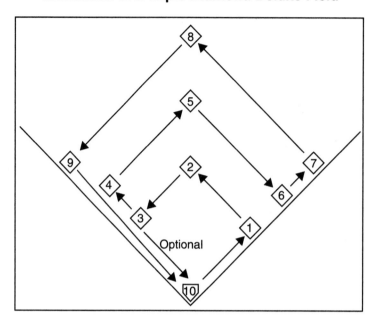

TWO BASE

Objectives:

◆ Score 11 runs before the opposition.

◆ Promote teamwork and cooperation.

Essentials:

◆ Field

◆ 2 bases, 1 bat, and 1 super-soft softball

◆ Face mask and chest protector

◆ Safety cone to mark the next batter's box if no backstops are present

Safety: **(See "Modified Softball" for the guidelines.)**

How to Play:

1. The rules of slow pitch softball apply to this game.

2. Form groups comprised of a catcher, batter, pitcher, and two outfielders.

3. The players will determine the distance between the two bases.

4. The pitcher must allow the batter to hit the ball.

5. Outs:

   a. A caught foul or fair fly.

   b. A force out at home.

    c. Sliding into a base.

    d. Throwing the bat more than four bat lengths from home plate.

    e. Scoring three runs in a row.

6. After the batter hits the ball, she or he must run to first base and back to home base before the catcher can receive the ball and tag the home plate.

7. When the batter is out, all participants will move up one position, with the batter going to the last outfielder position.

8. A player who catches a fly ball will exchange positions with the batter.

9. The first player to score 11 runs is victorious.

Student Tasks:

1. Catch a fly ball.

2. Score two or more runs during any at bat.

3. Throw the runner out at home.

4. Tag the base to put a runner out.

Variations:

1. Play for a predetermined amount of time.

2. Increase the numbers of runs needed to win.

3. Increase or decrease the number of runs in a row any one player may score.

4. Play with a vinyl-covered foam ball. Hitting the runner (below the waist) with the ball is also an out.

Illustration of Two Base

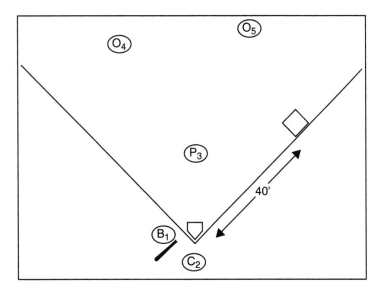

TWO BASE FOUR TEAM

Objectives:

◆ Score 15 runs before the opposition can.

◆ Promote teamwork and cooperation.

Essentials:

◆ Field

◆ 2 bases, 1 bat, and 1 super-soft softball

◆ Face mask and chest protector

◆ Safety cones to mark the next batter's box if no backstops are present.

Safety:

1. To prevent collisions when teammates are dashing to first and home at the same time, insist that they must pass left shoulder to left shoulder.

2. See "Modified Softball" for additional guidelines.

How to Play:

1. The rules of "Two Base" softball apply to this game.

2. Form teams comprised of two players each. Send four teams to an area with team A at bat, B at pitcher and catcher, C is at first base and short, and D at both out-fielders.

3. A batter making a hit and reaching first base may remain there until her or his partner hits.

4. The team receives one out for a force out at either base.

5. The batting team is retired:

   a. After two force-outs.

   b. When a fly ball is caught.

   c. For passing each other on the wrong side when both are running the bases.

   d. After scoring six consecutive runs.

6. All teams will rotate zones after two outs are acquired by the batting team.

7. When a team catches a fly ball, they will exchange zones with the batters.

8. The first team to score 15 runs is victorious.

Student Tasks:

1. Score five or more team runs during any at bat.

2. Throw a runner out at first and home base during the game.

© 2001 Parker Publishing Company

Variations:

1. Increase the number of runs needed to win.
2. Play for a given number of innings.
3. Create a round-robin tournament by mixing and matching the four mini teams. To do this, team #1 would join each team for one game.

Illustration of Two Base Four Team

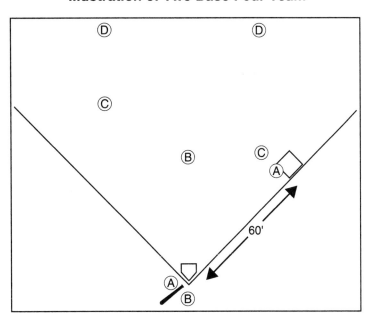

TWO BASE TWO BATTERS

Objectives:

◆ Score 13 runs before the opposition.
◆ Promote teamwork and cooperation.

Essentials:

◆ Field
◆ 4 bases, 1 bat, and 1 super-soft softball

◆ Face mask and chest protector
◆ Safety cones to mark the next batter's box if no backstops are present.

Safety: (See "Modified Softball" for the guidelines.)

How to Play:

1. The rules of "Two Base" softball apply to this game.
2. Form groups with two batters, catcher, pitcher, first base, and two outfielders.
3. The pitcher must allow the batter to hit the ball.
4. It is illegal to bunt the ball.
5. A participant is out:
   a. On any caught fly.
   b. On a force out at either base.
   c. For passing on the wrong side of an oncoming runner.
   d. After scoring four runs in a row.
   e. For throwing the bat more than four lengths from home plate.
6. A batter making a hit and reaching first base may remain there until the other person hits. The base runner does not have to run on a caught fly ball.
7. When the batter is out, all participants will move up one position, with the batter assuming the last outfielder position.
8. A player who catches a fly ball will switch positions with the batter.
9. The first player to score 13 runs is victorious.

Student Tasks:

1. Catch a fly ball.
2. Score three or more runs during any at bat.
3. During a game, throw a runner out at each of the bases.
4. Cause a force out at first and home during a game.

Variations:

1. Increase the number of runs needed to win.
2. Increase or decrease the number of runs any one player may score in a row.
3. Extend the first base distance. Allow two runs when a player runs down and back without stopping.
4. Play with a vinyl-covered foam ball. Hitting the runner (below the waist) with the ball is also an out.

Illustration of Two Base Two Batters

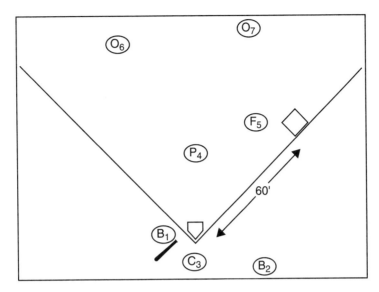

A VOID*

Objectives:

- ◆ Be the first player to score 15 points.
- ◆ Avoid landing in the center zone.
- ◆ Develop hand-and-eye coordination.
- ◆ Develop offensive and defensive strategies.

Essentials:

- ◆ Large room or gymnasium
- ◆ Tables
- ◆ 2 barriers (Use two nets, wooden 2 X 4s, foam, cardboard, etc.)
- ◆ Paddles
- ◆ Table tennis balls

How to Play:

1. The rules of table tennis apply to this game with a few modifications.
2. Divide the table into three zones. Each end zone will be four feet long. (See illustration below.)
3. Adjust the top of the net to measure three or four inches high.
4. It is illegal to hit the ball into the center zone.
5. The ball is only played in and from the end zones.
6. During the serve, the ball must land in each end zone before being played.
7. Each player will alternate serving three times in a row.
8. First player to reach 15 points (win by two) is the champion.

Student Tasks:

1. Use the forehand and backhand shots.
2. Put spin on the ball when hitting it.
3. Serve an ace.
4. After being behind by five or more points, rally to win the game.
5. When in a tournament, defeat a previously unbeaten player.

Variations:

1. Play a doubles match and obtain 21 points.
2. Use the "expedited" method of scoring. The receiving player counts out loud each returned stroke. After seven good returns, the point goes to the receiving player.

© 2001 Parker Publishing Company

---

*Created by Ken Lumsden, 2000.

3. Partners must exchange after hitting the bird once.

4. Leave the nets at regulation height.

5. Alter the size of the center area.

6. Create a tournament format.

Diagram of an A Void Ping Pong Table

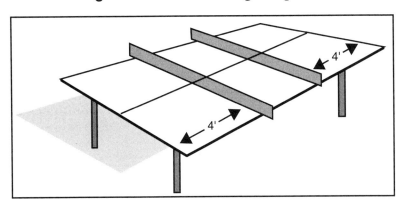

CHINA WALL

Objectives:

◆ Score 15 points before the opposition does.

◆ Improve ball control.

◆ Develop offensive and defensive strategies.

Essentials:

◆ Large area or gymnasium   ◆ 1 paddle for every participant

◆ Tables and nets   ◆ Table tennis balls

◆ 2 net extenders (Tape a small 12-inch wooden dowel to the net supports and then add either a second net, cardboard, strip of athletic tape or whatever, above the existing net. The top of the second barrier should be eight to 12 inches high.)

How to Play:

1. Other than the height of the net, all of the rules of table tennis apply to this game.

2. First player to score 15 points (must win by two) is the victor.

Student Tasks:

1. Use the forehand and backhand shots.

2. Put spin on the ball when hitting it.

3. Serve an ace.

4. After being behind by five or more points, rally to win the game.

Variations:

1. Play a doubles match and obtain 21 points.

2. Add a third net.

3. Use the "expedited" method of scoring. The receiving player counts out loud each returned stroke. After seven good returns, the point goes to the receiving player.

4. Create a tournament format.

Illustration of a China Wall Table Tennis Net Layout

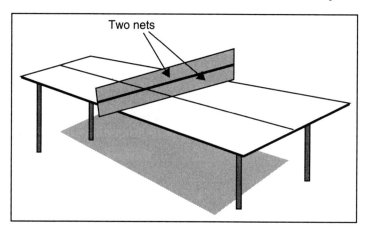

Two nets

© 2001 Parker Publishing Company

DOUBLE PADDLE

Objectives:

◆ Score 15 points before the opposition does.

◆ Develop the ability to play with either hand.

◆ Develop offensive and defensive strategies.

Essentials:

◆ Large area or gymnasium

◆ Tables and nets

◆ 2 paddles for every participant

◆ Table tennis balls

How to Play:

1. All of the rules of table tennis apply to this game.
2. Participants must hold a paddle in each hand while playing.
3. The ball must be hit with a different paddle each time.
4. First player to score 15 points (win by two) is the victor.

Student Tasks:

1. Use the forehand and backhand shots.
2. Put spin on the ball when hitting it.
3. Serve an ace.
4. After being behind by five or more points, rally to win the game.

Variations:

1. Play a doubles match and obtain 21 points first.
2. Allow the ball to be hit a maximum of two times in a row with the same hand.
3. Create a tournament format.

EXPEDITE

Objectives:

◆ Score 15 points before the opposition has a chance to.
◆ Shorten the time of a rally.
◆ Develop defensive strategies.

Essentials:

◆ Large area or gymnasium
◆ Ping pong tables and nets
◆ 1 paddle for every participant
◆ Table tennis balls

How to Play:

1. All of the rules of table tennis apply to this game except for the scoring during a long rally.

2. The "expedited" method of scoring is used. The receiving player counts out loud each returned stroke from one to seven. After seven good returns, the point goes to the receiving player.

3. First player to score 15 points is declared the winner.

Student Tasks:

1. Hit the ball two different ways (lob, forehand, backhand, smash) during any volley.

2. Put three different types of spin (right, left, over, or under) on the ball.

3. Send the ball to the outside corners of the opponent's end during a rally.

4. After being behind by five or more points, make a comeback and win the game.

Variations:

1. Change the number of returns needed to gain a point.

2. Play doubles with each player alternating hits of the ball.

PITCH OUT*

Objectives:

- ◆ Be the first player to eliminate all of the objects.
- ◆ Develop accuracy of ball placement.

Essentials:

- ◆ Large area or gymnasium
- ◆ Tables and nets
- ◆ 1 paddle for every participant
- ◆ Table tennis balls

- ◆ 5 matching pairs of pitch objects for each table (pencils, erasers, tightly wadded pieces of paper, dented ping pong balls, small blocks of wood, dominoes, etc.)

Created by Ken Lumsden, 1999.

TABLE TENNIS

How to Play:

1. All of the rules of table tennis apply to this game.

2. Players will strategically set five pitch objects anywhere desired on their side of the table.

3. All items must be set at least two feet away from the net and no less than six inches apart.

4. It is illegal to hit any pitch piece during a serve. If this happens, the guilty player must add one pitch piece (if any have been removed).

5. Each player will try to eliminate the pitch objects by hitting them during any rally. When this task is accomplished, the item is removed from the table and the successful player begins the next serve.

6. If during any rally a table tennis violation occurs, such as hitting the ball beyond the edge of the table or failing to return the ball, the responsible player will serve.

7. The first player to remove all of her/his items is the winner.

Student Tasks:

1. Avoid hitting the pitch object during the entire match.

2. Place the object so it is hit at least two times during the contest.

3. Hit two pitch objects on two successive rallies.

4. After being behind by three objects, win the game.

Variations:

1. After placing the object at one end, players will now switch sides and attempt to eliminate the objects that they just positioned. When objects are replaced, the opposition must replace them where directed.

2. Play a doubles match. Players must alternate hitting the ball and game is to 21 points (win by two).

3. Create a tournament format.

Illustration of a Pitch Out Table

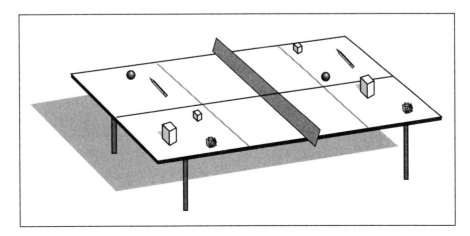

PITCH PONG*

Objectives:

◆ Score 15 points first.

◆ Develop ball placement accuracy.

Essentials:

◆ Large area or gymnasium

◆ Tables and nets

◆ 1 paddle for every participant

◆ Table tennis balls

◆ Pitch objects (pencils, erasers, tightly wadded pieces of paper, dented ping pong balls, small blocks or dowels of wood, dominoes set on end, etc.)

How to Play:

1. All of the rules of table tennis apply to this game.

2. Both pitch objects must be identical.

3. Players will strategically set their own pitch object anywhere desired on their side of the table.

4. It is illegal to hit the pitch item with the ball during play.

5. If the pitch piece is hit, the guilty player will lose two points.

6. The pitch object may be reset to any location after being hit or prior to the ball being served.

7. First player to score 15 points (must win by two) is the victor.

Student Tasks:

1. Avoid hitting the pitch object during the entire match.

2. Place the object so it is hit at least two times during the contest.

3. Serve an ace.

4. After being behind by five or more points, rally to win the game.

Variations:

1. Pitch objects cannot be reset unless hit.

2. When the pitch object is hit, two or three points are added to the score. The pitch item must be placed anywhere in an area within two feet of the end of the table, though.

3. Play a doubles match using two pitch objects on each end. Game is to 21 points (win by two).

4. Create a tournament format.

Created by Ken Lumsden, 1999.

© 2001 Parker Publishing Company

Example of a Pitch Pong Table Layout

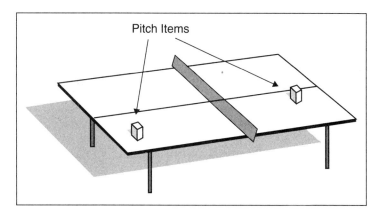

Pitch Items

THREE ZONE*

Objectives:

- ◆ Score 15 points prior to the opposition doing so.
- ◆ Develop ball control.

Essentials:

- ◆ Large room or gymnasium
- ◆ Paddles
- ◆ Tables
- ◆ Table tennis balls
- ◆ 2 nets about three to four inches high (wooden 2 X 4s, foam, cardboard, or whatever imaginable can be implemented)

How to Play:

1. The rules of table tennis apply to this game with a few modifications.
2. Divide the table into three equal sized zones (see illustration below).
3. Lower the top of the net to measure three or four inches high.
4. The ball must always bounce twice before being played.
5. The ball must first land in the center zone, then bounce in the end zone, before being played by the opposition. This is also true for the serve.
6. Each player will serve three points in a row before giving up the serve.
7. First player to reach 15 points (win by two) is the champion.

Created by Ken Lumsden, 2000.

© 2001 Parker Publishing Company

Student Tasks:

1. Use the forehand and backhand shots.
2. Put spin on the ball when hitting it.
3. Serve an ace.
4. After being behind by five or more points, rally to win the game.

Variations:

1. Play a doubles match and obtain 21 points.
2. Leave the nets at regulation height.
3. Alter the size of the center zone.
4. The ball must bounce in each zone before being played. (This is quite challenging.)
5. Create a tournament format.

Illustration of a Three Zone Table Layout

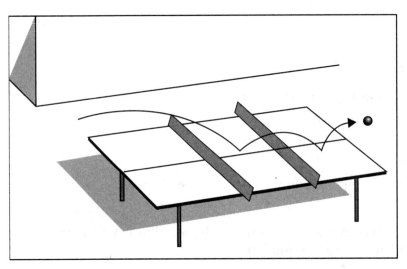

TEN-S-VOLLEY

Objectives:

- ◆ Score 15 points before the opposition can.
- ◆ Develop teamwork and cooperation.

Essentials:

- ◆ Tennis court and net
- ◆ 1 volleyball

How to Play:

1. The rules of volleyball apply to this game with some modifications.
2. Divide into teams composed of six players each and use the doubles court.
3. The serve is accomplished by the middle player in the back row hitting the ball underhanded to the middle teammate in the front row. The ball must bounce one time. The front player will then send the ball cleanly over the net.
4. The ball must always bounce once before being hit by another player.
5. A team receives "side out" or a point if the ball bounces twice.
6. Preventing the ball from coming over the net is prohibited since it must bounce.
7. The ball may be hit three times on a side. On the third hit, it must be returned.
8. The same person cannot hit the ball twice in a row.
9. Spiking is prohibited.
10. First team to score 15 points is the winner.

Student Tasks:

1. Score three points when serving.
2. Be part of a three hit.
3. Come from behind and win.

Variations:

1. Reduce the number of players on a team.
2. Make teams composed of two players and use the singles court.
3. The ball is playable after one or two bounces.
4. Allow a maximum of five hits on a side. Require that three or four different players (from the same team) must make contact with the ball before returning it over the net.
5. Give each player a paddle or racket and use a Tennis ball.
6. Make several teams and play a round robin tournament.

Illustration of Ten-S-Volley

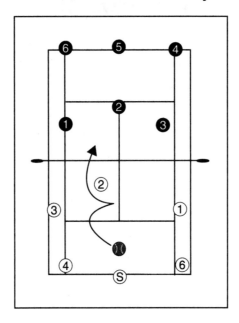

TENNIS GOLF

Objectives:

- ◆ Cover the course with the fewest hits.
- ◆ Develop hand and eye coordination relative to distance and accuracy.
- ◆ Understand the basic rules and terms of golf.

Essentials:

- ◆ Outdoor fields
- ◆ Tennis rackets
- ◆ Tennis balls (numbered)
- ◆ Course maps
- ◆ Pencils
- ◆ Score sheets (see the section "Golf" for forms)
- ◆ Pins (posts, walls, poles, cones, or buckets)

Terminology:

1.	Bogey	Number of strokes taken over the par
2.	Par	Average number of strokes
3.	Birdie	1 under par
4.	Eagle	2 under par
5.	Hole In One	Made or hit a pin with one shot

6.	Fore	Protect your head
7.	Pin	Object to be made or hit
8.	Away	Player farthest from the pin
9.	Lie	Position where the ball is resting
10.	Putt	Short stroke to the pin

How to Play:

1. Design a nine-hole course.
2. Use a "shotgun start" by sending players to different pins to begin the game.
3. The tennis ball can be hit with the racket in any manner.
4. Do not make distracting noises or motions when other players are hitting.
5. The player who had the lowest score on the previous hole determines each tee off. The lowest score will hit the ball first. In case of a tie, go back one, two, or three holes if necessary.
6. The golfer who is farthest from the hole will always hit first.
7. A player may not step past the lie of the previous hit when attempting the next swing.
8. No follow-through step is allowed within 30 feet of the pin.
9. Any unplayable lie can be relocated with a one-stroke penalty.
10. The player that covers the course with the least number of strokes is the winner.

Student Tasks:

1. Make a hole in one or an eagle.
2. Make a certain number of birdies during a round.
3. Attain back-to-back birdies.
4. Win two successive holes.
5. Come from behind and win a match.

Variations:

1. Allow the students to design a course.
2. Make teams of two or three students. After everyone has hit, determine the best lie. The entire team will now hit their next ball from this point.
3. Play the course in reverse starting with hole number 9 or number 18.
4. Players must alternate arms with each stroke.
5. Alternate each stroke with the forehand and backhand.

© 2001 Parker Publishing Company

ABOUT TETHERBALL

Objectives:

◆ Be the first player to wrap the rope around the pole.

◆ Develop hand-and-eye coordination.

Essentials:

◆ Large open area

◆ Steel pole set solid in ground (four to six inches in diameter by eight to ten feet high) or a heavy-based portable standard.

◆ Tetherball court (see diagram below)

◆ Inflated tetherball on nylon cord (ball should hang two feet above the ground)

How to Play:

1. Determine the player who serves first by playing the rock, paper, and scissors game.

2. One player assumes each zone and must remain there during play.

3. The server may hit the ball in either direction to begin play.

4. The opponent may not strike the ball until the second revolution around the pole. After this, the ball may be hit at anytime.

5. Only the hand is used when contacting the ball.

6. The ball cannot be caught or stopped.

7. It is illegal to touch the pole or cord during play.

8. A participant may not hit the ball while standing outside of her or his zone.

9. As the ball moves around the pole, each player attempts to wind the rope completely around the pole in the direction of play. The first player to do so is the winner.

Student Tasks:

1. Win by wrapping the rope in different directions.

2. Hit the ball four times in succession.

3. Win three games in a row.

4. Defeat an unbeaten player.

5. After losing to an individual, win the rematch at some point in time.

Variations:

1. The ball must be alternately hit with each hand.

2. Create a double-elimination tournament format.

3. Place a piece of tape somewhere on the nylon cord. First person to make the tape touch the pole, wins.

Diagram of a Tetherball Court

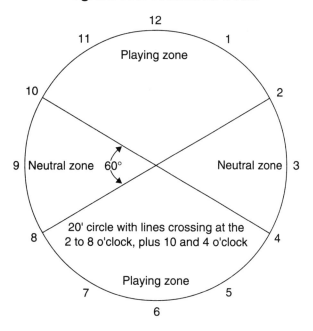

20' circle with lines crossing at the 2 to 8 o'clock, plus 10 and 4 o'clock

PADDLE TETHER

Objectives:

◆ Be the first player to wind the rope around the pole.

◆ Develop hand-and-eye coordination.

Essentials:

◆ Indoor play area

◆ Portable weighted standard

◆ Floor cones or floor tape to mark the circular boundaries (see "About Tetherball" for the dimensions)

◆ Tennis ball on nylon cord (The cord is threaded through ball and secured with a large knot so that it hangs one foot above the playing surface.)

◆ Wooden paddles (paddle ball, pickle ball, shuttle darts, etc.)

How to Play:

1. Determine the player who serves first by playing rock, paper, and scissors.

2. One player assumes each zone and must remain there during play.

3. The server may hit the ball with the paddle in either direction to begin play.

4. The opponent may not smash the ball until the second spiral around the pole. After this, the ball may be hit at any time.

5. Only the paddle is used when contacting the ball.

6. The ball cannot be caught or stopped.

7. It is illegal to touch the pole or cord during play.

8. A participant may not hit the ball while standing outside of the hitting zone.

9. As the ball moves around the pole, each player attempts to wind the rope completely around the pole in his or her direction of play. The first player to do so is the winner.

Student Tasks:

1. Serve in opposite directions during several games.

2. Hit the ball four times in succession.

3. Win three games in a row.

4. Defeat an unbeaten player.

5. After losing to an individual, win the rematch at some point in time.

Variations:

1. Use a different type of ball.

2. Use a different type of paddle or racket.

3. Players must use their weak arm during a game.

4. Place a piece of tape somewhere on the nylon cord. First person to make the tape touch the pole, wins.

5. Create a double-elimination tournament format (see Part II, Organization for Tournaments, for forms).

Illustration of Paddle Tether

TEAM TETHERBALL

© 2001 Parker Publishing Company

Objectives:

◆ Be the first player to wind the rope around the pole.

◆ Develop hand-and-eye coordination.

◆ Promote teamwork.

Essentials:

◆ Indoor or outdoor play area

◆ Fixed or portable standard

◆ Floor cones or floor tape to mark the boundaries

How to Play:

1. The rules of tetherball apply with a few modifications.

2. Divide into teams composed of two players each.

3. Determine the team that serves first with the rock, paper, and scissors game.

4. One player from each team assumes an alternate court zone on the opposite sides and must remain there during play.

5. The server may hit the ball in either direction to begin play.

6. The receiver may not strike the ball until the second revolution.

7. During play, the ball must be alternately hit by teammates.

8. As the ball moves around the pole, each team attempts to wind the rope completely around the pole in the team's direction of play. The first team to do so is the winner.

9. Winners stay and take on a new set of challengers.

Student Tasks:

1. Hit the ball three times in succession.

2. Win three games in a row.

3. Defeat any unbeaten team.

4. After losing to a team, win a rematch.

Variations:

1. Place a piece of tape somewhere on the nylon cord. First team to make the tape touch the pole, wins.

2. A team must exit after winning three games in a row.

3. Allow any player to hit the ball at any time.

4. Create a tournament format.

Depiction of Team Tetherball

ABOUT TUG-OF-WAR

Objectives:

- ◆ Pull the center indicator past the team cone.
- ◆ Keep the center indicator closer to the team cone when time expires.
- ◆ Develop teamwork and cooperation.

Essentials:

- ◆ Open area
- ◆ 1 tug-of-war rope (50, 75, or 100 feet long) with a center indicator
- ◆ 3 field cones (lines on a football field may be substituted)

How to Play:

1. Set the two outer markers (team cones) about 15 feet apart.
2. Make two teams composed of five players each.
3. Teams will go to opposite ends and take a slight strain on the rope so that its center indicator is positioned halfway in between the two cones.
4. On a signal, each team will attempt to pull the gauge past the team's cone in order to win.
5. For safety reasons, teams or players may not intentionally let go of the rope.
6. If, after a set amount of time, neither team is able to pull the indicator beyond their cone, then the team that has the pointer closer to the team's cone is the winner.

Student Tasks:

1. Be the last person in line (anchor).
2. Come from behind and win the match.
3. Win two or more contests in a row.

Variations:

1. Alter the number of players on a team.
2. Change the distance of the pull requirement.
3. The first person on either team must be pulled across a common line.
4. Make the center area muddy.
5. Create several teams and compete in a round-robin tournament. Each win is worth one point. The team that accumulates the most points is the winner.
6. Create several teams and compete in a round-robin tournament. Change the scoring so that pulling the center indicator past the team's cone is worth two

points or keeping the center indicator beyond the center cone (closer to the team's cone) is worth one point when time expires. The team with the highest point total is the winner.

Illustration of Tug-of-War

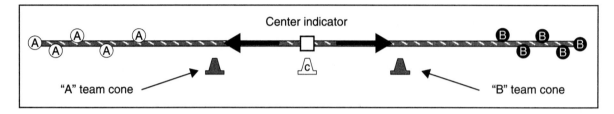

"A" team cone   "B" team cone

ADD ON

© 2001 Parker Publishing Company

Objectives:

◆ Keep the center indicator of a rope on the team's side after all of the members have been added.

◆ Develop teamwork and cooperation.

Essentials:

◆ Open area

◆ 1 tug-of-war rope (50, 75, or 100 feet long) with a center indicator

◆ 3 field cones (lines on a field may be substituted)

◆ Stopwatch

How to Play:

1. Draw a line or set a cone on the field.

2. Make two teams composed of eight players each.

3. Each team will form a single file line at equal distances from the ends of the rope.

4. One player from each team will step forward, grab the rope, and take a slight strain so that the center indicator is positioned directly above the cone or line.

5. On a signal, each opponent will attempt to pull the gauge to her/his side of the field.

6. Teams or players may not intentionally let go of the rope, for safety reasons.

7. At predetermined time intervals (10 seconds), the first person in each line will rush to the rope and join in.

8. Continue this procedure until everyone has attached to the rope.

9. Wait about 30 seconds and whichever team has the center of the rope on its side of the field is victorious.

TUG-OF-WAR

Student Tasks:

1. Cause the indicator to move in a positive direction after bonding to the rope.
2. Come from behind and win the match.

Variations:

1. Divide the entire class in half. Allow two new players each time. As two arrive, one must leave and return to the end of the line.
2. Create several teams and compete in a round-robin tournament. Each win is worth one point. The team that accumulates the most points is the winner.

Illustration of Add On

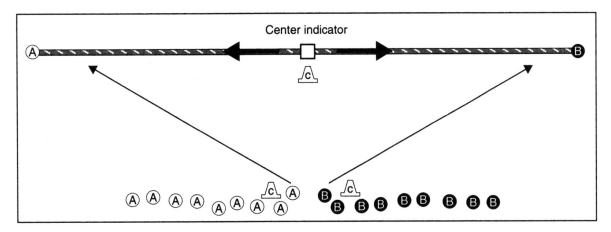

DRAG RACE

Objectives:

◆ Score more points than the opposition is able to.
◆ Cross the finish line ahead of the competition.
◆ Develop teamwork and cooperation.

Essentials:

◆ Open area
◆ 2 tug-of-war ropes (50, 75, or 100 feet long)
◆ 2 identical heavy objects (bags of sand, football blocking sleds, or cars)
◆ 4 field cones
◆ Round-robin bracket sheet

TUG-OF-WAR

How to Play:

1. Use the cones and mark the start and finish lines about 60 feet apart. (The yard lines of a football field may also be used.)

2. Divide the class into six equal teams.

3. On a signal, both teams will simultaneously pull the object across the finish line as fast as possible.

4. Record each team's win by giving them one point.

5. Continue the races until each team has challenged every other team.

6. Team members must rotate positions with each new pull.

7. The entire crew must face the same direction when pulling.

8. When finished, tally up the scores to determine the winner. Highest score wins.

Student Tasks:

1. Win three races in a row.

2. Defeat a previously unbeaten crew.

3. Finish in the top three.

Variations:

1. Require that a certain number of team members must sit out each time. Players may not rest two times in a row.

2. Modify the distance.

3. Use an eight-team double elimination bracket (see Part II, Organization for Tournaments, for forms).

4. Award two points when beating any team by two or more seconds.

Diagram of Drag Race

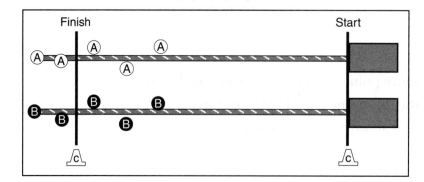

Sample Score Sheet for Drag Race

Team #	Wins	Match Schedule			
1		Round 1	1 vs 2	3 vs 4	5 vs 6
2		Round 2	1 vs 3	2 vs 5	4 vs 6
3		Round 3	1 vs 5	3 vs 6	2 vs 4
4		Round 4	1 vs 6	4 vs 5	2 vs 3
5		Round 5	1 vs 4	2 vs 6	3 vs 5
6					

FOUR-WAY MIX-UP

Objectives:

◆ Score more points than the opposition by pulling the center indicator closer to or beyond the team cone.

◆ Develop teamwork and cooperation.

Essentials:

◆ Open area

◆ 2 tug-of-war ropes (100 feet long) with a center indicator

◆ 5 field cones

How to Play:

1. Place the four outer markers (team cones) about 15 feet apart to form a crossing pattern.

2. Create eight teams and combine two teams each new contest (see score sheet below).

3. Teams will go to opposite ends and take a slight strain on the rope so that its center indicator is positioned halfway in between the team cones.

4. On a signal, each team will attempt to pull the indicator past its team cone.

5. Each contest will last for one minute.

6. Teams or players may not intentionally let go, for safety reasons.

7. One point is given for having the center indicator closest to the team's cone when time expires.

8. Two points are awarded for pulling the indicator past the team's cone before time expires.

Student Tasks:

1. Be the last person (anchor) on the rope.
2. Score in three successive matches.
3. Score two points.

Variations:

1. Change the distance of the pull requirement.
2. Add more time to each pull.

Illustration of Four-Way Mix-Up (Schedule A)

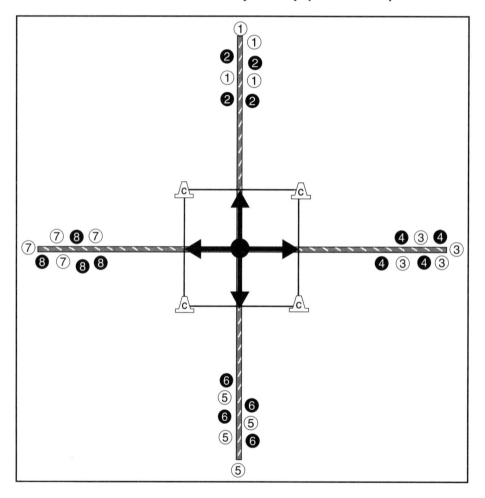

Sample Score Sheet for Four-Way Mix-up

Team Number
(record team points of each match)

1	2	3	4	5	6	7	8

Schedule

A	Rope "A"	1+2 vs 5+6	Rope "B"	3+4 vs 7+8
B	Rope "A"	1+3 vs 4+7	Rope "B"	2+5 vs 6+8
C	Rope "A"	1+5 vs 3+8	Rope "B"	3+7 vs 4+6
D	Rope "A"	1+7 vs 3+6	Rope "B"	2+4 vs 5+8
E	Rope "A"	1+8 vs 4+5	Rope "B"	2+3 vs 6+7
F	Rope "A"	1+6 vs 2+7	Rope "B"	3+5 vs 4+8
G	Rope "A"	1+4 vs 3+8	Rope "B"	2+6 vs 5+7

TAFFY PULL

Objectives:

◆ Knock over an object before the opposition does.

◆ Create teamwork and cooperation.

Essentials:

◆ Large open area

◆ 1 tug-of-war rope

◆ 2 bowling pins

◆ 1 floor cone

How to Play:

1. Make equal-sized teams.

2. Place a bowling pin five feet from each end of the rope.

3. Teams will go to opposite ends and take a slight strain on the rope so that the center indicator is positioned above the middle cone.

4. On a signal, each team will pull the rope so that the last person (anchor) can reach out with one hand and knock over the bowling pin.

5. For safety reasons, players may not intentionally let go of the rope.

6. Play the best two out of three to determine a winner.

TUG-OF-WAR

Student Tasks:

1. Be the anchor.
2. Come from behind and win.

Variations:

1. Create a double elimination tournament with small teams composed of two or three players each.
2. Compete in a singles match.
3. Create a "Four-Way Rope." Tie two ropes together, make four teams, and pull at 90-degree angles.

Illustration of Taffy Pull

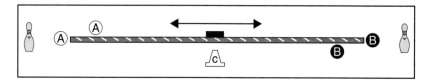

Diagram of Four-Way Taffy Pull

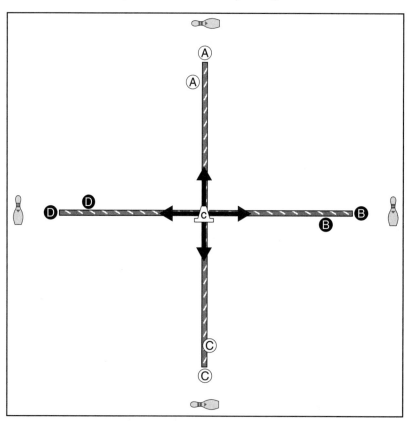

TINY TUG-OF-WAR

Objectives:

- Pull the opponent's last person across a line.
- Win two out of three contests.
- Build strength and power.
- Develop teamwork and cooperation.

Essentials:

- Large open area with mats on the floor (wrestling room works well)
- Stopwatch

How to Play:

1. Form groups composed of two or three players each.
2. Designate a line that cannot be crossed by the last person on either team.
3. The two front players (leaders) will grab their opponent's wrists.
4. Each teammate will lock her/his arms around the waist of the person in front.
5. A team is disqualified for purposely letting go.
6. Winners are declared by:
   a. Pulling the last person over the line.
   b. Forcing the opposition to let go or break apart.
   c. Causing the other team to lose balance and fall down.
   d. Holding any member of the opposition beyond the centerline when time expires (20 seconds).
7. Rotate positions and repeat the contest.
8. In order to be crowned champions, a team must win two out of three contests.

Student Tasks:

1. Defeat two different units.
2. Out pull an undefeated group.

Variations:

1. Use a 12 foot long by 1/2" thick rope.
2. Pull while on the knees.

Illustration of a Tiny Tug-of-War Match

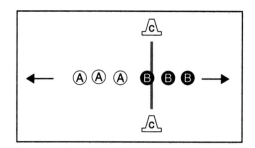

TOW TRUCK

Objectives:

- ◆ Score more points than the adversary does.

- ◆ Pull the center marker of a rope past the team marker before time elapses.

- ◆ Pull the center indicator closer to the team marker when time expires.

- ◆ Develop teamwork and cooperation.

Essentials:

- ◆ Open area
- ◆ 1 tug-of-war rope (50, 75, or 100 feet long) with a center indicator
- ◆ 3 field cones (lines on a football field may be substituted)

How to Play:

1. The rules of tug-of-war apply to this game.
2. Place the two outer markers (team cones) about 15 feet apart.
3. Make two teams by dividing the class in half.
4. Within each team, form smaller groups composed of three players on each.
5. A different threesome will play each new match.
6. Each match will last for 30 seconds.
7. The team that wins must be the first to send three new players into the arena. The losing team will now decide on which new threesome will be the challengers.
8. One point is given for having the center indicator closest to the team cone when time expires.
9. Two points are awarded for pulling the indicator past the team cone before time expires.
10. Continue this process until everyone has competed.
11. The team with the highest score wins.

Student Tasks:

1. Be the last person in line (anchor).

2. Come from behind and win the match.

Variations:

1. First team to reach a predetermined number of points is the winner.

2. Alter the number of players on a team.

3. Change the distance of the pull requirement.

4. Allow a threesome to win two matches before exiting.

5. A threesome will stay until they are defeated.

Illustration of Tow Truck

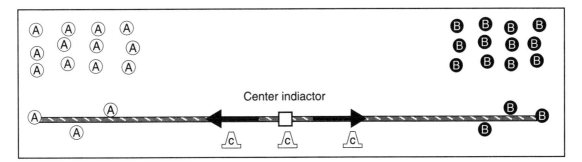

TUGBOAT

Objectives:

◆ Pull an object over a required distance in the shortest amount of time.

◆ Develop teamwork and cooperation.

Essentials:

◆ Open area

◆ 1 tug-of-war rope (50, 75, or 100 feet long)

◆ Heavy object (bags of sand tied together, football blocking sled, or a car)

◆ 4 field cones

◆ Stopwatch

◆ Score sheet

How to Play:

1. Use the cones and mark the start and finish lines about 60 feet apart. (The yard lines of a football field may also be used.)

2. Make several teams composed of five players each.

3. Each team will pull the object a required distance in the shortest time possible.

4. Record each team's time on the score sheet.

5. Repeat the process three times.

6. Team members must rotate positions with each new pull.

7. The entire team must face in the same direction when pulling.

8. When finished, combine the three times. The team with the lowest time is the winner.

Student Tasks:

1. Pull the object faster each time.

2. Win by one or more seconds over the next set of competitors.

3. Finish in the top three.

Variations:

1. Alter the number of players on a team.

2. Change the distance of the pull requirement.

3. Pull the object up a slight incline.

Diagram of Tugboat

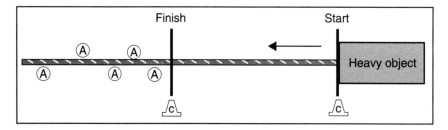

Sample Score Sheet for Tugboat

	Team 1	Team 2	Team 3	Team 4	Team 5	Team 6	Team 7	Team 8
Time Pull #1								
Time Pull #2								
Time Pull #3								
Total Time								

WHIRLPOOL

Objectives:

◆ Have the lowest score when the competition ends.

◆ Cause an opponent to receive five points.

Essentials:

◆ Open area

◆ Hanging rope or upright football blocking pad

How to Play:

1. Assemble into groups of four players of about the same size.

2. Form a circle around the center object by holding the hands or wrists with the combatants on each side.

3. Attempt to pull any player into the hanging rope.

4. Every time a participant touches the rope, one point is earned.

5. Any player that intentionally lets go of another player's wrist or hand will receive one point.

6. The person with the lowest score, when any of the other players finally accumulates five points, is the winner.

Student Tasks:

1. Win the contest.

2. Finish with the second-lowest score.

3. Have three or less points when any other player obtains five.

Variations:

1. When a player has been pulled into the rope for the second time, that player is eliminated. The last person left is the winner.

2. Make teams composed of two or three players. When forming the circle, make sure that the teams are alternately distributed around the rope.

Diagram of Whirlpool

ADDICTED

Objectives:

- ◆ Score 15 points before the opposition does.
- ◆ Promote teamwork.

Essentials:

- ◆ Volleyball court
- ◆ 1 volleyball

How to Play:

1. The rules of volleyball apply to this event.
2. The ball can be hit a maximum of six times on a side.
3. The ball must be volleyed a number of times equal to, or one more than, the opposition's previous volley.
4. Participants may hit the ball twice in a row during a possession.
5. The first team to score 15 points wins.

Student Tasks:

1. Serve three in a row.
2. Be involved in a three hit composed of a bump, set, and spike.
3. Be involved in a three hit composed of a bump, set, and return volley.
4. Bump or set the ball a certain number of times.
5. Spike the ball.
6. Block a shot.

Variations:

1. Use a beach ball.
2. Teams must add one extra hit each time the ball is volleyed to their side.
3. After any player serves three in a row, the team must rotate to a new server.

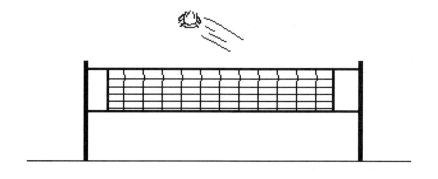

VOLLEYBALL

AIR MAIL

Objectives:

◆ Cause the opposition to lose their 15 points first.

◆ Promote teamwork and cooperation.

Essentials:

◆ Gymnasium or outside court

◆ Volleyball

◆ Score board or paper to record the team points

◆ 4 volleyball nets

◆ 5 standards

How to Play:

1. The rules of volleyball apply to this contest.
2. Form four equal teams.
3. Each team begins with 15 points.
4. Any error by a team will cost them one point.
5. The team that loses a point will serve to any court to initiate play.
6. The contest is over when any team drops to zero. The team with the most points left is the winner.

Student Tasks:

1. Serve three unplayable balls.
2. Be part of a three-hit combination.
3. Bump or set the ball a certain number of times.
4. Spike the ball.
5. Rally the ball that puts a team out.

Variations:

1. Use a beach ball.
2. Allow unlimited hits on a side.
3. After a player serves three in a row, the team must rotate to a new server.
4. Change the scoring. The team that hit the ball into the court of the team that blundered will gain a point.

Illustration of Air Mail Floor Plan

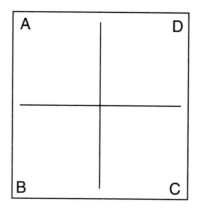

BATTLE OF THE GENDERS

Objectives:

- ◆ Score more points than the opponent does in a given amount of time.
- ◆ Develop team play.
- ◆ Reinforce fair play and sportsmanship.

Essentials:

- ◆ 3 volleyball courts
- ◆ 3 volleyballs

How to Play:

1. The rules of volleyball apply to this game.
2. Divide the girls into three equal teams. Do likewise with the boys.
3. Send each of the six teams to a different court and play a round-robin tournament. Under this structure, the games will have girls against girls, boys versus boys, and girls pitted against boys.
4. Each game will be for a designated time period. The team that is ahead when time expires wins.
5. Any tie is settled by a one-point sudden death playoff. An error by either team spells defeat.
6. The best overall team record wins the tournament.

Student Tasks:

1. Be involved in a three hit composed of a bump, set, and spike.
2. Be involved in a three hit composed of a bump, set, and return volley.

3. Serve the ball three times in a row.

4. During a sudden death playoff, hit the ball that causes the defense to make an error.

Variations:

1. Use trainer volleyballs or beach balls.

2. Use the "expedited" method of scoring. The receiving team counts out loud each returned hit. After five good returns, the point goes to the receiving team.

3. Play a sixth volleyball game by locating all of the girls opposite all of the boys (mass action). A different server is required for each serve.

4. Sag the nets six or more inches.

Illustration of Court Rotation for Battle of the Genders

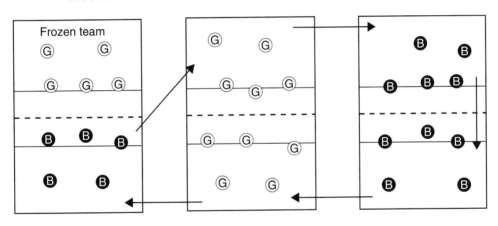

CLASS VOLLEY

Objectives:

◆ Rally two volleyballs for as long as possible.

◆ Develop teamwork.

Essentials:

◆ Large play area

◆ 3 volleyballs

◆ Stopwatch

How to Play:

1. Scatter the entire class around the playing area. Participants may move about freely.

2. All hits must be legal. The ball may not be played off of a wall.

3. Begin by tossing the first ball into the group and starting the timer. After 10 seconds have elapsed, toss the second ball, and after 10 more seconds, toss the third ball into the crowd.

4. Time stops when the last of the three volleyballs hits the floor.

5. Give the class several opportunities to improve. Record their longest time.

Student Tasks:

1. When a ball is dead, move to another group and help them with the rally.

2. Be the player that makes the hit to improve the class record.

3. Improve, as a class, three times in a row.

Variations:

1. Allow players to hit the ball two or more times in a row.

2. Add four or five balls to the contest.

3. Use beach balls.

4. Post times and compete against other classes for top honors.

5. Set a class goal for two or more minutes.

Illustration of Five Ball Class Volley

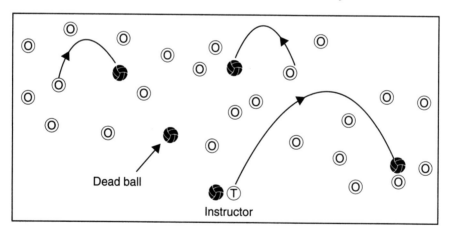

EXIT STAGE RIGHT

Objectives:

♦ Score more points than the opposition does.

♦ Transfer the entire team to the opposite court.

♦ Develop ball-control skills.

VOLLEYBALL

Essentials:

- ◆ Volleyball court
- ◆ 1 volleyball

How to Play:

1. Break the class into groups of six or seven players.
2. The whole team starts on one side of the volleyball net.
3. Each player volleys the ball to another player and then departs under the net to the opposite side.
4. The last player to handle the ball must hit it over the net.
5. Score one point for each time a team is successful.
6. Play 10 sessions and the team with the most points is the winner.

Student Tasks:

1. Be the last person to hit the ball over the net.
2. In a three-game series, never make a mistake.

Variations:

1. Use a beach ball.
2. Attempt to get the entire team over and back.
3. Place a different team on each side. Both squads must switch sides.
4. Add more contestants to a side.
5. Players must hit the ball on two different occasions (not consecutively) before evacuating.

Illustration of a Player Hitting and then Leaving

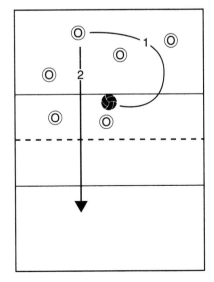

FIFTY-TWO

Objectives:

- ◆ Score 15 points first.
- ◆ Play a game where everyone can be successful.
- ◆ Develop team play.

Essentials:

- ◆ Volleyball court
- ◆ Beach ball

How to Play:

1. The rules of volleyball apply to this game with a few modifications.
2. Divide into equal teams.
3. Each team may volley the ball up to five times when it is on their side.
4. Any player may hit the beach ball two times in a row.
5. The beach ball may be spiked on the first hit when receiving serve.
6. First team to score 15 points wins.

Student Tasks:

1. Be involved in a three hit composed of a bump, set, and spike.
2. Be involved in a three hit composed of a bump, set, and return volley.
3. Set the ball to yourself, then immediately hit or spike it over the net.
4. Be involved in a volley that totals up to five hits.
5. Be the one that hits the ball over the net on the fifth volley.

Variations:

1. Play to 11 points.
2. Use regular volleyballs.
3. When a player double-hits the ball, the second hit may not be spiked.
4. Sag the net six or more inches.

Depiction of Team A Hitting the Ball Five Times in Fifty-Two

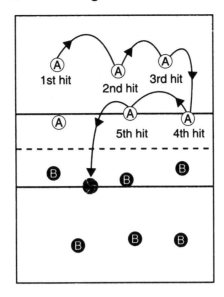

HALF VOLLEY

Objectives:

◆ Score 15 points before the opposition can.

◆ Develop teamwork.

Essentials:

◆ Volleyball court

◆ Volleyball

◆ Floor cones, heavy twine, or floor tape (for marking boundaries)

◆ Antenna or foam pipe insulation

How to Play:

1. The rules of volleyball will apply to this game with some exceptions.

2. Assemble teams with two players each.

3. Divide a standard volleyball court in half from baseline to baseline. Play two separate games on one court (see illustration).

4. Place the antenna at the middle of the net.

5. Games will last for three to four minutes.

6. Play a round-robin format.

7. Each game will be for a designated time period. The team that is ahead when time expires, wins.

8. Any tie is settled by a one-point (rally scoring) sudden death playoff. Any error by either team will be disastrous.

9. The best overall team record wins the tournament.

Student Tasks:

1. Serve an unplayable ball.

2. Be part of a bump, set, spike.

3. Bump or set the ball to each teammate.

Variations:

1. Use a beach ball.

2. After any player serves three in a row, the players must rotate and employ a new server.

3. Place three players on a team.

4. Shrink the court by designating the 10-foot line is now the baseline.

5. Allow only underhand serves.

6. Create a tournament format.

Illustration of the Floor Plan for Half Volley

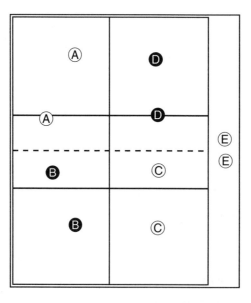

HANDS OFF

Objectives:

- ◆ Score 11 points before the other team is able to.
- ◆ Develop total body reflexes and coordination.

Essentials:

- ◆ Badminton courts and nets
- ◆ Beach ball

How to Play:

1. Divide into teams composed of three or more players each.
2. Any part of the body, other than the hands, may be used to hit the ball.
3. Only one arm may be used when contacting the ball.
4. The ball can be hit three consecutive times by the same person.
5. The ball may be volleyed six times per side.
6. Serves will be performed one step behind the front service line.
7. First team to 11 points is victorious.

Student Tasks:

1. Serve three in a row.
2. Be involved in a three hit composed of a bump, set, and spike.
3. Be involved in a three hit composed of a bump, set, and return volley.
4. Use either the head, knee, or elbow to get the ball over the net.

Variations:

1. Use volleyball nets and courts. Sag the nets if desired (see illustration).
2. Use a volleyball.
3. Prohibit the use of any part of the arms.

Illustration of the Sagging Volleyball Net

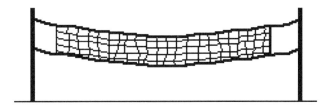

HOT AIR BALLOON

Objectives:

- ◆ Score 7 points before the opposition does.
- ◆ Promote teamwork.

Essentials:

- ◆ Badminton courts
- ◆ Any size round balloon

How to Play:

1. The rules of volleyball apply to this contest.
2. Make teams with two players on each.
3. Spiking on the serve is not allowed.
4. The serve must be hit with a bump or pass. After the initial hit anything goes as long as it is not a carry or open-handed lift.
5. First team to reach seven points is declared the winner.

Student Tasks:

1. Be involved in a three hit composed of a bump, set, and spike.
2. Bump or set the balloon a certain number of times during a game.
3. Bump or set the balloon to each teammate during a contest.
4. Spike the balloon for a point.

Variations:

1. Sag the volleyball nets. The boundaries are inside of the ten-foot line.
2. Allow players to hit the balloon two or three times in a row.
3. Use volleyball courts and sagging nets. Divide each court in half so more games can be played.
4. Use the "expedited" method of scoring. The receiving team counts out loud each returned stroke. After five good returns, the point goes to the receiving team.
5. Play a tournament format.

Illustration of a Badminton Net as a Divider for Hot Air Balloon

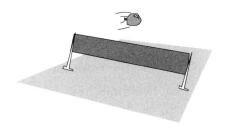

NO PEEK

Objectives:

◆ Score 15 points before the other team does.

◆ Develop player alertness and quick reactions.

Essentials:

◆ Indoor or outdoor volleyball court

◆ Volleyball

◆ Sheet of black plastic ground cover for the net. (Drape it over the net so that it almost touches the floor. It works well, is cheap, and lasts for years.)

How to Play:

1. The rules of volleyball apply to this game.

2. Cover the net with the large plastic sheet.

3. Make teams and disperse them to their respective sides.

4. The game goes as usual except the players are never sure when, or from where the ball is going to be returned.

5. First team to reach 15 points wins.

Student Tasks:

1. Be involved in a three hit composed of a bump, set, and spike.

2. Be involved in a three hit composed of a bump, set, and return volley.

3. Bump or set the ball to each teammate during a contest.

4. Spike the ball for a point.

5. Block a ball from coming over the net.

Variations:

1. Use a beach ball.
2. Allow five hits on a side.
3. After a player serves three in a row, the team must rotate to a new server.
4. Allow one player to hit the ball two times in a row.
5. Require only underhand serves.
6. Prohibit spiking.

Illustration of a Black Plastic Sheet Used for No Peek

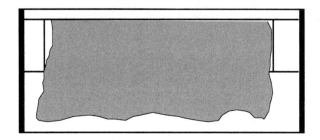

ONE BOUNCE

Objectives:

◆ Score 15 points before the adversaries can.
◆ Develop passing skills.
◆ Promote teamwork.

Essentials:

◆ Volleyball court
◆ 1 volleyball

How to Play:

1. The rules of volleyball apply to this contest.
2. Divide into teams composed of four players.
3. Only underhand serves are allowed.
4. Only bumps or passes may be used when hitting the ball.
5. The ball must bounce on the floor one time before it can be hit.
6. First team to 15 points wins.

Student Tasks:

1. Pass the ball to a location where the other team is unable to make contact.

2. Bounce the ball to every teammate during a match.

3. Come from behind and win a game.

4. Require everyone on a side to volley-bounce the ball before it may be returned. Allow five or six hits per side when this is done.

Variations:

1. Require that the ball must be volleyed a minimum of two times per side.

2. Use the "expedited" method of scoring. The receiving team counts out loud each returned stroke. After seven good returns, the point goes to the receiving team.

3. Use a high-bounce playground ball.

4. Allow players to strike the ball before it hits the floor, as well as after.

Illustration of One Bounce

TEAMSTERS

Objectives:

◆ Score 15 points before the opposition does.

◆ Promote team unity.

Essentials:

◆ Volleyball court

◆ 1 volleyball

How to Play:

1. The rules of volleyball apply with a few adjustments.

2. Divide into two teams with six players on each.

3. Three of the players from each team form a mini team and take the court while the others remain at the side. Teams stay on the same side of the net and are standing by to substitute.

4. Every time a mini team loses the serve (side out), it is rotated to the sideline.

5. A team is replaced after it serves three times in a row.

6. Score 15 points (win by two) and become victorious.

Student Tasks:

1. Pass to everyone on the mini team.

2. Be part of a given number of three hits.

3. Come from behind and win a game.

Variations:

1. Use a beach ball.

2. Create four-person mini teams.

3. Play a round-robin tournament by mixing and matching the mini teams.

Illustration of Micro Groups for Teamsters

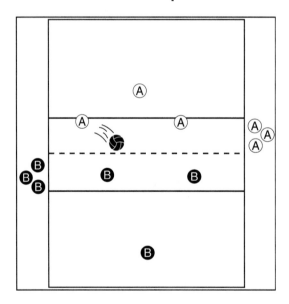

© 2001 Parker Publishing Company

Objectives:

◆ Score 15 points before the opposition is able to.

◆ Stay in the A court as long as possible.

◆ Combine forces and eliminate the leaders.

VOLLEYBALL

Essentials:

- Gymnasium or outside court
- 1 volleyball
- 2 flip scoreboard
- 4 volleyball nets
- 5 standards

How to Play:

1. The rules of volleyball will apply to this game.
2. Form five equal teams.
3. The A court must always serve to start a game and may serve to any court.
4. Any team that makes a mistake will leave the playing floor. The vanquished team returns to the start and remains there for one point.
5. Any team that puts another team out will receive a point.
6. Every team behind the expelled team will move up one court.
7. First team to score 15 points wins the contest.

Student Tasks:

1. Be involved in a three hit composed of a bump, set, and spike.
2. Be involved in a three hit composed of a bump, set, and return volley.
3. Bump or set the ball a certain number of times during a game.
4. Bump or set the ball to each teammate during a contest.
5. Spike the ball for a point.

Variations:

1. Use a beach ball.
2. Allow five or more volleys per side.
3. After a player serves three in a row, the team must rotate to a new server.

Illustration of VIP Rotation

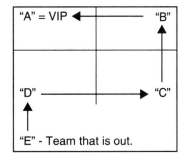

ABOUT WALL BALL

Objectives:

♦ Score 11 points before the opposition does.

♦ Hit a ball within the boundaries in such a way that an opponent is unable to do the same.

♦ Develop agility and ball control.

Essentials:

♦ Large indoor or outdoor area with a wall

♦ Medium-size playground ball

♦ 2 floor cones or floor spots

How to Play:

1. Two opponents will compete against one another.

2. Set up the court and boundaries (see illustration).

3. The ball must contact the wall first, before being played by the adversary.

4. The ball may be struck in any manner with the hand or fist. It may never be caught and held with the open hand, though.

5. The ball is served from the middle of the court to start a game or after a point is scored.

6. The person who scores will serve next.

7. The ball must land in bounds when it contacts the wall and floor.

8. An opponent may play the ricochet in the air or after the first bounce.

9. The ball is not allowed to bounce twice.

10. Immediately after contacting the ball, the hitter must:

    a. Get out of an opponent's way.

    b. Give an opponent clean sight of the ball.

    c. Allow an opponent to play the ball to any part of the wall.

    d. Not create visual or audible disturbances.

11. Failure to comply with the above regulations will result in a redo.

12. First player to score 11 points (ahead by two) is the champion.

Student Tasks:

1. Defeat three other challengers.

2. Score four consecutive points.

3. Hit the ball before it bounces to the floor on three successive returns.

4. Come from behind and win.

© 2001 Parker Publishing Company

Variations:

1. Use a different type of ball, such as a volleyball.

2. Place a line horizontally across the wall about three feet high. The ball must hit above this line every time.

3. Alter the number of points needed to win.

4. Make teams with two players each. Alternate hits amongst players.

5. Create a "Do or Die" format. Form a line with six or seven participants. First player to win one point stays and takes on a new challenger. The challenger will always serve to start the game. Players who lose return to the end of the line.

Example of a Wall Ball Court

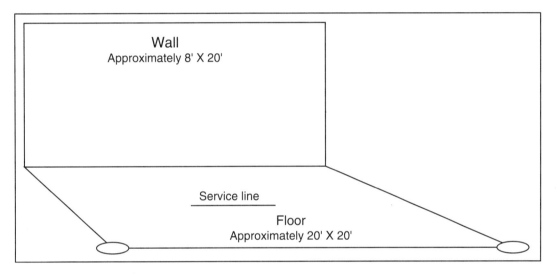

CORNER BALL

Objectives:

◆ Score 11 points before an opponent does.

◆ Hit the ball against two walls in such a manner that an opponent is unable to return it.

Essentials:

◆ Any indoor or outdoor corner with a fairly high ceiling

◆ Medium-size playground ball

◆ 1 floor cone or floor spot (used as a boundary marker)

WALL BALL

How to Play:

1. All of the rules of wall ball will apply to this game with a few exceptions.
2. Two opponents are needed.
3. Set up the court and boundaries in the corner of two walls (see illustration).
4. The ball is served from the floor cone or floor spot.
5. Players will alternate serving the ball two times in a row.
6. The ball must first bounce against both walls before being played.
7. The receiver may play the ball while it is in the air or after the first bounce from the floor.
8. First player to score 11 points (ahead by two) is the champion.

Student Tasks:

1. Defeat three players in a row.
2. Come from behind and win.
3. Hit the ball before it bounces to the floor on three successive returns.
4. Score four consecutive points.

Variations:

1. Use a different type of ball, such as volleyball.
2. Place a line horizontally across the wall about three feet high. The ball must hit above this line the first time it hits the wall.
3. Play to 15 points (win by two). Serve three times in a row.
4. Divide the court down the middle with a centerline. When the ball lands in the right or left court, it must be returned to that same wall first. If it hits on the line, then the hitter can hit the ball to either wall (see illustration).
5. Create a "Do or Die" format. Form a line with six or seven participants. First player to win two points, stays and takes on a new challenger. The challenger will always serve to start the game. Challengers who get beaten return to the end of the line.

Illustration of a Corner Ball Court Layout with a Centerline

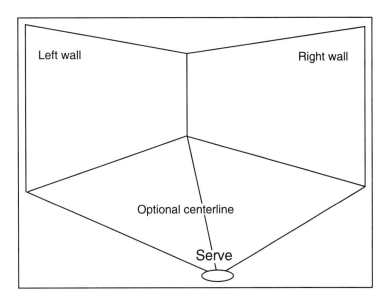

FLOOR BALL

Objectives:

- ◆ Score 11 points before an opponent does.
- ◆ Hit the ball within the boundaries in such a manner that an opponent is unable to play it.

Essentials:

- ◆ Large indoor or outdoor area with a wall
- ◆ Medium-size playground ball
- ◆ 2 floor cones or floor spots (used as boundary markers)

How to Play:

1. The rules of wall ball apply to this game with modifications.
2. Two opponents will compete.
3. The ball may be struck in any manner with the hands either held together or apart.
4. The ball may not be caught and held.
5. The ball is served from the middle of the court.
6. The ball must remain in bounds whenever it contacts the wall and floor.
7. The ball must first bounce against the floor and then the wall, before being played.

8. The receiver may play the ball either from the wall or after it rebounds from the floor.

9. The ball is not allowed to bounce twice on the floor at any time.

10. Immediately after contacting the ball, the hitter must:

    a. Get out of an opponent's way.

    b. Give an opponent clean sight of the ball.

    c. Allow an opponent to play the ball to any part of the wall.

    d. Not create visual or audible disturbances.

11. Failure to comply with the above regulations will result in a do over.

12. First player to score 11 points (ahead by two) is the champion.

Student Tasks:

1. Defeat three other challengers.

2. Score four consecutive points.

3. Hit the ball before it bounces to the floor on three successive occasions.

4. Come from behind and win.

Variations:

1. Use a different type of ball, such as volleyball.

2. Participants must switch hands each time the ball is touched.

3. Make teams with two players each. Alternate hits amongst players.

4. Create a "Do or Die" format. Form a line with six or seven participants. First player to win one point stays and takes on a new challenger. The challenger will always serve to start the game. When defeated, players return to the end of the line.

Illustration of When the Ball Can Be Hit in Floor Ball

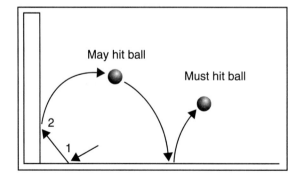

WALL BALL

WALL SPEED BALL

Objectives:

◆ Remain in the game when time expires.

◆ Eliminate the other players.

◆ Develop quick thinking and fast reactions.

Essentials:

◆ Indoor or outdoor wall

◆ 1 small bouncing type ball (tennis ball, handball, etc.)

How to Play:

1. The playing area may or may not have definitive boundaries.

2. Divide into groups composed of eight players each.

3. Four players will enter the playing area. The four others will form a single file line at the side of the court.

4. One player begins the competition by throwing the ball against the wall. The ball must always hit the wall first.

5. The thrower is eliminated if:

   a. The tossed ball hits the ground prior to hitting the wall.

   b. The thrown ball strikes the wall and is caught by another player before it hits the playing surface.

6. If the ricocheting ball touches another player at any time, be it a bounce or failed catching attempt, that hit player must sprint to and touch the wall before another player grabs the ball and throws it against the wall. If the thrown ball touches the wall before the sprinter does, she/he is eliminated and will go to the end of the line. The first person in line will now enter the game.

7. It is illegal to intentionally impede a thrown ball from striking the wall.

8. If a ball double touches a player, she/he is out. An example would be a player who drops an attempted catch and then is touched by the ball again.

9. The game is played for a given amount of time. The four players who are still in the game when time expires are all winners.

Student Tasks:

1. Banish two or more players.

2. Beat the ball to the wall two times.

3. Dispose of a previously unbeaten player.

4. Never be put out.

Variations:

1. Create groups with more or fewer players.

2. Only four players will compete. The objective is to eliminate the opposition and be the last player.

3. Each time a player is eliminated, that player will receive one point. Play to a pre-determined number of points. As soon as any player hits that predetermined benchmark, the individual with the lowest score, wins.

4. Use two balls and the same rules. (This can be quite challenging.)

Example of Wall Speed Ball

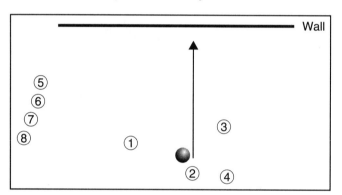

BOULDER COURSE

Objectives:

- Score the maximum points possible.
- Provide safe climbing without the use of safety ropes.
- Learn the proper techniques of climbing.
- Develop body strength and balance.
- Enhance decision-making skills.

Essentials:

- Inside wall
- Climbing surface
- Hand and foot placements
- Safety mat
- Powdered hand gypsum (optional)

How to Build:

1. The wall can be somewhat expensive but well worth the time, effort, and money. This could be an all-school project, with the industrial arts classes designing and building the wall.

Illustration of Attaching the Tabbed Hold Nut

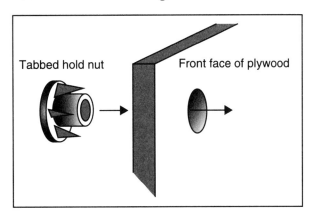

2. The course can incorporate two or three panels in a row that tilt out at the top (6 to 12 inches) from the existing wall. Each panel can have a different tilt, too. This innovation will produce a difficult section to traverse.

3. On either end of the wall, a low overhang, that resembles a cave, can be added. Holds will also be attached to the underside of this overlay.

4. The top of the climbing wall should not be higher than eight feet from the floor. The span of the wall should be at least forty feet long but can extend to any length desired.

5. First, make the framework for the plywood by securing 2″ X 4″ lumber to the existing wall with lag bolts.

6. Next drill 16 or more holes in each 4′ X 8′ plywood panel at various locations. From the backside of the plywood, fasten a "tabbed hold nut" into each of the holes (see illustration). Be sure to *double* secure each threaded nut with panel glue. This insures that the nut will not be pushed out when the handholds and footholds are relocated.

7. Using screw nails, secure the plywood panels to the framework.

8. Paint the surface, being careful not to get any paint into the threads of the hold nuts. (Sprinkling sand onto the wet paint will add extra traction.)

9. Lastly, attach the holds to the panels at strategic locations and have a great time.

Safety:

1. Never allow students to scale directly above or go over the top of another climber.

2. Teach students that when they know they are going to drop, to slightly push away from the wall. This action prevents hitting the holds with the body while on the way down to the mat.

3. When students land on the mat, they should keep the knees slightly bent to absorb the shock.

How to Play:

1. Start at one end of the boulder course and attempt to cross the entire wall without touching the mat on the floor.

2. One point is scored for each panel of the wall that is successfully negotiated.

3. Participants will be given two tries to complete the course.

4. Only the attached handholds and footholds may be used.

5. It is illegal to grab onto or hold the top of the wall.

6. Climbers that receive a perfect score are labeled experts.

Student Tasks:

1. Navigate the course without an error.

2. Do not remain stationary for more than ten seconds.

3. Utilize a new hold every three seconds.

4. Perform a complete body spiral.

Variations:

1. Design different courses along the wall by placing difficult holds at strategic locations. Designate each course by placing colored dots next to the holds that must be used. The following colors could represent:

   Yellow   Easy

   Blue   Risky

   Red   Difficult

2. Form teams and keep score.

3. Go down and back.

4. Reach a designated spot on the wall within a prescribed time limit.

5. Allow the students to design a course.

Example of a Boulder Course layout*

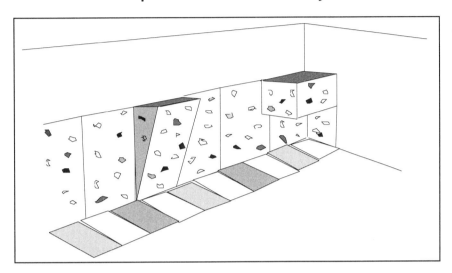

Similar to a course created by Sean Bagshaw, 2000.

ABOUT WASHERS

Objectives:

- ◆ Score 11 points before the opposition does.
- ◆ Develop hand-and-eye coordination.
- ◆ Introduce a lifelong activity.
- ◆ Provide a possible mini-activity within other units.

Essentials:

- ◆ Field or open area
- ◆ 2 washer boxes for every two to four players
- ◆ 8 large fender washers per contest

How to build a plywood washer box:

1. The box has an inside diameter of 16"X 16". The bottom is ½" thick plywood cut 19" X 19". The sides are built from 2 X 4s. (Plywood could also be used.)

2. The center is a black PVC pipe connector, 5" to 6" in diameter and height. It is attached to the middle of the box with four steeply angled wood screws. Any type of a soft plastic container could be substituted as long as it is fairly durable and easily replaced. (A metal can is not recommended because it is easily distorted and could possibly produce sharp edges over time.)

3. Eight fender washers (2¾" to 3" in diameter) are needed. Paint four one color and the other four a contrasting color.

4. Note: Boxes can also be made from oversized pet feeders, large plastic food storage containers, cut down plastic buckets, or anything that is preferably not metal. Check at any hardware store.

© 2001 Parker Publishing Company

Illustration of a Washer Box

Box	PVC	Washer box

Terminology:

1. Canner	Washer winds up in container
2. Angel	Both washers end up in the can
3. Hanger	Washer that extends over the hole from above
4. Inning	After both players have pitched

WASHERS

How to Play:

1. Set the boxes seven large steps apart (approximately 21 feet).

2. The first player begins by tossing four washers, one at a time, into the box.

3. A thrower stands beside either side of the box and is allowed one step. All throws are underhand. The washer may be released so that it rotates backward, forward, or flat like a flying disc.

4. After the first player has finished pitching, the second player follows.

5. Washers landing outside of the box are voided.

6. All washers landing inside the box are worth one point.

7. Any washer that stays in the center (can) is worth three points.

8. Opposing washers that land in the same area are canceled.

9. Point winner of each inning throws first. When no points are awarded, the player that threw first in the previous inning throws second.

10. First player to reach 11 points wins.

Student Tasks:

1. Make three washers score during an inning.

2. Cancel an opponent's canner.

3. Nullify out an opponent's score.

4. Throw two canners during a game.

Variations:

1. Play to 15 or 21 points.

2. Play with a partner. Partners are located at opposite boxes.

3. Play a doubles tournament.

4. Exchange the metal washers with plastic hockey pucks and play indoors. (Other washer substitutes can be invented, too.)

Scoring Examples

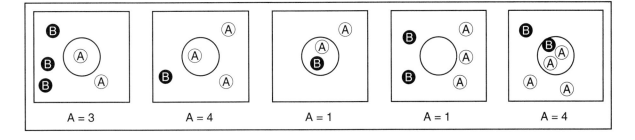

Washers Being Played by Pairs

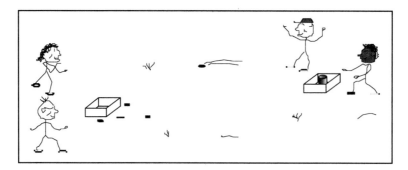

DOUBLE FEATURE*

Objectives:

◆ Score 15 points before the opposition is able to.

◆ Improve hand-and-eye coordination.

◆ Create challenging and risky situations.

Essentials:

◆ Large area

◆ Set of washer boxes

◆ 8 washers

How to Play:

1. The rules of washers apply to this game.

2. Mark a common throwing line on the playing area. Take seven large steps and place the first box. Take two more normal steps and place the second box. The boxes should now be about four to five feet apart.

3. All players will throw from a common pitching line.

4. Point values double when a washer lands in the second box.

5. First player to obtain 15 points is the winner.

Student Tasks:

1. Score in both boxes during any inning.

2. Throw a canner in both boxes during the contest.

Created by Ken Lumsden, 1998.

© 2001 Parker Publishing Company

3. Bounce a washer (from the first box) into the second box for a score.

4. Neutralize all of the opponent's washers.

Variations:

1. Stagger the second box to the right or left of the first one (see second illustration).

2. Use four boxes and form teams with two members each (see third illustration).

3. Exchange the metal washers with plastic hockey pucks and play indoors.

Illustration of Layout for Double Feature

Diagram of Staggered Boxes for Double Feature

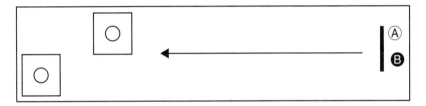

Diagram of Double Feature using Four Boxes and Partners

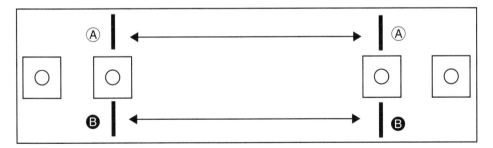

FLUSH PIT WASHERS

Objectives:

◆ Score 21 points before the opposition does.

◆ Develop hand-and-eye coordination.

Essentials:

- ◆ Any outdoor area
- ◆ 2 thin soft plastic containers (butter, cottage cheese, dip, etc.)
- ◆ 4 washers (each pair contrasting or distinguishable)
- ◆ Measuring device two feet long (string, stick, etc.)

How to Play:

1. The rules of "horseshoes" apply to this game with a few modifications.
2. Bury two plastic containers so that the tops are flush with the ground about 10 paces (30 feet) apart.
3. Opponents start at the same end and try to toss the washers into or closer to the hole than the competitor.
4. A washer must be within two feet of the hole before it can be scored.
5. The first contestant pitches two washers, and then the opponent does the same (an inning).
6. Point winner of each inning pitches first in the following inning (hammer). In case of a tie, the player who pitched last in that inning will pitch first in the following inning.
7. The pitcher must start even with the container and is allowed one step during the release.
8. No heckling the person that is pitching.
9. No player shall touch any washer until points of that inning have been agreed upon.
10. No player may go to the other container or be informed of the position of washers prior to the end of the inning.
11. Players that are not pitching must remain behind and opposite the thrower.
12. Scoring:
    a. Only one player scores each inning.
    b. A "Canner" is worth three points.
    c. A "Hanger" is valued at two points.
    d. Closest washer to the container scores one point.
    e. Two washers closer than the opponent's washers, count two points.
    f. One canner and closest washer of the same player score four points.
    g. If each player has a canner, the next closest washer (if within two feet of the can) scores one point.
    h. All equals count as ties and no points are awarded.
13. First player to reach 21 points is the winner.

Student Tasks:

1. Have both washers score.
2. Get a canner.
3. Cancel an opponent's canner.
4. Throw two canners in a row (angel).

Variations:

1. Change the distance between the containers.
2. Remove the two-foot scoring boundary so that all washers have the potential to count.
3. Play a doubles or mixed-doubles tournament.
4. Play a double-elimination tournament.
5. Play any of the other washer games using the buried containers instead of washer boxes.

Example of the Buried Container for Flush Pit Washers

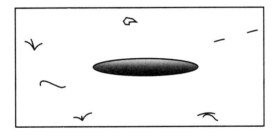

MOUNT WASHINGTON

Objectives:

◆ Reach the summit of Mount Washington and win two games in a row.
◆ Develop hand-and-eye coordination.

Essentials:

◆ Large open area
◆ 6 or more sets of washer boxes and washers.

How to Play:

1. The rules of washers apply to this contest.
2. To start play, assign groups of two individuals to the various sets of boxes. Both players toss from the same end.

3. The challenger will always throw first.

4. Tally the score after each player has thrown four washers.

5. The challenger will lose in the event of a tie.

6. The defeated player will remain and take on a new challenger.

7. The winner will advance one set of boxes toward the peak and wait for the next turn to challenge.

8. Once at the final set of boxes, the winner must defeat two opponents in a row to be successful at reaching the peak of Mount Washington.

9. After a player has won back-to-back games, both the winner and the defeated player return to the first set of boxes (base camp).

10. A player who is defeated at the last set of boxes (summit) must return to the start (base camp) and begin the ascent all over.

Student Tasks:

1. Win one game at the summit boxes.

2. Win four games in a row at the lower boxes.

3. Defeat any past "champion" while at a lower set of boxes.

Variations:

1. Use "Flush Pit" containers and rules.

2. In the event of a tie, competitors will alternate throwing one washer at a time in a sudden death playoff.

3. Require individuals to defeat three or more players to reach the peak.

4. Play games with only two washers each.

5. Make doubles teams. Send one player from each team to opposite ends.

6. Exchange the metal washers with plastic hockey pucks and play indoors. Other washer substitutes can be invented, too.

Illustration of Movement for Mount Washington

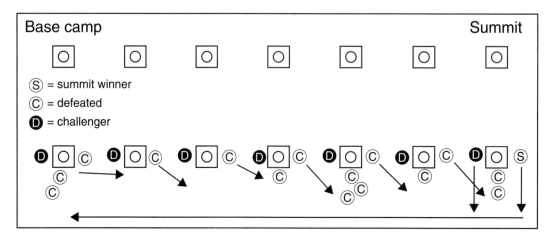

THREE-WAY WASHERS*

Objectives:

- ◆ Score 21 points before the opposition can.
- ◆ Develop hand-and-eye coordination.

Essentials:

- ◆ Large open area
- ◆ 2 sets of washer boxes
- ◆ 16 washers

How to Play:

1. The rules of washers apply to this game.
2. Place one box at each corner of a rectangle that is eight paces long by six paces wide (see diagram).
3. Create teams comprised of four players.
4. Send a team member to each box. Everyone will possess two washers. After the two opposing players at the same pit have thrown, tally the score, and continue the process in a clockwise manner.
5. The washers may be thrown to any of the other three boxes.
6. Washers that land inside the closest box or can are worth one point and three points.
7. Washers ending up in the box and can eight paces away, are double values.
8. Washers that wind up in the pit and can on the far side, receive triple points.
9. First team to score 21 points wins.

Student Tasks:

1. Rest a washer in the opposite box.
2. Cancel out both of the opposition's washers.
3. Toss two washers and have them both score.
4. Toss a canner in the middle distance pit.
5. Throw the washer that is a game winner.
6. Come from eight or more points behind and tie, go ahead, or win.

Created by Ken Lumsden, 1999.

Variations:

1. Change the number of points needed to win.

2. Change the distance of the pits to five and seven paces.

3. Have two-member teams play from opposite ends. Each player will toss four washers instead of two.

4. Lay out a parallelogram with the boxes but use only two-member teams. (See last illustration below.)

5. Exchange the metal washers with plastic hockey pucks and play indoors. Other washer substitutes can be invented, too.

Illustration of Four Members per Team for Three-Way Washers

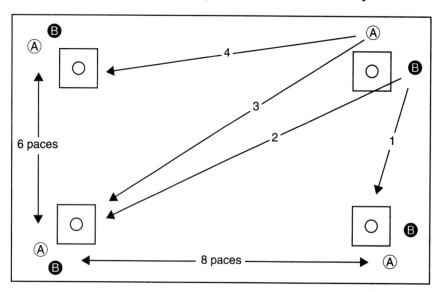

Illustration of a Parallelogram Layout for Three-Way Washers

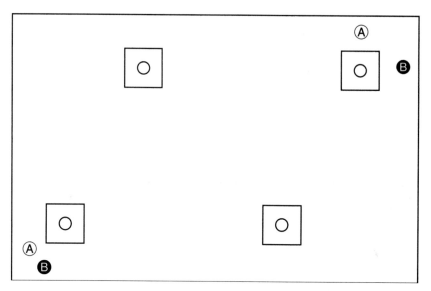

TWO PITCH UNLIMITED

Objectives:

- ◆ Score 21 points before the opposition does.
- ◆ Develop hand-and-eye coordination.

Essentials:

- ◆ Field or open area
- ◆ 2 washer pits
- ◆ 8 large fender washers

How to Play:

1. The rules for washers apply to this game with a few modifications.
2. Players will alternate back and forth after every two pitches.
3. After all eight washers have been thrown, tally the score.
4. All washers that land in the box or can will score. Points are never nullified.
5. The first player to reach 21 points is declared the winner.

Student Tasks:

1. Score four or more points in one inning.
2. Come from five points behind and go ahead or win a contest.
3. During a match, make two or more canners.

Variations:

1. Allow players to determine the number of points needed to win.
2. In order to win, a player must be ahead by two or more points.
3. Pick a partner and play against another pair.
4. Create any tournament format.
5. Exchange the metal washers with plastic hockey pucks and play indoors. Other washer substitutes can be invented, too.

Examples of Various Two Pitch Unlimited Scoring Scenarios

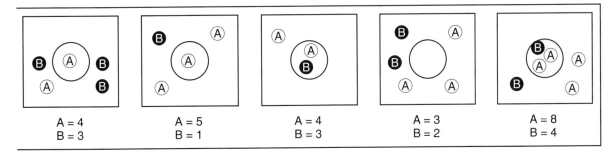

WASHOUT*

Objectives:

- ◆ Score 21 points before the opposition is able to.
- ◆ Avoid scoring exactly 13 points.
- ◆ Create strategies that enable your opponent to have 13 points.

Essentials:

- ◆ Large area
- ◆ Set of washer boxes
- ◆ 8 washers

How to Play:

1. The rules of washers apply to this game.
2. When a player ends an inning with 13 points, that score will return to seven.
3. First person to reach 21 points is the winner.

Student Tasks:

1. Cause your opponent's score to be 13 points at the end of an inning.
2. Toss a canner during the game.
3. Score with three or four washers during an inning.

Variations:

1. Add two numbers that may not be acquired.
2. Allow a person to wind up with 13 points if a canner is present.
3. Exchange the metal washers with plastic hockey pucks and play indoors. (Other washer substitutes can be invented, too.)

Example of Scoring for Washout

1 2 3 4 5 6 7 8 9 10 11 12 (13) 14 15 16 17 18 19 20

© 2001 Parker Publishing Company

Created by Ken Lumsden, 1999.

WEIGHT TRAINING

ABOUT WEIGHT TRAINING

Objectives:

- Understand the benefits of weight training.
- Develop the skills of proper weight training.

Essentials:

- Weight room
- Weight cards printed for each student.

Terminology:

1. Repetitions — The number of times you lift without resting (15)
2. Sets — A group of repetitions that include a rest (2-3)
3. Range of motion — Muscle works from the beginning to the end (ROM)
4. Weight — Pounds that are used
5. Dumbbell — A short bar that is held with one hand
6. Barbell — A long bar that is held with both hands
7. Universal — A fixed machine that includes many stations
8. Isometric — Muscle fibers stay the same length
9. Concentric — Muscle fibers shorten
10. Eccentric — Muscle fibers lengthen

Body Shaping and Toning:

1. Use low weight and high reps.
2. 12 to 15 repetitions with weights.
3. Two to three sets of repetitions.

Body Building: (MAXING) *(Not recommended for middle-school-aged students for safety reasons.)*

1. Use high weight and low reps.
2. Three to five repetitions.
3. Three to four sets of repetitions.

Benefits of Weight Training:

1. Daily activities become easier.
2. Helps prevent injury.
3. Severity of an injury is lessened.

4. Performance is enhanced and improved.

5. Increases muscle tone.

6. Increases lean muscle mass.

7. Muscle burns more energy than fat.

8. Allows body shaping (smaller waist, firm arms and legs).

9. Builds self-esteem and confidence.

10. Reduces stress.

11. Allows one to meet others and make new friends.

Safety:

1. Younger individuals should never MAX OUT.

2. You should be able to lift the weight 12 to 15 times.

3. Go through the entire range of motion (ROM).

4. Movements should be smooth and not jerky.

5. Breathe out when effort is needed to move the weights.

6. Never "horse around" with the weights.

7. Always use a spotter with the bench press.

8. Keep fingers away from the machine and plates.

9. Never misuse the equipment.

10. Check to see that the area is clear when using free weights.

11. Look over equipment for damage or loose items before using.

12. Replace the equipment to the racks.

BODY MASS INDEX

Objectives:

◆ Correctly calculate body mass.

◆ Determine adipose tissue content.

Essentials:

◆ Paper with formula

◆ Pencil

How to:

1. Give each student a formula sheet (see sample).

2. To determine body mass index:

    a. First, multiply the student's weight (a) in pounds by 703 to attain (b).

    b. Second, convert the student's height into inches squared (c). (Use table.)

    c. Finally, divide (c) into (b) to get the body mass index (BMI).

3. Example—John weighs 150 pounds and is 5 feet 7 inches tall:

    a. First, multiply 150 X 703 = 105,450.

    b. Second, 5'7" = 67" X 67" = 4,489. (See height conversion scale.)

    c. Finally, 105,450 ˜ 4,489 = 23.49 Body Mass Index (BMI).

4. Scale:

    a. 21 - 22   Healthiest

    b. 25 +   Overweight

    c. 30 +   Obese

Student Tasks:

1. Calculate proper body mass index.
2. Calculate the proper body mass index for each family member.

WEIGHT TRAINING

Illustration of Height Conversion Scale

Height	Inches	Squared (c)	Height	Inches	Squared (c)
4' - 6"	54	2916	4' - 6.5"	54.5	2970
4' - 7"	55	3025	4' - 7.5"	55.5	3080
4' - 8"	56	3136	4' - 8.5"	56.5	3192
4' - 9"	57	3249	4' - 9.5"	57.5	3306
4' - 10"	58	3364	4' - 10.5"	58.5	3422
4' - 11"	59	3481	4' - 11.5"	59.5	3540
5' - 0"	60	3600	5' - 0.5"	60.5	3660
5' - 1"	61	3721	5' - 1.5"	61.5	3782
5' - 2"	62	3844	5' - 2.5"	62.5	3906
5' - 3"	63	3969	5' - 3.5"	63.5	4032
5' - 4"	64	4096	5' - 4.5"	64.5	4160
5' - 5"	65	4225	5' - 5.5"	65.5	4290
5' - 6"	66	4356	5' - 6.5"	66.5	4422
5' - 7"	67	4489	5' - 7.5"	67.5	4556
5' - 8"	68	4624	5' - 8.5"	68.5	4692
5' - 9"	69	4761	5' - 9.5"	69.5	4830
5' - 10"	70	4900	5' - 10.5"	70.5	4970
5' - 11"	71	5041	5' - 11.5"	71.5	5112
6' - 0"	72	5184	6' - 0.5"	72.5	5256
6' - 1"	73	5329	6' - 1.5"	73.5	5402
6' - 2"	74	5476	6' - 2.5"	74.5	5550
6' - 3"	75	5625	6' - 3.5"	75.5	5700
6' - 4"	76	5776	6' - 4.5"	76.5	5852
6' - 5"	77	5929	6' - 5.5"	77.5	6006
6' - 6"	78	6084	6' - 6.5"	78.5	6162

Formula Sheets for Calculating Body Mass Index

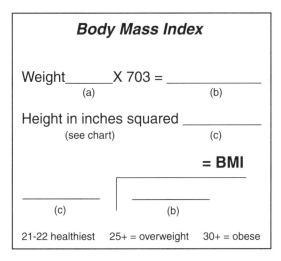

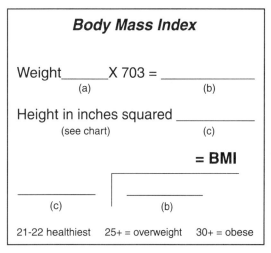

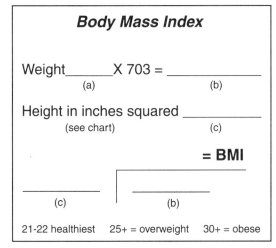

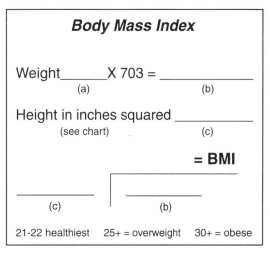

Station Number

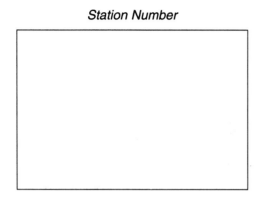

ABDOMINAL MACHINE

Benefits: abdominal

◆ Grasp the straps so that the arms go across the chest.

◆ Keep the head against the support.

◆ Do not push on the foot supports.

◆ Pull the torso forward using the waist.

Station Number

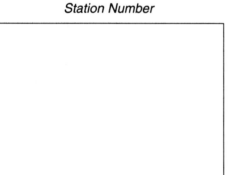

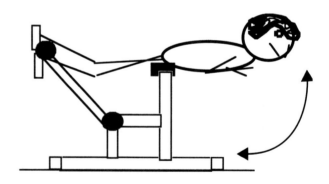

BACK EXTENSIONS

Benefits: lower back

◆ Lock one foot over and one under the support.

◆ Cross the arms on the chest.

◆ Lift the back parallel to the floor.

Station Number

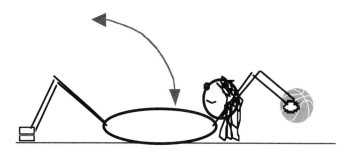

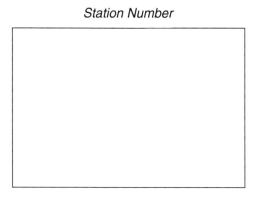

BALL CRUNCHES

Benefits: abdominal

- ◆ Sit with knees bent and toes to the wall.
- ◆ Place ball on floor above the head.
- ◆ Curl up and toss the ball against the wall, catch it, and return to the starting position.
- ◆ Repeat 15 to 20 times.

Station Number

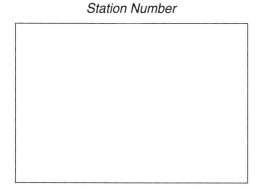

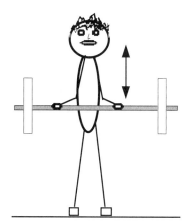

BARBELL CURLS

Benefits: biceps

- ◆ Tilt the pelvis slightly.
- ◆ Do not use your back to lift.
- ◆ Keep the knees slightly bent.
- ◆ Move slowly in both directions.

Station Number

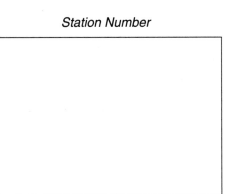

CABLE CURLS

Benefits: biceps

- ◆ Tilt the pelvis slightly.
- ◆ Do not use your back to lift.
- ◆ Keep the knees slightly bent.
- ◆ Move slowly in both directions.

Station Number

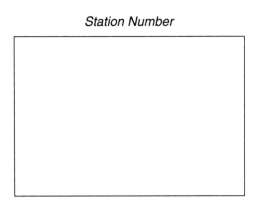

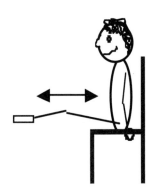

CHAIR KICK OUTS

Benefits: abdominal

- ◆ Sit on chair in a tucked position.
- ◆ Hold on to the chair seat with both hands.
- ◆ Extend and return the legs while keeping the stomach sucked in.
- ◆ Keep the back straight.

Station Number

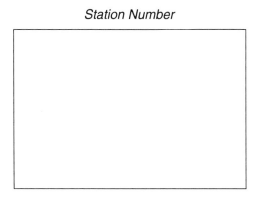

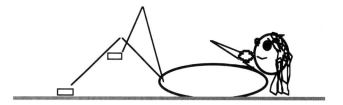

CROSS-OVER CRUNCHES

Benefits: abdominal

- ◆ Place one foot on the floor, cross the other foot over the knee.
- ◆ Cross the arms on the chest.
- ◆ Perform a crunch while bringing the opposite elbow toward the crossed leg.
- ◆ Do 15 to 20 and then switch sides.

Station Number

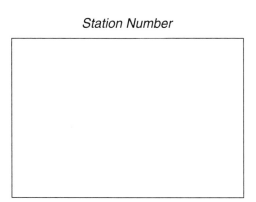

Instructions:
1. Attempt to do six sets in a given amount of time.
2. Each missed dot will add 1/10 of a second to the final time.

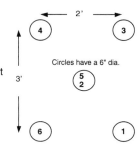

DOT HOPS

Benefits: lower body and cardiovascular

- ◆ Left foot only: 1, 2, 3, 4, 5, and 6.
- ◆ Repeat with right foot, then both feet.
- ◆ Always face forward: spread feet at ends, keep together at center.
- ◆ Same as above except jump and turn at both ends.

Station Number

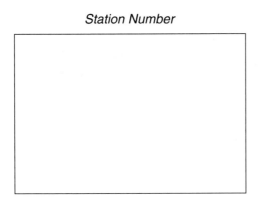

DUMBBELL CURLS

Benefits: biceps

- Tilt the pelvis slightly.
- Do not use the back when lifting.
- Keep the knees slightly bent.
- Each arm alternates during lifting.

Station Number

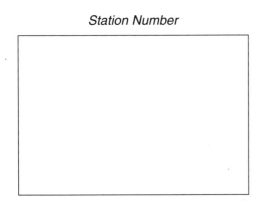

HANGING KNEE-UPS

Benefits: hand and abdominal

- Face away from the bar.
- Grab the bar and hang.
- Raise and lower the knees level with the waist.

Station Number

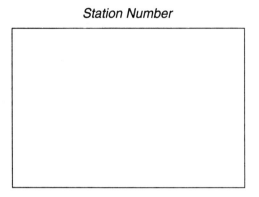

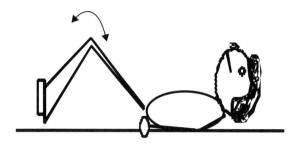

HIP ROLLS

Benefits: oblique

◆ Lie on the floor with hands under rear.

◆ Place both feet on the floor with the knees bent.

◆ Lower legs to right until upper thigh touches, return to start position, and repeat to the left side.

◆ Bend only at the waist.

Station Number

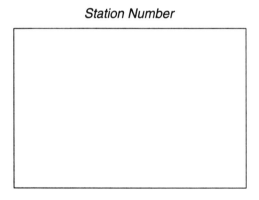

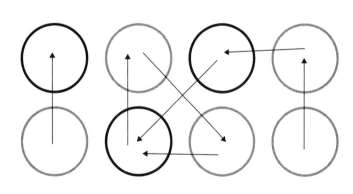

HULA HOOP HOPS

Benefits: lower body and cardiovascular

◆ Remain in the maze the entire time without touching the hula-hoops.

◆ Use a single leg hop.

◆ Use a double leg hop.

◆ Alternate the feet every two hops.

Station Number

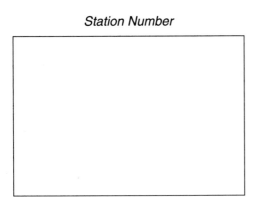

INCLINE CRUNCHES

Benefits: abdominal

- ◆ Secure the board for the proper angle.
- ◆ Hook feet under the toeholds.
- ◆ Keep the knees bent.
- ◆ Keep the arms folded on the chest.
- ◆ Do sit-ups to the desired height.

Station Number

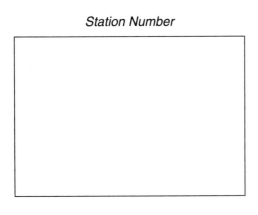

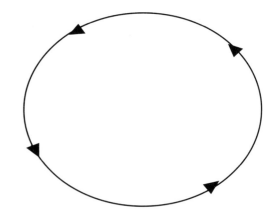

JOG

Benefits: cardiovascular

- ◆ Jog around the outside perimeter of the open area.
- ◆ Do not interfere with any of the other individuals.
- ◆ Use two dumbbells if desired.

Station Number

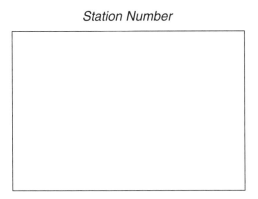

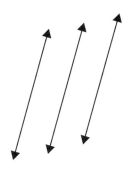

JUMP REACH

Benefits: cardiovascular and lower body

◆ Jump as high and as quickly as possible 15 times.

  OR

◆ Stand next to a wall, reach up and establish a start mark.

◆ Jump three times.

◆ Determine the highest mark.

Station Number

KNEELING CURLS

Benefits: biceps

◆ Kneel on left knee with dumbbell in right hand. Right knee is bent at a 45-degree angle. Left hand is on the hip.

◆ Do not support arm against leg.

◆ Raise weight to shoulder height while keeping upper arm stationary.

Station Number

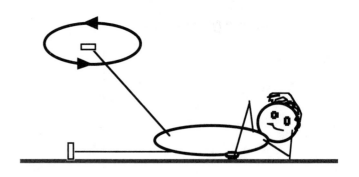

LEG CIRCLES

Benefits: upper leg and hip

- Lie on one side and support the torso with the arms.
- Keep the bottom leg on the floor.
- Top leg is lifted up high with toes pointed.
- Make circles with the entire leg.
- Repeat the process with the opposite leg.

Station Number

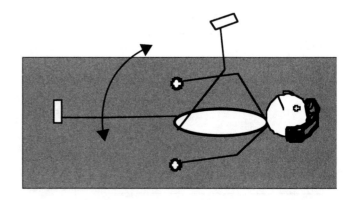

LEG CROSSOVER

Benefits: oblique and hip

- Lie on back with hands wide on floor for support, while keeping the shoulders flat.
- Swing one straightened leg over the other as far as possible.
- Return to the start and repeat with the other leg.

Station Number

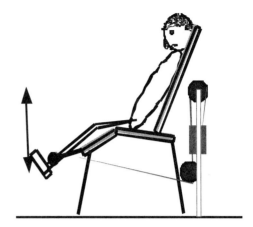

LEG EXTENSIONS

Benefits: quads

- ◆ Hold on to the chair seat with both hands.
- ◆ Point the toes up.
- ◆ Do not lock the knees.

Station Number

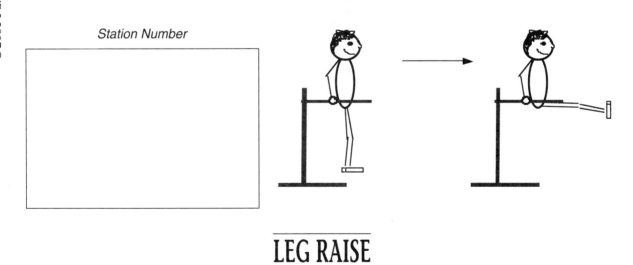

LEG RAISE

Benefits: lower abdominal

- ◆ Face out on the dip stand.
- ◆ Raise the legs parallel to the floor.
- ◆ Return to the starting position.
- ◆ May lift only one leg at a time.

Station Number

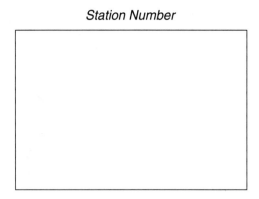

LINE HOPS

Benefits: legs and cardiovascular

◆ Do as many jumps as possible for ten seconds at each station.

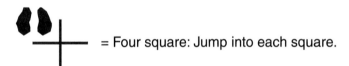 = Four square: Jump into each square.

= Heel click: Jump and click the heels together.

= Spinners: Jump and face in the opposite direction with alternate right and lefts turns.

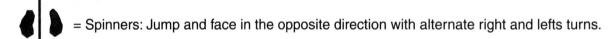 = Bunny hops: jump forward and backward.

= Cross step: Start with the legs crossed then jump and cross them on opposite sides.

= Side hop: Jump sideways back and forth.

WEIGHT TRAINING

Station Number

LUNGES

Benefits: quadriceps

- ◆ The barbell rests on the shoulders with both feet even.
- ◆ Step forward keeping the front knee behind the toe and the back straight.
- ◆ Drop the back knee toward the floor.
- ◆ Reverse the procedure and alternate the legs.

Station Number

MACHINE TOE PRESS

Benefits: gastrocnemius and ankle

- ◆ Keep the hips under the body.
- ◆ Do not lock the knees.
- ◆ Push weight up with the shoulders.
- ◆ Stand tall with half of the foot on the pad.
- ◆ Lift with only the toes and ankles.

© 2001 Parker Publishing Company

Station Number

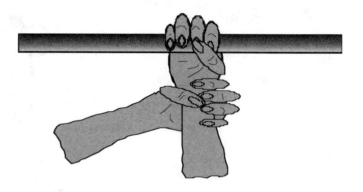

ONE ARM PULL-UPS

Benefits: biceps and shoulder

- The palm may face either direction.
- The free hand grabs the other wrist.
- Chin must go over the bar.
- Arm goes fully extended on the return.

Station Number

PEC DECK

Benefits: anterior deltoid, pectorals major and minor

- Keep the back straight.
- Position upper arms parallel to the floor.
- Press forward at elbows and upper arms (not the hands).

Station Number

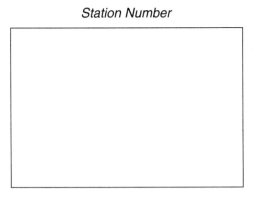

PRESS DOWNS

Benefits: triceps

- ◆ Keep the knees slightly bent.
- ◆ Elbows should remain at the sides.
- ◆ Use a narrow grip on the bar.
- ◆ Extend the arms fully when pushing down.

Station Number

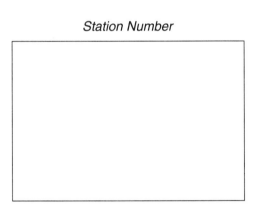

SEATED CURLS

Benefits: biceps

- ◆ Sit on the bench with a dumbbell in hand.
- ◆ Place the other hand on the knee.
- ◆ Lift and lower the weight while keeping the upper arm vertical to the floor.

Station Number

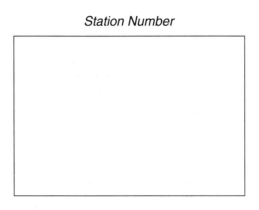

SEATED TWISTS

Benefits: oblique

◆ Place the barbell on shoulders or against the chest.

◆ Keep the back straight and the head up.

◆ Twist to the right and left at the waist.

Station Number

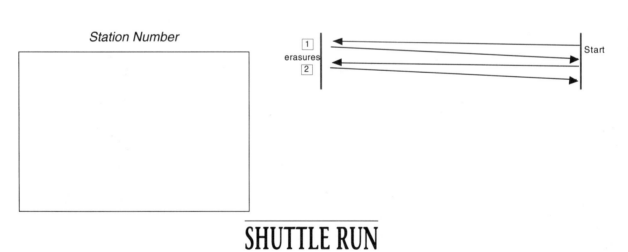

SHUTTLE RUN

Benefits: cardiovascular and lower body

◆ Use the stopwatch that is provided.

◆ Sprint down and grab the first eraser (or foam cut into squares). Bring it back to the start line and set it down.

◆ Go get the second eraser, return and when crossing the finish, stop the time.

◆ Rest for 10 seconds and attempt to better the first time.

Station Number

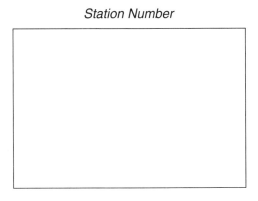

SIDE BEND

Benefits: oblique

◆ Hold the dumbbell with the palm up. Place the opposite hand on the waist.

◆ Keep the back straight.

◆ Bend as far to the right and left as possible.

◆ Change hands and repeat.

Station Number

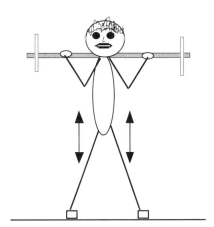

SQUATS

Benefits: quadriceps, hamstring, and buttock

◆ Keep the back straight.

◆ Use a wide stance with the feet slightly uneven for balance.

◆ Bend the knees out but not past the toes.

Station Number

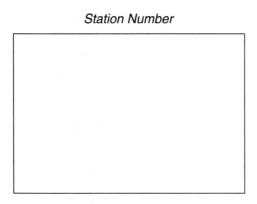

STANDING TOE PRESS

Benefits: gastrocnemius and ankle

- ◆ Keep the hips under the body.
- ◆ Do not lock the knees.
- ◆ Hold both dumbbells at the side.
- ◆ Stand tall with half of the foot on the pad.
- ◆ Lift only with the toes and ankles.

Station Number

STANDING TWISTS

Benefits: obliques

- ◆ Place the barbell on the shoulders or against the chest.
- ◆ Keep the back straight with the knees slightly bent, and head up.
- ◆ Twist right and left only at the waist.

WEIGHT TRAINING

Station Number

STEP-UPS

Benefits: legs and cardiovascular

- ◆ Step up on the box and then back down.
- ◆ Use a quick pace.
- ◆ Alternate the lead foot each time.

© 2001 Parker Publishing Company

Station Number

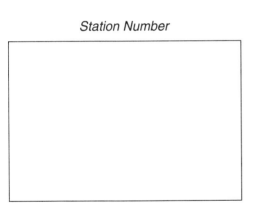

TRICEPS EXTENDS

Benefits: triceps

- ◆ Start with both hands behind the head with the elbows bent.
- ◆ Straighten the arms over the head, then return.

Station Number

WRIST CURLS

Benefits: lower arm and shoulder

- ◆ Grip the dowel and extend the arms parallel to the floor.
- ◆ Roll the weight that is attached to the rope up and down in both twisting directions.

FREE ROAM WEIGHTS

Objectives:

♦ Design a work out.

♦ Choose an area of the body to improve.

♦ Properly fill out and maintain a weight card.

Essentials:

♦ Weight room and equipment

♦ Weight cards

♦ Pencils

♦ Clipboards

♦ Music

How to Play:

1. Stretch and warm the joints and muscles before participation.

2. Students will decide to work on either the upper body, lower body, or cardiovascular system.

3. The goal is to get two or three sets finished in the allotted time.

4. To begin, each student goes to a different station with a scorecard, pencil, and clipboard and follows the instructions on the station card.

5. After completing the exercise, the participant will freely roam to the next station.

6. If more than one person is waiting at a desired station, the student must move to another location and return later.

7. Individual weight cards will be filled out after each exercise.

Student Tasks:

1. Complete the entire workout.

2. Show an improvement in one or more areas during the course.

3. Correctly fill out the weight card.

Variations:

1. Participants may work out with a partner.

2. Weight cards are not required.

Sample Free Roam Weight Scorecard

Weight Training Scorecard

Name: _____
Period: _____
Target Heart Rate: ____ to ____ beats per minute.

Type of Exercise	Day 1			Day 2			Day 3			Day 4			Day 5		
	lbs	rep	set	lbs	rep	set	lbs	rep	set	lbs	rep	set	lbs	rep	set
Sample: Arm Curls	25	15	3												

MUSCLE MYSTERY

Objectives:

- ◆ List the muscle or muscles that are strengthened during a given exercise.
- ◆ Describe a piece of strength-conditioning equipment.
- ◆ While participating in a specific sport or activity, list the possible gains by improving the strength of a certain muscle.

Essentials:

- ◆ Weight room
- ◆ Weight equipment
- ◆ Muscle chart
- ◆ Student handout
- ◆ Pencils

Terminology:

1.	Repetitions	Number of times a weight is lifted without resting (15)
2.	Sets	A group of repetitions that include a rest
3.	Range of motion	Muscle works from the beginning to the end (ROM)
4.	Weight	Pounds that are used
5.	Dumbbell	A short bar that is held with one hand
6.	Barbell	A long bar that is held with both hands
7.	Universal	A fixed machine that includes many stations
8.	Isometric	Muscle fibers stay the same length
9.	Concentric	Muscle fibers shorten
10.	Eccentric	Muscle fibers lengthen

How to Play:

1. Students will pair up and receive a worksheet and a pencil.
2. Each pair will go to a piece of equipment and fill in the blanks on the worksheet.
3. The blanks include:
   a. Type of equipment being used.
   b. Name of exercise.
   c. Muscle or muscles being worked.
   d. Benefits of strengthening a muscle for a chosen sport.
4. After completing the four stations, turn in the paper to be graded.
5. Scoring: (Each blank is worth five points.)
   a. 90%   A
   b. 80%   B

© 2001 Parker Publishing Company

c. 70%   C

d. 60%   D

Student Tasks:

1. Complete four exercises in the allotted time.

2. Score 80 percent or higher on the worksheet.

3. Using the muscle chart, locate four different muscles.

Variations:

1. Each pair of students could give a short oral and visual presentation on one of the chosen stations.

2. Give a written test that covers all of the muscles, terms, and stations used during the course.

Example Student Form for Muscle Mystery
Muscle Mystery Worksheet

Names: 1)
              2)

Date:

Period:

Station #1:

a) Type of equipment being used: 1)

b) Name of exercise: 2)

c) Muscle/s being worked: 3)

d) Improvement of this muscle would help in the sport of: 4)

e) By improving: 5)

Station #2:

f) Type of equipment being used: 1)

g) Name of exercise: 2)

h) Muscle/s being worked: 3)

i) Improvement of this muscle would help in the sport of: 4)

j) By improving: 5)

Station #3:

k) Type of equipment being used: 1)

l) Name of exercise: 2)

m) Muscle/s being worked: 3)

n) Improvement of this muscle would help in the sport of: 4)

o) By improving: 5)

Station #4:

p) Type of equipment being used: 1)

q) Name of exercise: 2)

r) Muscle/s being worked: 3)

s) Improvement of this muscle would help in the sport of: 4)

t) By improving: 5)

BENEFITS OF WEIGHT TRAINING

- Daily activities become easier
- Aids in the prevention of injuries
- Severity of an injury is lessened
- Performance enhanced and improved
- Increases muscle tone
- Increases lean muscle mass
- Muscle burns more energy than fat
- Allows body shaping
- Builds self-esteem and confidence
- Reduces stress
- Meet people and make friends

SAFETY IN WEIGHT TRAINING

- Younger individuals should never MAX OUT.

- Lift the weight 12 to 15 times.

- Go through the entire range of motion (ROM).

- Movements should be smooth and not jerky.

- Exhale when effort is needed to move the weights.

- Never "horse around" with the weights.

- Always use a spotter with the bench press.

- Keep fingers away from the machine and plates.

- Never misuse the equipment.

- Check that the area is clear when using free weights.

- Check equipment for damage or loose items before using.

- Replace the equipment to the racks.

FOOT WRESTLING

Objectives:

- ◆ Score five points before the opposition does.
- ◆ Step on the top of an opponent's foot.
- ◆ Develop quickness and agility.

Essentials:

- ◆ Large open area
- ◆ Every participant must wear shoes for safety reasons.

How to Play:

1. Participants will pick a foe to do battle against.
2. Each player must continuously hold the opponent's hands.
3. Players will attempt to lightly step on the top of the opponent's foot.
4. One point is tallied for each successful hit.
5. First player to score five points is the winner.

Student Tasks:

1. After lifting one foot, score with the opposite.
2. Defeat two different players.
3. Defeat an opponent by three or more points.
4. Trounce a previously unbeaten player.

Variations:

1. Require more or fewer hits to win.
2. Create a double-elimination tournament (see Part II, "Organization," for forms).

Illustration of Foot Wrestling

Splat

KNEESLES

Objectives:

♦ Defeat an opponent by causing the kneepad to touch the shoe.

♦ Develop speed, quickness, and strength.

Essentials:

♦ Large matted area (wrestling room)

♦ Knee pads

♦ Stopwatch

How to Play:

1. Pair up everyone in class.

2. Competitors should be about the same size.

3. Each player will place one kneepad directly over the kneecap on either leg.

4. A player may not touch this kneepad during the competition.

5. Wrestlers must compete from the knees or on the mat at all times. (Standing is not allowed.)

6. All matches will last for 90 seconds.

7. The first player to move her or his opponent's kneepad down the leg and against the shoe wins.

8. If neither combatant is successful when time expires, the player whose kneepad is farthest from the shoe wins.

Student Tasks:

1. Remove the kneepad from two different players.

2. Defeat a previously undefeated wrestler.

3. Defeat two different players in a row.

Variations:

1. Each player has two kneepads.

2. Attempt to remove the pad from the leg.

3. A wrestler must win two out of three matches in order to be victorious.

4. Create a weight division tournament.

Illustration of Players with Knee Pads for Kneesles

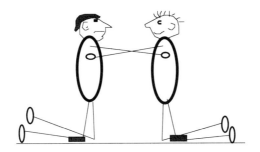

TAG TEAM

Objectives:

- ◆ Eliminate the opposing team by stepping on the tops of their feet first.
- ◆ Avoid getting stepped on.
- ◆ Develop a strategy.

Essentials:

- ◆ Large open area
- ◆ Shoes must be worn by every participant

How to Play:

1. Participants will first pair up and then challenge any other twosome to a match.
2. Players will form a circle by continuously holding the opponent's hands. (Teammates will be opposite each other.)
3. Players will attempt to lightly step on the top of either opponent's foot.
4. One point is tallied for each successful hit.
5. Any player that gets tapped five times is eliminated.
6. First team to eliminate both of the opponents is the champion.

Student Tasks:

1. Defeat two different teams.
2. Defeat a team by three or more points.
3. Trounce a previously unbeaten pair.

Variations:

1. While in the circle, teammates will be next to each other (see illustration).

2. Create teams with three or four players each. One or two players will wait on the outside. Players who are eliminated will be replaced with a teammate.

3. Require more or fewer touches to win.

4. Form a round-robin tournament.

Illustration of Tag Team

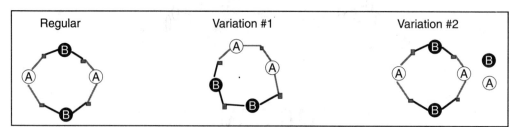

PART II
ORGANIZATION FOR
TOURNAMENTS

* Arrangement Variations

  Distribution of Students

  Rotating Teams

* Team Rosters

  Team Record Sheets for 4 to 13 player teams

* Tournaments

  Tournament Formats – Blank, ready-to-use charts
      for single or double elimination

* Team Organizer – Chart

  Easy-to-use formula for combining classes
      or any number of students for tournaments

ARRANGEMENT VARIATIONS

Benefits:

1. Organization becomes fast and simple.

2. Student excitement increases while boredom decreases due to the available variety of methods and limitless combinations.

3. The "loser syndrome" is virtually eliminated because teams can be reconfigured daily.

4. Expediting the team-choosing process expands playing time.

5. Allows for several shorter games, which in turn averts lopsided scores.

6. Provides for multiple activities within any unit where teams are required.

DISTRIBUTING STUDENTS

I. Line Dispersal

1. The essentials are a large area and visible numbers that represent each team.

2. This method of forming teams is excellent when used by a single teacher or when two or more instructors combine classes. This process is repeated daily, thus permanent teams are not required.

3. The students will form two single-file lines, one of girls and one of boys. When two or more classes are combined, allow everyone to pick a partner before lining up. This reduces the time required to establish the teams.

4. Assign the first player/pair a team number to report to and direct them to sit behind that number in a straight line. As the second person or pair steps forward, do the same. Alter the dispersion number order so that students will not seek to stand a chosen number of spaces behind another player or duo that they want to be with. Continue this process until everyone has been assigned a team.

5. When there are not enough pairs to make all of the teams equal, split the remaining twosomes and assign each individual to a unit.

6. Once assigned, students are not allowed to switch teams.

Illustration of a Line Dispersal

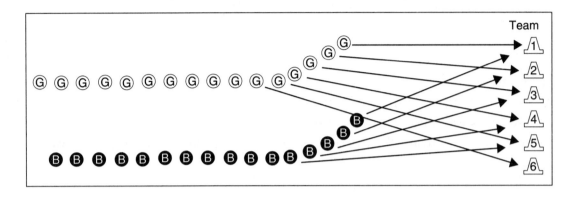

II. One Extra Team

1. The essentials are a large area, visible numbers that represent each team, and a team roster and record sheet. The vast array of forms is located at the end of this section.

2. Determine the number of teams needed to play the game and then create one extra one. (Example: The unit is softball. There are 40 students in the class. Each team needs 10 players on a side. Make five teams, instead of four, composed of eight players each.)

3. On the first day, sit all five teams in a single file line behind their respective team number. Team #1 stands up and comes to the front of the class. Split up team #1 by sending two players to the four other teams (see illustration below).

4. Play a round-robin schedule or win versus win and loss versus loss.

5. On the second day, the same process is used, but this time disperse the players from team #2 to the various other teams.

6. Continue the process for five days and then play a tournament based on each individual team record.

Diagram of One Extra Team

Step 1–Day#1

1. ① ① ① ① ① ① ① ①
2. ❷ ❷ ❷ ❷ ❷ ❷ ❷ ❷
3. ③ ③ ③ ③ ③ ③ ③ ③
4. ❹ ❹ ❹ ❹ ❹ ❹ ❹ ❹
5. ⑤ ⑤ ⑤ ⑤ ⑤ ⑤ ⑤ ⑤

Step 2–Day #1

1.
2. ❷ ❷ ❷ ❷ ❷ ❷ ❷ ❷ ① ①
3. ③ ③ ③ ③ ③ ③ ③ ③ ① ①
4. ❹ ❹ ❹ ❹ ❹ ❹ ❹ ❹ ① ①
5. ⑤ ⑤ ⑤ ⑤ ⑤ ⑤ ⑤ ⑤ ① ①

Step 1–Day #2

1. ① ① ① ① ① ① ① ①
2. ❷ ❷ ❷ ❷ ❷ ❷ ❷ ❷
3. ③ ③ ③ ③ ③ ③ ③ ③
4. ❹ ❹ ❹ ❹ ❹ ❹ ❹ ❹
5. ⑤ ⑤ ⑤ ⑤ ⑤ ⑤ ⑤ ⑤

Step 2–Day #2

1. ① ① ① ① ① ① ① ① ❷ ❷
2.
3. ③ ③ ③ ③ ③ ③ ③ ③ ❷ ❷
4. ❹ ❹ ❹ ❹ ❹ ❹ ❹ ❹ ❷ ❷
5. ⑤ ⑤ ⑤ ⑤ ⑤ ⑤ ⑤ ⑤ ❷ ❷

III. Month

1. Determine the number of players needed for each team.

2. Beginning with January 1, fill the first team with all participants who were born in January, February, March, and so on.

3. When more than enough students step forward after a month is announced, select the player(s) with the earliest birthday first.

4. Fill the second and remaining teams by sequencing through the calendar.

5. A second variation is to have everyone who was born on the first day of any month step forward. Once team #1 has been filled, progress to the next day. When more students approach than are required to satisfy the team limit, select the first alphabetically.

IV. Height

1. Line the students up by height from the tallest to the shortest.

2. Determine the number of players needed for each team.

3. Start at either end, but stay in sequence when dividing the students. (Note: The teams that are shorter in stature are just as competitive because of their speed and quickness.)

ROTATING TEAMS

I. Round Robin

1. This format is used when several short games are played. Freeze one team at a corner location. Play several games. With each new contest, all of the other teams will rotate one field clockwise (Example A).

2. Example A allows for each team to compete against every other group. Seven games can be played before the order starts to repeat.

3. Example B provides for five different games before the order replicates itself.

Example A of a Round-Robin Rotation using Eight Teams

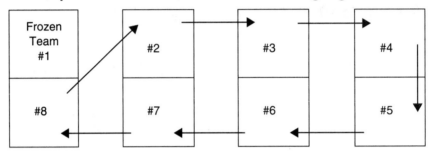

Example B of a Round-Robin Rotation using 10 Teams

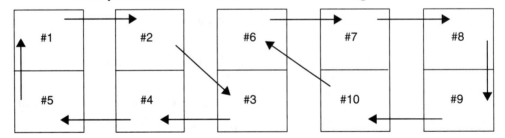

II. Winner Versus Winner

1. This method can be used when only two games are played during the period.

2. After the first game, pit the winners versus winners and the vanquished versus vanquished for the second game.

3. Optional: The team that wins both games will receive two bonus points. After losing its first, the team that wins the second game will receive one bonus point.

4. The example below shows that both #1 and #2 won their first game and will play each other the second game.

Example of a Winner Versus Winner Rotation

Game 1

1	2
3	4

Game 2

1 Winner	3 Lost
2 Winner	4 Lost

III. Team Size Variations

1. This rotation sequence is used to change the number of players on a team from game to game. This adaptation will also allow for more than one type of activity to be performed.

2. The first illustration (Diagram A) requires six teams. Each team must be composed of two, four or six players, since they will be split in half on B and D. Six different rotations can be played before the games repeat.

3. The second illustration (Diagram B) also requires the same team makeup. With this rotation sequence, all three playing areas will have a different number of players on each team. Notice that #1 rejoins on the lower half of Court C after the first game.

4. Additional playing areas and teams can be added to either format.

Diagram A of Team Size Variations

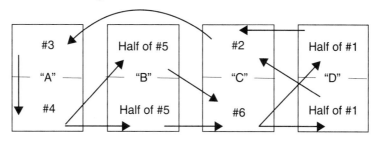

Diagram B of Team Size Variations

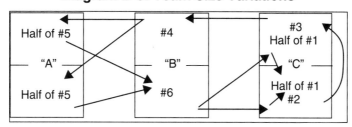

IV. Crisscross

1. This format might be used when two or more classes are combined. Two different games are played during the same period. Each team will compete in both types of game.

2. Pit the winners versus winners and the vanquished versus vanquished for the second game.

3. The team that wins both games will receive two bonus points and the team that wins the second game (after losing the first) will receive one bonus point.

4. In the example below, at the conclusion of the first game, the winners of Rogue's Gallery on field #1 and #4, would play a second game of Double Diamond on field #2. The winners of the first game of Double Diamond on field #2 and #3 would play a second game of Rogue's Gallery on field #1. The losing teams would do likewise on the opposite fields.

Depiction of a Crisscross Rotation after the First Game

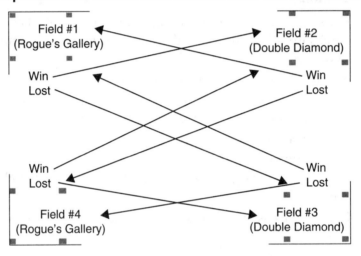

V. Free Space

1. This pattern can be used when:

   a. There is not enough equipment or area available. (The "free space" could be the stage when inside.)

   b. Rest time is required.

   c. Referees are needed.

   d. Skill practice is necessary.

   e. Teams need time to plan a strategy.

2. Always create an uneven number of teams and rotate in a round-robin format.

3. As the various teams rotate to the "free space," they are at liberty to perform any of the actions above (a–e).

Illustration of the Free Space Rotation

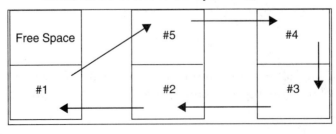

VI. Flag Distribution

1. This system allows for a quick, simple, and cost effective way in which to change team identification colors. It also works well in almost any team sport.

2. Use football flags instead of pinnies for all team games. Only two different colors of flags are needed. (The shirt must be tucked in at the hips though.)

3. Place an extra batch of football flags in two buckets located in between the end and adjoining fields (see illustration).

4. Players will only exchange flags when they rotate at each end of the playing area.

Illustration of Buckets for Flag Distribution

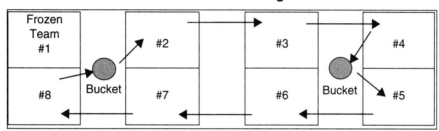

4-Team Record Sheet

Unit: _____ _____ Period:

Team	Roster	Record	Team	Roster	Record
1		W	**3**		W
		T			T
2		W	**4**		W
		T			T

Notes:

SCHEDULE		
1	**2**	**3**
1 vs 2	1 vs 3	1 vs 4
3 vs 4	2 vs 4	2 vs 3

All Or Nothing Championship Brackets
(To determine placement: Win = 2   Tie = 1)

Gold	**Silver**
___ vs ___	___ vs ___
1st 2nd	3rd 4th

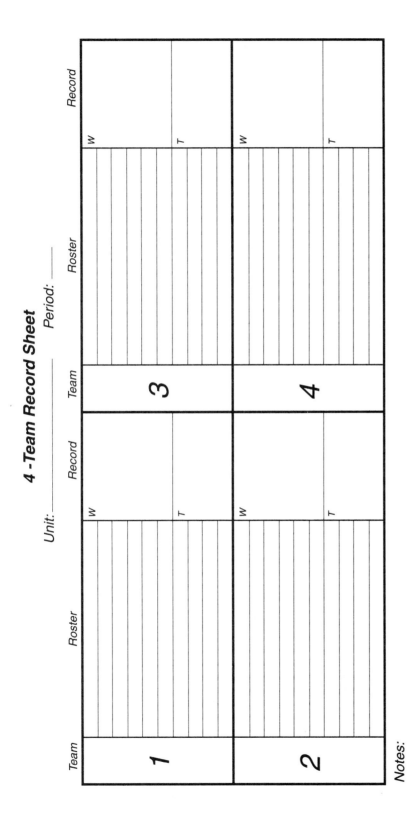

4 -Team Record Sheet

Unit: _____   Period: _____

Team	Roster	Record W / T
1		
2		
3		
4		

SCHEDULE

1	2	3
1 vs 2	1 vs 3	1 vs 4
3 vs 4	2 vs 4	2 vs 3

All Or Nothing Championship Brackets

(To determine placement: Win = 2   Tie = 1)

Gold

_____ vs _____
1st   2nd

Silver

_____ vs _____
3rd   4th

Notes:

ROTATING TEAMS

5 -Team *(Mix 'n' Match)* **Record Sheet**

Unit: _____ Period: _____

Team	Roster	Record	Team	Roster	Record
1		W / T	**4**		W / T
2		W / T	**5**		W / T
3		W / T	Notes:		

SCHEDULE

Day/Team Out	1	2	3	4	5
Game 1	2 vs 3	1 vs 3	1 vs 2	1 vs 2	1 vs 2
	4 vs 5	4 vs 5	4 vs 5	3 vs 5	3 vs 4
Game 2	2 vs 4	1 vs 4	1 vs 4	1 vs 3	1 vs 3
	5 vs 3	3 vs 5	2 vs 5	2 vs 5	2 vs 4
Game 3	2 vs 5	1 vs 5	1 vs 5	1 vs 5	1 vs 4
	3 vs 4	3 vs 4	2 vs 4	2 vs 3	2 vs 3

Championship Brackets

(To determine placement: Win = 2   Tie = 1)

Gold   **Silver**

____ vs ____   ____ vs ____

1st   2nd   3rd   4th

Add ____ anywhere.

5th

ROTATING TEAMS

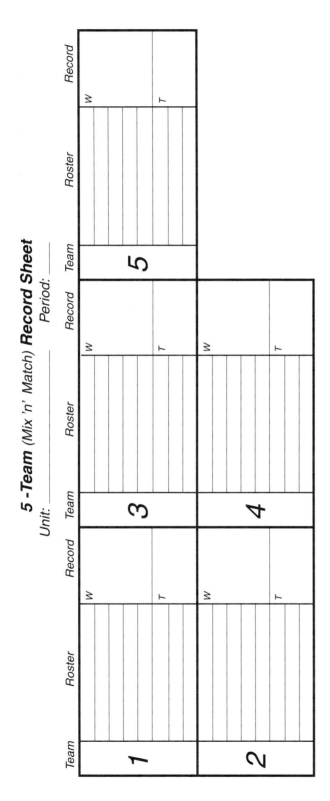

5-Team (Mix 'n' Match) Record Sheet

Unit: _____ Period: _____

SCHEDULE

Day/Team Out	1	2	3	4	5
Game 1	2 vs 3	1 vs 3	1 vs 2	1 vs 2	1 vs 2
	4 vs 5	4 vs 5	4 vs 5	3 vs 5	3 vs 4
Game 2	2 vs 4	1 vs 4	1 vs 4	1 vs 3	1 vs 3
	5 vs 3	3 vs 5	2 vs 5	2 vs 5	2 vs 4
Game 3	2 vs 5	1 vs 5	1 vs 5	1 vs 5	1 vs 4
	3 vs 4	3 vs 4	2 vs 4	2 vs 3	2 vs 3

Championship Brackets

(To determine placement: Win = 2 Tie = 1)

Gold

_____ vs _____
1st   2nd

Silver

_____ vs _____
3rd   4th

Add _____ anywhere.
        5th

© 2001 Parker Publishing Company

6 -Team Record Sheet

Unit: _____ Period: _____

Team	Roster	Record		Team	Roster	Record	
1		W		4		W	
		T				T	
2		W		5		W	
		T				T	
3		W		6		W	
		T				T	

Notes:

SCHEDULE

1	2	3	4	5
1 vs 2	1 vs 3	1 vs 5	1 vs 6	1 vs 4
3 vs 4	2 vs 5	2 vs 4	2 vs 3	2 vs 6
5 vs 6	4 vs 6	3 vs 6	4 vs 5	3 vs 5

Championship Brackets

(To determine placement: Win = 2   Tie = 1)

Gold		Silver		Bronze	
____ vs ____		____ vs ____		____ vs ____	
1st 2nd		3rd 4th		5th 6th	

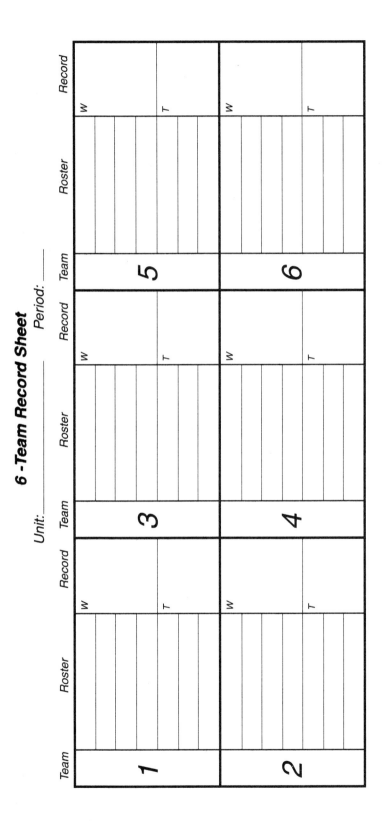

6 - Team Record Sheet

Unit: _____   Period: _____

Team	Roster	Record
1		W T
2		W T
3		W T
4		W T
5		W T
6		W T

SCHEDULE

1	2	3	4	5
1 vs 2	1 vs 3	1 vs 5	1 vs 6	1 vs 4
3 vs 4	2 vs 5	2 vs 4	2 vs 3	2 vs 6
5 vs 6	4 vs 6	3 vs 6	4 vs 5	3 vs 5

Championship Brackets

(To determine placement: Win = 2 Tie = 1)

Gold   Silver   Bronze

____ vs ____   ____ vs ____   ____ vs ____
1st   2nd   3rd   4th   5th   6th

7 -Team *(Mix 'n' Match)* **Record Sheet**

Unit: _____   Period: _____

Team	Roster	Record	Team	Roster	Record
1		W / T	5		W / T
2		W / T	6		W / T
3		W / T	7		W / T
4		W / T	Notes:		

Day and Team Out			**SCHEDULE**			
1	**2**	**3**	**4**	**5**	**6**	**7**
2+4 vs 6+7	1+6 vs 3+ 4	5+6 vs 2+7	1+7 vs 2+5	3+7 vs 4+6	2+3 vs 1+5	4+5 vs 1+3
2+4 vs 3+5	1+6 vs 5+ 7	5+6 vs 1+4	1+7 vs 3+6	3+7 vs 1+2	2+3 vs 4+7	4+5 vs 2+6
6+7 vs 3+5	3+4 vs 5+ 7	2+7 vs 1+4	2+5 vs 3+6	4+6 vs 1+2	1+5 vs 4+7	1+3 vs 2+6
1	**2**	**3**	**4**	**5**	**6**	**7**
2+4 vs 6+7	1+6 vs 3+ 4	5+6 vs 2+7	1+7 vs 2+5	3+7 vs 4+6	2+3 vs 1+5	4+5 vs 1+3
3 vs 5	5 vs 7	1 vs 4	3 vs 6	1 vs 2	4 vs 7	2 vs 6

Round Robin Championship Brackets
(To determine placement: Win = 2   Tie = 1)

____ + ____ vs ____ + ____ vs ____ + ____   Add ____ anywhere.
1st   6th   2nd   5th   3rd   4th   7th

7-Team (Mix 'n' Match) Record Sheet

Unit: _____   Period: _____

Team	Roster	Record
1		W ___ T ___
2		W ___ T ___
3		W ___ T ___
4		W ___ T ___
5		W ___ T ___
6		W ___ T ___
7		W ___ T ___

Notes:

SCHEDULE

Day and Team Out						
1	**2**	**3**	**4**	**5**	**6**	**7**
2+4 vs 6+7	1+6 vs 3+4	5+6 vs 2+7	1+7 vs 2+5	3+7 vs 4+6	2+3 vs 1+5	4+5 vs 1+3
2+4 vs 3+5	1+6 vs 5+7	5+6 vs 1+4	1+7 vs 3+6	3+7 vs 1+2	2+3 vs 4+7	4+5 vs 2+6
6+7 vs 3+5	3+4 vs 5+7	2+7 vs 1+4	2+5 vs 3+6	4+6 vs 1+2	1+5 vs 4+7	1+3 vs 2+6
1	**2**	**3**	**4**	**5**	**6**	**7**
2+4 vs 6+7	1+6 vs 3+4	5+6 vs 2+7	1+7 vs 2+5	3+7 vs 4+6	2+3 vs 1+5	4+5 vs 1+3
3 vs 5	5 vs 7	1 vs 4	3 vs 6	1 vs 2	4 vs 7	2 vs 6

Round Robin Championship Brackets

(To determine placement: Win = 2 Tie = 1)

_____ + _____ vs _____ + _____ vs _____ + _____   Add _____ anywhere.
1st   6th   2nd   5th   3rd   4th   7th

ROTATING TEAMS

8 -Team Record Sheet

Unit: _____   Period: _____

Team	Roster	Record	Team	Roster	Record
1		W T	**5**		W T
2		W T	**6**		W T
3		W T	**7**		W T
4		W T	**8**		W T

Notes:

SCHEDULE

1	2	3	4	5	6	7
1 vs 2	1 vs 3	1 vs 5	1 vs 7	1 vs 8	1 vs 6	1 vs 4
3 vs 4	2 vs 5	2 vs 8	2 vs 4	2 vs 3	2 vs 7	2 vs 6
5 vs 6	4 vs 7	3 vs 7	3 vs 6	4 vs 5	3 vs 5	3 vs 8
7 vs 8	6 vs 8	4 vs 6	5 vs 8	6 vs 7	4 vs 8	5 vs 7

All Or Nothing Championship Brackets

(To determine placement: Win = 2   Tie = 1)

First		Second		Third		Fourth	
___ vs ___		___ vs ___		___ vs ___		___ vs ___	
1st 2nd		3rd 4th		5th 6th		7th 8th	

ROTATING TEAMS

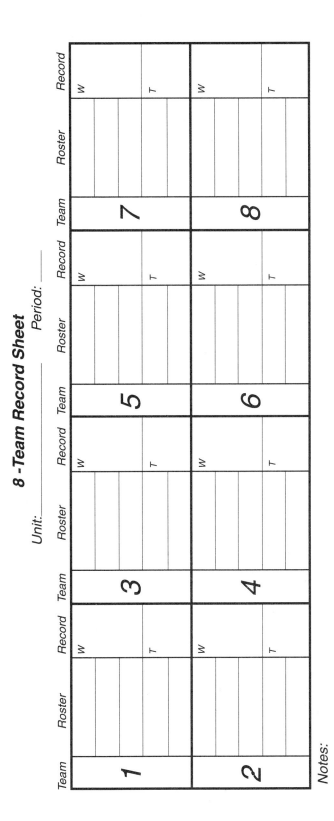

8 -Team Record Sheet

Unit: _____ Period: _____

Team	Roster	Record
1		W T
2		W T
3		W T
4		W T
5		W T
6		W T
7		W T
8		W T

Notes:

SCHEDULE

1	2	3	4	5	6	7
1 vs 2	1 vs 3	1 vs 5	1 vs 7	1 vs 8	1 vs 6	1 vs 4
3 vs 4	2 vs 5	2 vs 8	2 vs 4	2 vs 3	2 vs 7	2 vs 6
5 vs 6	4 vs 7	3 vs 7	3 vs 6	4 vs 5	3 vs 5	3 vs 8
7 vs 8	6 vs 8	4 vs 6	5 vs 8	6 vs 7	4 vs 8	5 vs 7

All Or Nothing Championship Brackets

(To determine placement: Win = 2 Tie = 1)

First		Second		Third		Fourth	
____ vs ____		____ vs ____		____ vs ____		____ vs ____	
1st	2nd	3rd	4th	5th	6th	7th	8th

ROTATING TEAMS

9 -Team *(Mix 'n' Match)* **Record Sheet**

Unit: _____   Period: _____

Team	Roster	Record	Team	Roster	Record	Team	Roster	Record
1		W / T	**4**		W / T	**7**		W / T
2		W / T	**5**		W / T	**8**		W / T
3		W / T	**6**		W / T	**9**		W / T

Notes:

SCHEDULE

Day and Team Out								
1	**2**	**3**	**4**	**5**	**6**	**7**	**8**	**9**
2+3 vs 4+5	1+6 vs 4+8	1+7 vs 5+9	1+5 vs 3+7	1+4 vs 2+6	1+8 vs 4+9	1+9 vs 5+8	1+3 vs 2+5	1+2 vs 3+4
6+7 vs 8+9	3+9 vs 5+7	2+8 vs 4+6	2+9 vs 6+8	3+8 vs 7+9	2+7 vs 3+5	2+4 vs 3+6	4+7 vs 6+9	5+6 vs 7+8
2+3 vs 8+9	1+6 vs 5+7	1+7 vs 4+6	1+5 vs 6+8	1+4 vs 7+9	1+8 vs 3+5	1+9 vs 3+6	1+3 vs 6+9	1+2 vs 7+8
4+5 vs 6+7	4+8 vs 3+9	5+9 vs 2+8	3+7 vs 2+9	2+6 vs 3+8	4+9 vs 2+7	5+8 vs 2+4	2+5 vs 4+7	3+4 vs 5+6
2+3 vs 6+7	1+6 vs 3+9	1+7 vs 2+8	1+5 vs 2+9	1+4 vs 3+8	1+8 vs 2+7	1+9 vs 2+4	1+3 vs 4+7	1+2 vs 5+6
8+9 vs 4+5	5+7 vs 4+8	4+6 vs 5+9	6+8 vs 3+7	7+9 vs 2+6	3+5 vs 4+9	3+6 vs 5+8	6+9 vs 2+5	7+8 vs 3+4

Champîonship Brackets

(To determine placement: Win = 2   Tie = 1)

First Place				**Second Place**					
____ + ____	vs	____ + ____		____ + ____	vs	____ + ____		Add ____ anywhere.	
1st 4th		2nd 3rd		5th 8th		6th 7th		9th	

9-Team (Mix 'n' Match) Record Sheet

Unit: _____   Period: _____

Team	Roster	Record		Team	Roster	Record		Team	Roster	Record
1		W		4		W		7		W
		T				T				T
2		W		5		W		8		W
		T				T				T
3		W		6		W		9		W
		T				T				T

SCHEDULE

Day and Team Out	1	2	3	4	5	6	7	8	9
	2+3 vs 4+5	1+6 vs 4+8	1+7 vs 5+9	1+5 vs 3+7	1+4 vs 2+6	1+8 vs 4+9	1+9 vs 5+8	1+3 vs 2+5	1+2 vs 3+4
	6+7 vs 8+9	3+9 vs 5+7	2+8 vs 4+6	2+9 vs 6+8	3+8 vs 7+9	2+7 vs 3+5	2+4 vs 3+6	4+7 vs 6+9	5+6 vs 7+8
	2+3 vs 8+9	1+6 vs 5+7	1+7 vs 4+6	1+5 vs 6+8	1+4 vs 7+9	1+8 vs 3+5	1+9 vs 3+6	1+3 vs 6+9	1+2 vs 7+8
	4+5 vs 6+7	4+8 vs 3+9	5+9 vs 2+8	3+7 vs 2+9	2+6 vs 3+8	4+9 vs 2+7	5+8 vs 2+4	2+5 vs 4+7	3+4 vs 5+6
	2+3 vs 6+7	1+6 vs 3+9	1+7 vs 2+8	1+5 vs 2+9	1+4 vs 3+8	1+8 vs 2+7	1+9 vs 2+4	1+3 vs 4+7	1+2 vs 5+6
	8+9 vs 4+5	5+7 vs 4+8	4+6 vs 5+9	6+8 vs 3+7	7+9 vs 2+6	3+5 vs 4+9	3+6 vs 5+8	6+9 vs 2+5	7+8 vs 3+4

Championship Brackets

(To determine placement: Win = 2   Tie = 1)

First Place

1st ____ + ____ 4th   vs   ____ 2nd + ____ 3rd

Second Place

____ 5th + ____ 8th   vs   ____ 6th + ____ 7th

Add ____ 9th ____ anywhere.

ROTATING TEAMS

10 -Team Record Sheet

Unit: _____   Period: _____

Team	Roster	Record		Team	Roster	Record	
1		W		**6**		W	
		T				T	
2		W		**7**		W	
		T				T	
3		W		**8**		W	
		T				T	
4		W		**9**		W	
		T				T	
5		W		**10**		W	
		T				T	

Notes:

SCHEDULE

1	2	3	4	5	6	7	8	9
1 vs 2	1 vs 3	1 vs 5	1 vs 7	1 vs 9	1 vs 10	1 vs 8	1 vs 6	1 vs 4
3 vs 4	2 vs 5	3 vs 7	5 vs 9	7 vs 10	8 vs 9	6 vs 10	4 vs 8	2 vs 6
5 vs 6	4 vs 7	2 vs 9	3 vs 10	5 vs 8	6 vs 7	4 vs 9	2 vs 10	3 vs 8
7 vs 8	6 vs 9	4 vs 10	2 vs 8	3 vs 6	4 vs 5	2 vs 7	3 vs 9	5 vs 10
9 vs 10	8 vs 10	6 vs 8	4 vs 6	2 vs 4	2 vs 3	3 vs 5	5 vs 7	7 vs 9

All Or Nothing Championship Brackets

(To determine placement: Win = 2   Tie = 1)

First		Second		Third		Fourth		Fifth	
___ vs ___		___ vs ___		___ vs ___		___ vs ___		___ vs ___	
1st	2nd	3rd	4th	5th	6th	7th	8th	9th	10th

10 -Team Record Sheet

Unit: _____   Period: _____

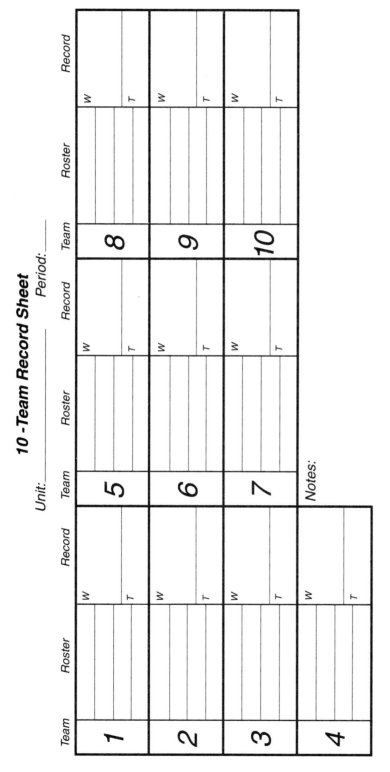

Team	Roster	Record		
1		W		T
2		W		T
3		W		T
4		W		T
5		W		T
6		W		T
7		W		T
8		W		T
9		W		T
10		W		T

Notes:

SCHEDULE

1	2	3	4	5	6	7	8	9
1 vs 2	1 vs 3	1 vs 5	1 vs 7	1 vs 9	1 vs 10	1 vs 8	1 vs 6	1 vs 4
3 vs 4	2 vs 5	3 vs 7	5 vs 9	7 vs 10	8 vs 9	6 vs 10	4 vs 8	2 vs 6
5 vs 6	4 vs 7	2 vs 9	3 vs 10	5 vs 8	6 vs 7	4 vs 9	2 vs 10	3 vs 8
7 vs 8	6 vs 9	4 vs 10	2 vs 8	3 vs 6	4 vs 5	2 vs 7	3 vs 9	5 vs 10
9 vs 10	8 vs 10	6 vs 8	4 vs 6	2 vs 4	2 vs 3	3 vs 5	5 vs 7	7 vs 9

All Or Nothing Championship Brackets

(To determine placement: Win = 2   Tie = 1)

First	Second	Third	Fourth	Fifth
___ vs	___ vs	___ vs	___ vs	___ vs
1st ___ 2nd	3rd ___ 4th	5th ___ 6th	7th ___ 8th	9th ___ 10th

11 -Team *(Mix 'n' Match)* **Record Sheet**

Unit: _____   Period: _____

Team	Roster	Record		Team	Roster	Record	
1		W		**7**		W	
		T				T	
2		W		**8**		W	
		T				T	
3		W		**9**		W	
		T				T	
4		W		**10**		W	
		T				T	
5		W		**11**		W	
		T				T	
6		W		Notes:			
		T					

SCHEDULE

Day and Team Out

1	2	3	4	5	6
4+7 vs 9+11	1+6 vs 7+10	2+10 vs 6+8	1+9 vs 2+7	1+3 vs 6+7	3+10 vs 7+9
2+5 vs 8+10	3+4 vs 8+9	4+11 vs 5+9	3+5 vs 8+11	4+8 vs 10+11	2+11 vs 5+8
3 vs 6	1 vs 5	1 vs 7	6 vs 10	2 vs 9	1 vs 4

7	8	9	10	11
1+11 vs 2+6	2+3 vs 6+9	2+4 vs 6+11	3+11 vs 5+6	5+7 vs 1+10
4+5 vs 9+10	1+5 vs 4+10	1+8 vs 3+7	1+2 vs 7+8	4+6 vs 3+9
3 vs 8	7 vs 11	5 vs 10	4 vs 9	2 vs 8

First Place Bracket   **Second Place Bracket**

(To determine placement: Win = 2   Tie = 1)

____ + ____ vs ____ + ____   ____ + ____ vs ____ + ____

1st   4th   2nd   3rd   6th   9th   7th   8th

Add ____ here.   Add ____ here.   Add ____ anywhere.

5th   10th   11th

11-Team (Mix 'n' Match) *Record Sheet*

Unit: _____   Period: _____

Team	Roster	Record	W	T	Team	Roster	Record	W	T	Team	Roster	Record	W	T
1					5					9				
2					6					10				
3					7					11				
4					8					Notes:				

SCHEDULE

Day and Team Out

1	2	3	4	5	6
4+7 vs 9+11	1+6 vs 7+10	2+10 vs 6+8	1+9 vs 2+7	1+3 vs 6+7	3+10 vs 7+9
2+5 vs 8+10	3+4 vs 8+9	4+11 vs 5+9	3+5 vs 8+11	4+8 vs 10+11	2+11 vs 5+8
3 vs 6	1 vs 5	1 vs 7	6 vs 10	2 vs 9	1 vs 4

7	8	9	10	11
1+11 vs 2+6	2+3 vs 6+9	2+4 vs 6+11	3+11 vs 5+6	5+7 vs 1+10
4+5 vs 9+10	1+5 vs 4+10	1+8 vs 3+7	1+2 vs 7+8	4+6 vs 3+9
3 vs 8	7 vs 11	5 vs 10	4 vs 9	2 vs 8

First Place Bracket

(To determine placement: Win = 2   Tie = 1)

1st ____ + ____ vs ____ + ____ 3rd
   4th   2nd
   Add ____ 5th here.

Second Place Bracket

6th ____ + ____ vs ____ + ____ 8th
   9th   7th
   Add ____ 10th here.

Add ____ 11th anywhere.

ROTATING TEAMS

12 -Team Record Sheet

Unit: _____   Period: _____

Team	Roster	Record		Team	Roster	Record	
1		W		**7**		W	
		T				T	
2		W		**8**		W	
		T				T	
3		W		**9**		W	
		T				T	
4		W		**10**		W	
		T				T	
5		W		**11**		W	
		T				T	
6		W		**12**		W	
		T				T	

© 2001 Parker Publishing Company

SCHEDULE

1	2	3	4	5	6	7	8	9	10	11
1 vs 2	1 vs 3	1 vs 5	1 vs 7	1 vs 9	1 vs 11	1 vs 12	1 vs 10	1 vs 8	1 vs 6	1 vs 4
3 vs 4	2 vs 5	2 vs 9	2 vs 12	2 vs 8	2 vs 4	2 vs 3	2 vs 7	2 vs 11	2 vs 10	2 vs 6
5 vs 6	4 vs 7	3 vs 7	3 vs 11	3 vs 10	3 vs 6	4 vs 5	3 vs 5	3 vs 9	3 vs 12	3 vs 8
7 vs 8	6 vs 9	4 vs 11	4 vs 10	4 vs 6	5 vs 8	6 vs 7	4 vs 9	4 vs 12	4 vs 8	5 vs 10
9 vs 10	8 vs 11	6 vs 12	5 vs 9	5 vs 12	7 vs 10	8 vs 9	6 vs 11	6 vs 10	5 vs 11	7 vs 12
11 vs 12	10 vs 12	8 vs 10	6 vs 8	7 vs 11	9 vs 12	10 vs 11	8 vs 12	7 vs 5	7 vs 9	9 vs 11

All Or Nothing Championship Brackets
(To determine placement: Win = 2   Tie = 1)

First	Second	Third	Fourth	Fifth	Sixth
___ vs ___	___ vs ___	___ vs ___	___ vs ___	___ vs ___	___ vs ___
1st 2nd	3rd 4th	5th 6th	7th 8th	9th 10th	11th 12th

12 -Team Record Sheet

Unit: _____   Period: _____

Team	Roster	Record		Team	Roster	Record		Team	Roster	Record	
		W				W				W	
1		T		**5**		T		**9**		T	
2		W		**6**		W		**10**		W	
		T				T				T	
3		W		**7**		W		**11**		W	
		T				T				T	
4		W		**8**		W		**12**		W	
		T				T				T	

SCHEDULE

1	2	3	4	5	6	7	8	9	10	11
1 vs 2	1 vs 3	1 vs 5	1 vs 7	1 vs 9	1 vs 11	1 vs 12	1 vs 10	1 vs 8	1 vs 6	1 vs 4
3 vs 4	2 vs 5	2 vs 9	2 vs 12	2 vs 8	2 vs 4	2 vs 3	2 vs 7	2 vs 11	2 vs 10	2 vs 6
5 vs 6	4 vs 7	3 vs 7	3 vs 11	3 vs 10	3 vs 6	4 vs 5	3 vs 5	3 vs 9	3 vs 12	3 vs 8
7 vs 8	6 vs 9	4 vs 11	4 vs 10	4 vs 6	5 vs 8	6 vs 7	4 vs 9	4 vs 12	4 vs 8	5 vs 10
9 vs 10	8 vs 11	6 vs 12	5 vs 9	5 vs 12	7 vs 10	8 vs 9	6 vs 11	6 vs 10	5 vs 11	7 vs 12
11 vs 12	10 vs 12	8 vs 10	6 vs 8	7 vs 11	9 vs 12	10 vs 11	8 vs 12	7 vs 5	7 vs 9	9 vs 11

All Or Nothing Championship Brackets

(To determine placement: Win = 2 Tie = 1)

First		Second		Third		Fourth		Fifth		Sixth	
	vs		vs		vs		vs		vs		vs
1st	2nd	3rd	4th	5th	6th	7th	8th	9th	10th	11th	12th

ROTATING TEAMS

13 -Team *(Mix 'n' Match)* Record Sheet

Unit: _____   Period: _____

Team	Roster	Record		Team	Roster	Record	
1		W		**8**		W	
		T				T	
2		W		**9**		W	
		T				T	
3		W		**10**		W	
		T				T	
4		W		**11**		W	
		T				T	
5		W		**12**		W	
		T				T	
6		W		**13**		W	
		T				T	
7		W		Notes:			
		T					

© 2001 Parker Publishing Company

SCHEDULE

1	2	3	4	5	6	7	8	9	10	11	12	13
2 vs 13	1 vs 3	2 vs 4	3 vs 5	4 vs 6	5 vs 7	6 vs 8	7 vs 9	8 vs 10	9 vs 11	10 vs 12	11 vs 13	1 vs 12
5 vs 10	6 vs 11	7 vs 12	8 vs 13	1 vs 9	2 vs 10	3 vs 11	4 vs 12	5 vs 13	1 vs 6	2 vs 7	3 vs 8	4 vs 9
3 vs 12	4 vs 13	1 vs 5	2 vs 6	3 vs 7	4 vs 8	5 vs 9	6 vs 10	7 vs 11	8 vs 12	9 vs 13	1 vs 10	2 vs 11
7 vs 8	8 vs 9	9 vs 10	10 vs 11	11 vs 12	12 vs 13	1 vs 13	1 vs 2	2 vs 3	3 vs 4	4 vs 5	5 vs 6	6 vs 7
4 vs 11	5 vs 12	6 vs 13	1 vs 7	2 vs 8	3 vs 9	4 vs 10	5 vs 11	6 vs 12	7 vs 13	1 vs 8	2 vs 9	3 vs 10
6 vs 9	7 vs 10	8 vs 11	9 vs 12	10 vs 13	1 vs 11	2 vs 12	3 vs 13	1 vs 4	2 vs 5	3 vs 6	4 vs 7	5 vs 8

Championship Brackets

Gold	**Silver**	**Bronze**		
___+___ vs ___+___	___+___ vs ___+___	___+___ vs ___+___	Add ___	anywhere.
1st 4th 2nd 3rd	5th 8th 6th 7th	9th 12th 10th 11th	13th	

13 -Team (Mix 'n' Match) *Record Sheet*

Unit: _____ Period: _____

Team	Roster	W	T	Record	Team	Roster	W	T	Record	Team	Roster	W	T	Record
1					6					10				
2					7					11				
3					8					12				
4					9					13				
5					Notes:									

SCHEDULE

1	2	3	4	5	6	7	8	9	10	11	12	13
2 vs 13	1 vs 3	2 vs 4	3 vs 5	4 vs 6	5 vs 7	6 vs 8	7 vs 9	8 vs 10	9 vs 11	10 vs 12	11 vs 13	1 vs 12
5 vs 10	6 vs 11	7 vs 12	8 vs 13	1 vs 9	2 vs 10	3 vs 11	4 vs 12	5 vs 13	1 vs 6	2 vs 7	3 vs 8	4 vs 9
3 vs 12	4 vs 13	1 vs 5	2 vs 6	3 vs 7	4 vs 8	5 vs 9	6 vs 10	7 vs 11	8 vs 12	9 vs 13	1 vs 10	2 vs 11
7 vs 8	8 vs 9	9 vs 10	10 vs 11	11 vs 12	12 vs 13	1 vs 13	1 vs 2	2 vs 3	3 vs 4	4 vs 5	5 vs 6	6 vs 7
4 vs 11	5 vs 12	6 vs 13	1 vs 7	2 vs 8	3 vs 9	4 vs 10	5 vs 11	6 vs 12	7 vs 13	1 vs 8	2 vs 9	3 vs 10
6 vs 9	7 vs 10	8 vs 11	9 vs 12	10 vs 13	1 vs 11	2 vs 12	3 vs 13	1 vs 4	2 vs 5	3 vs 6	4 vs 7	5 vs 8

Championship Brackets

Gold
1st ___ vs ___ 2nd + ___ 3rd ___ 4th

Silver
5th ___ vs ___ 6th + ___ 7th ___ 8th

Bronze
9th ___ vs ___ 10th + ___ 11th ___ 12th Add ___ anywhere. ___ 13th

ROTATING TEAMS

Single Elimination (8 Team)

Unit: _____ *Period:* _____

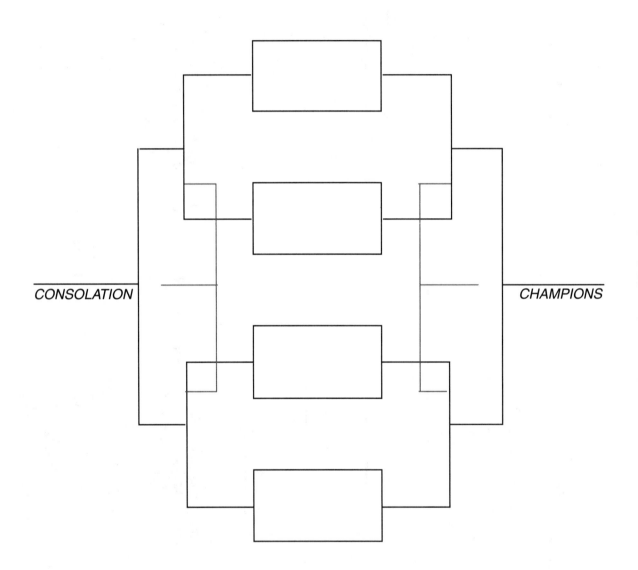

CONSOLATION   CHAMPIONS

Single Elimination (16 Team)

Unit:　　　　　　　　　　　*Period:*

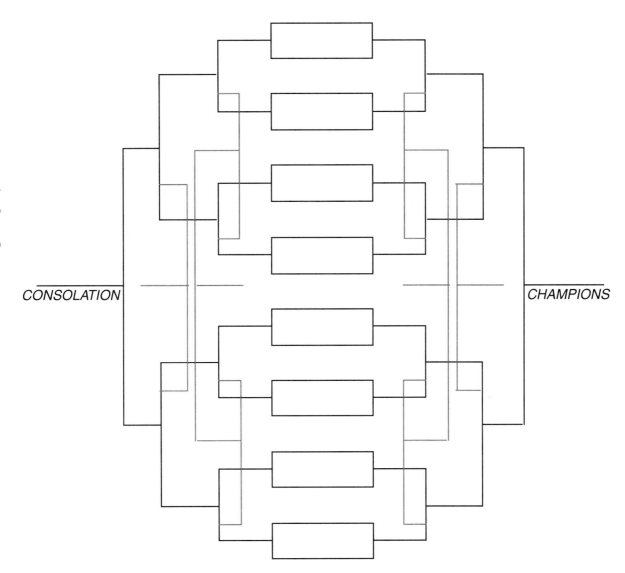

CONSOLATION　　　　　　　　　　　　　　　CHAMPIONS

Double Elimination (4 Team)

Unit: _____

Date: _____

Period: _____

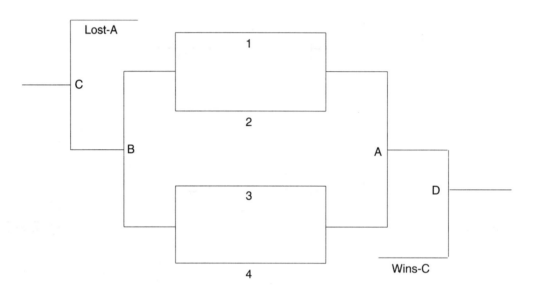

If winner of C wins the first game here, then one more game will be played.

Final Standings			
Place		*No#*	*Name*
1st	*Won D*		
2nd	*Lost D*		
3rd	*Lost C*		
4th	*Lost B*		

ROTATING TEAMS

Double Elimination (8 Team)

Unit: _____
Date: _____
Period: _____

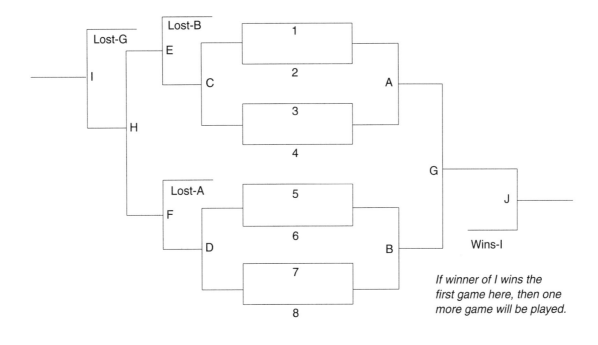

*If winner of I wins the
first game here, then one
more game will be played.*

Final Standings

Place		No#	Name
1st	Won J		
2nd	Lost J		
3rd	Lost I		
4th	Lost H		
5th	Won K		
6th	Lost K		
7th	Won L		
8th	Lost L		

ROTATING TEAMS

Double Elimination (16 Team)

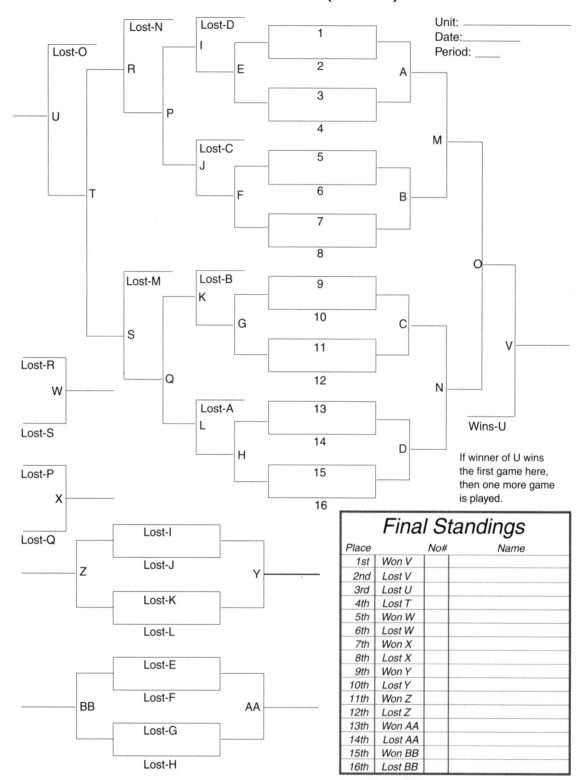

Unit: _____
Date:_____
Period: _____

If winner of U wins
the first game here,
then one more game
is played.

Final Standings

Place		No#	Name
1st	Won V		
2nd	Lost V		
3rd	Lost U		
4th	Lost T		
5th	Won W		
6th	Lost W		
7th	Won X		
8th	Lost X		
9th	Won Y		
10th	Lost Y		
11th	Won Z		
12th	Lost Z		
13th	Won AA		
14th	Lost AA		
15th	Won BB		
16th	Lost BB		

TEAM ORGANIZER*

Directions:

Total up the combined number of students. Move right to a given number. The bold value is ideal. The minus and plus values represent the number of teams that will have an unequal amount.

© 2001 Parker Publishing Company

TOTAL NUMBER OF STUDENTS

No#	AVERAGE NUMBER OF PLAYERS PER TEAM							No #	AVERAGE NUMBER OF PLAYERS PER TEAM						
	4	**5**	**6**	**7**	**8**	**9**	**10**		**4**	**5**	**6**	**7**	**8**	**9**	**10**
41	10+1	8+1		6-2			4-2	81	20+1	16+1	14-3	12-3	10+1		8+1
42	10+2	8+2		6-1			4-1	82	20+2	16+2	14-2	12-2	10+2		8+2
43				**6**			**4**	83			14-1	12-1	10+3		8+3
44				6+1	6-4		4+1	84			**14**	**12**	10+4		8+4
45			8-3	6+2	6-3		4+2	85			14+1	12+1			8+5
46	12-2		8-2	6+3	6-2			86	22-2		14+2	12+2		10-4	
47	12-1		8-1		6-1			87	22-1		14+3	12+3		10-3	
48	**12**	10-2	**8**		**6**			88	**22**	18-2				10-2	
49	12+1	10-1	8+1		6+1			89	22+1	18-1				10-1	
50	12+2	**10**	8+2		6+2	6-4		90	22+2	**18**				**10**	
51		10+1	8+3		6+3	6-3		91		18+1				10+1	
52		10+2			6+4	6-2		92		18+2			12-4	10+2	
53				8-3		6-1		93			16-3		12-3	10+3	
54	14-2			8-2		**6**		94	24-2		16-2		12-2	10+4	
55	14-1			8-1		6+1	6-5	95	24-1		16-1	14-3	12-1		10-5
56	**14**			**8**		6+2	6-4	96	**24**		**16**	14-2	**12**		10-4
57	14+1		10-3	8+1		6+3	6-3	97	24+1		16+1	14-1	12+1		10-3
58	14+2	12-2	10-2	8+2		6+4	6-2	98	24+2	20-2	16+2	**14**	12+2		10-2
59		12-1	10-1	8+3			6-1	99		20-1	16+3	14+1	12+3		10-1
60		**12**	**10**		8-4		**6**	100		**20**		14+2	12+4		**10**
61		12+1	10+1		8-3		6+1	101		20+1		14+3			10+1
62	16-2	12+2	10+2		8-2		6+2	102	26-2	20+2					10+2
63	16-1		10+3		8-1		6+3	103	26-1						10+3
64	**16**				**8**		6+4	104	**26**					12-4	10+4
65	16+1				8+1		6+5	105	26+1		18-3			12-3	10+5
66	16+2				8+2			106	26+2		18-2			12-2	
67				10-3	8+3			107			18-1			12-1	
68		14-2		10-2	8+3	8-4		108		22-2	**18**		14-4	**12**	
69		14-1	12-3	10-1		8-3		109		22-1	18+1	16-3	14-3	12+1	
70	18-2	**14**	12-2	**10**		8-2		110	28-2	**22**	18+2	16-2	14-2	12+2	
71	18-1	14+1	12-1	10+1		8-1		111	28-1	22+1	18+3	16-1	14-1	12+3	
72	**18**	14+2	**12**	10+2		**8**		112	**28**	22+2		**16**	**14**	12+4	
73	18+1		12+1	10+3		8+1		113	28+1			16+1	14+1		
74	18+2		12+2			8+2		114	28+2			16+2	14+2		
75			12+3			8+3	8-5	115				16+3	14+3		12-5
76					10-4	8+4	8-4	116					14+4		12-4
77					10-3		8-3	117			20-3				12-3
78	20-2	16-2			10-2		8-2	118	30-2	24-2	20-2				12-2
79	20-1	16-1			10-1		8-1	119	30-1	24-1	20-1				12-1
80	**20**	**16**			**10**		**8**	120	**30**	**24**	**20**				**12**

*Created by Ken Lumsden, 2000.

PART III
EASY ASSESSMENTS

* Assessment Format

   How I Got My Grade – Key

   How I Got My Grade – Student handout

* Sample Roll Call

   10-Day Roll Call

   15-Day Roll Call

* Sample Inverted Grade Scale

   10-Day Inverted Grade Scale

   15-Day Inverted Grade Scale

* Sample Final Term Grade

   Final Term Grade

* Unified Units Grade Scale

* About Accountability Statement

   Accountability Statement Form

* About Deficiency Report

   Physical Education Deficiency Report

* Motivators

   Ticket Takers

   Lunch Bunch

ASSESSMENT FORMAT

Students are graded strictly on their effort in class and the ability to follow the rules and procedures set forth by the class guidelines. Students will be held accountable for their own actions. They are not graded on how many, how far, how fast, or how high they can perform a task. The instructor does not give each student a grade based on a personal evaluation or standardized test, but instead assigns the grade based on each student's accountability and effort. Thus, the grade is earned, not given.

Each student begins class with zero points and can earn a maximum of five (5) points by the end of the period. Points are never taken away; instead, points are not awarded when undesirable behaviors or actions occur. Think of it as if it were a job on the outside. Each student (worker) has no points (money) at the beginning of class (work) and will earn points (money) at the end of the period (day). A student (carpenter) who forgets her or his attire (hammer and saw), will not be active (build), and will forfeit the right to accumulate any points (money). Students can earn bonus points (overtime) for performing extra tasks.

How I Got My Grade (Key), is presented so that the instructor will understand what the abbreviations represent and the point values of each. Only these abbreviations are placed on the *10- or 15-Day Roll Call* sheets. Once the abbreviations and their point values are learned, it becomes a breeze to record each student's conduct and final grade. Remember, points are never taken away. However, for the ease of determining the final grade in each unit, the deficiency values are tallied, then changed to a negative number. These abbreviations will also allow for quick reference when writing deficiency reports and are quite valuable during parent conferences.

How I Got My Grade is handed out to every student at the beginning of each term. It is reviewed and any desired additions or rewrites by the students (if any) are recorded. This eliminates any surprises or gray areas, and informs students of what is expected of them to attain the grades they desire. If and when a student has a "bad day", there is the possibility of bringing the grade back up by earning bonus points during the unit. Keep in mind, under this prescribed plan, it takes two bonus points to equal one grade point (B+ to an A-). The final grade is determined from the percentage of the total points attained out of the total points possible.

Using the redesigned and clipboard-friendly *10- or 15-Day Roll Call* sheet, the teacher and students record actions and behaviors, whether beneficial or adverse, that are demonstrated daily. These edits will be used for determining the final unit grade. Since a grade is formulated on the number of days present, the total points possible may differ from student to student due to illnesses, vacations, excused field trips, or the like. Some teachers prefer to have students make up missed days by doing activities outside of class. That is the instructor's option.

Using the newly created *Inverted Grade Scale* sheet, you can quickly arrive at the final grade. Unit grades are recorded on the *Final Term Grade* sheet, then averaged together using the *Unified Units Grade Scale* sheet to determine the final term or semester grade.

This grading method is simple, fast, fair, and allows each student to be in charge of the grade she or he aspires to obtain.

HOW I GOT MY GRADE (KEY)
(Instructor's Guide)

I can earn a maximum of 5 points each day in P.E.

I will earn 0 points for:
Non-dressed/non-active (Nd) = -5
Unexcused absence (U) = -5
Being insubordinate (I) = -5
Fighting (F) = -5
Destroying school property or equipment (D) = -5

I can only earn a maximum of 2 points for:
Non-dressed/active (Nd3) = -3
Cutting class (C) = -3

I can only earn a maximum of 3 points for:
Being partially dressed (Pd) = -2
Reduced effort during an activity (E) = -2
Being tardy to class (T) = -2

I can only earn a maximum of 4 points for:
Performing hazardous or unsafe acts (H) = -1
Showing poor sportsmanship (S) = -1
Belittling or putting others down (B) = -1
Intentionally breaking class or game rules (R) = -1
Displaying or voicing obscenities (V) = -1
Arguing with others for any reason (A) = -1

I can earn from 1 to 2 bonus points for: (2 bonus points = 1 grade point.)
Extra effort (assisting the teacher, helping a student, etc.) (++) = +1
Performing a predetermined goal (such as a task, number of, routine, or correctly answering a question) (++) = +1

My grade is based on a percentage of the total points possible:
A = 90%
B = 80%
C = 70%
D = 60%
NP = 59% and below

HOW I GOT MY GRADE

(Student handout)

I can earn a maximum of 5 points each day in P.E.

I will earn 0 points for:
Non-dressed/non-active
Unexcused absence
Being insubordinate
Fighting
Destroying school property

I can only earn a maximum of 2 points for:
Non-dressed/active (example: walked four times around the track)
Cutting class

I can only earn a maximum of 3 points for:
Being partially dressed (only shirt or shorts)
Reduced effort during an activity
Being tardy to class

I can only earn a maximum of 4 points for:
Performing unsafe acts
Showing poor sportsmanship
Putting others down
Intentionally breaking class or game rules
Displaying or voicing obscenities
Arguing with others for any reason

I can earn from 1 to 2 bonus points for: (2 bonus points = 1 grade raise)
Showing extra effort (assisting the teacher, helping a student, etc.)
Performing a predetermined goal (such as a task, number of, routine, or correctly answering a question)

My grade is based on a percentage of the total points possible:
A   = 90%
B   = 80%
C   = 70%
D   = 60%
NP = 59% and below

SAMPLE ROLL CALL

Unit Records

Activity: Floor Hockey

Begins: March 10
Ends: March 21

GOALS key:
- E: Deflect a scoring attempt (2)
- D: Cause a shutout
- C: Pass to three teammates
- B: Assist in a score (2)
- A: Be a goalie (3)

#	Class Roster	H	P	G	1	2	3	4	5	6	7	8	9	10	#	A	B	C	D	E
1	Abel, Shirley	10	+2	A											1	+	++	+		
2	Burns, Camille	9	-7	B			R		Ab		S R		Nd		2	+	+			
3	Campbell, Sam	10	-12	C		T	Nd			R	V	B	R	S	3					
4	Cochran, Bruce	6	0	A							Ab	Ab	Ab	Ab	4		+		+	

(Day # columns 1–10; GOALS columns A–E; BONUS section at far right)

Directions:

1. Fill in the information needed for Activity, Begins, Ends, and Class Roster.

2. Write in any skills or tasks needed in the *GOALS* section. When a student successfully completes a goal or task (can be more than once if so desired), she/he will mark it with a "+". The *BONUS* section is for miscellaneous "+" marks such as student help, knowing the answer to a question, "Play of the Day," refereeing, helping another classmate, taking roll, etc.

3. The *Day #* is for taking roll and recording deficiencies such as not dressing down, rules violation, sportsmanship, tardy, etc.

4. At the completion of the unit, tally up the total number of days each student was present in the *# Days Here* (H) column.

5. Using the *How I Got My Grade (Key)*, tally up each student's violations and "+" marks, then mark the total in the *Pts.* (P) column.

6. Finally, place the final grade in the *Grade* (G) column. Use the *Inverted Grade Scale* sheet to determine the final unit grade. (See *Sample Inverted Grade Scale* for Camille Burns' grade.)

SAMPLE ROLL CALL

461

© 2001 Parker Publishing Company

10-Day Unit Records

Activity: _____

Begins: _____
Ends: _____

No.	Class Roster	Here	Pts	Grade	Day # 1	2	3	4	5	6	7	8	9	10
1														
2														
3														
4														
5														
6														
7														
8														
9														
10														
11														
12														
13														
14														
15														
16														
17														
18														
19														
20														
21														
22														
23														
24														
25														
26														
27														
28														
29														
30														
31														
32														
33														
34														
35														
36														
37														

GOAL GRADE: A B C D E

BONUS: A B C D E

15-Day Unit Records

Activity: _____

Begins: _____

Ends: _____

Day #

No.	Class Roster	Here	Pts	Grade	1	2	3	4	5	6	7	8	9	10	11	12	13	14	15
1																			
2																			
3																			
4																			
5																			
6																			
7																			
8																			
9																			
10																			
11																			
12																			
13																			
14																			
15																			
16																			
17																			
18																			
19																			
20																			
21																			
22																			
23																			
24																			
25																			
26																			
27																			
28																			
29																			
30																			
31																			
32																			
33																			
34																			
35																			
36																			
37																			

GOALS: A B C D E

BONUS

SAMPLE INVERTED GRADE SCALE

	Days Present In Class															
	1	2	3	4	5	6	7	8	⑨	10	11	12	13	14	15	
A+ 110%	+1	+2	+2	+2	+3	+3	+4	+4	+5	+5	+6	+6	+7	+7	+8	**A+** 12
A 92%			-1	-1	-2	-2	2	-3	-3	-4	-4	-4	-5	-5	-6	**A** 11
A- 90%		-1		-2		-3	-4	-4	-4	-5	-5	-5 -6	-6	-6 -7	-7	**A-** 10
B+ 88%					-3		-5		-5	-6	-6	-7	-7	-8	-8 -9	**B+** 9
B 82%			-2	-3	-4	-4 -5	-6 -7	-5 -6 -7	-7	-7 -8 -9	-7 -8 -9	-8 -9 -10	-8 -9 -10 -11	-9 -10 -11 -12	-10 -11 -12 -13	**B** 8

Directions:

1. Use the *Sample Roll Call* sheet.

2. Example of Camille Burns: She was present 9 days. Her total was -7.

3. Using the *Inverted Grade Scale* sheet above, go to the top, locate the 9 days present column and follow it down until the -7 is found. Next move to the far right column and find the letter grade of "B." Notice that the "B" has a point value of 8. This number will be written down on the Final Term Grade sheet.

4. Once this system is used, it will be found to be simple, accurate, and fast. An entire class can be graded in two to three minutes.

INVERTED GRADE SCALE (10-DAY)

	Days Present In Class										
	1	2	3	4	5	6	7	8	9	10	
A+ 110%	+1	+2	+2	+2	+3	+3	+4	+4	+5	+5	**A+** 12
A 92%			-1	-1	-2	-2	-2	-3	-3	-4	**A** 11
A- 90%		-1		-2		-3	-4	-4	-4	-5	**A-** 10
B+ 88%					-3		-5		-5	-6	**B+** 9
B 82%			-2	-3	-4	-4 -5	-6 -7	-5 -6 -7	-6 -7 -8	-7 -8 -9	**B** 8
B- 80%	-1	-2	-3	-4	-5	-6	-8	-8	-9	-10	**B-** 7
C+ 78%										-11	**C+** 6
C 72%			-4	-5	-6 -7	-7 -8	-9 -10	-9 -10 -11	-10 -11 -12	-12 -13 -14	**C** 5
C- 70%		-3		-6		-9	-11	-12	-13	-15	**C-** 4
D+ 68%					-8		-12		-14	-16	**D+** 3
D 62%			-5	-7	-9	-10 -11	-13 -14	-13 -14 -15	-15 -16 -17	-17 -18 -19	**D** 2
D- 60%	-2	-4	-6	-8	-10	-12	-15	-16	-18	-20	**D-** 1
NP 59%	-3	-5	-7	-9	-11	-13	-16	-17	-19	-21	**NP** 0

INVERTED GRADE SCALE (15-DAY)

INVERTED GRADE SCALE (15-DAY)

	\	\	\	\	\	\	\	\	\	\	\	\	\	\	\	
							Days Present In Class									
	1	**2**	3	**4**	5	**6**	7	**8**	9	**10**	11	**12**	13	**14**	15	
A+ *110%*	+1	**+2**	+2	**+2**	+3	**+3**	+4	**+4**	+5	**+5**	+6	**+6**	+7	**+7**	+8	**A+** *12*
A *92%*			-1	**-1**	-2	**-2**	-2	**-3**	-3	**-4**	-4	**-4**	-5	**-5**	-6	**A** *11*
A- *90%*		**-1**		**-2**		**-3**	-4	**-4**	-4	**-5**	-5	**-5** **-6**	-6	**-6** **-7**	-7	**A-** *10*
B+ *88%*					-3		-5		-5	**-6**	-6	**-7**	-7	**-8**	-8 -9	**B+** *9*
B *82%*			-2	**-3**	-4	**-4** **-5**	-6 -7	**-5** **-6** **-7**	-6 -7 -8	**-7** **-8** **-9**	-7 -8 -9	**-8** **-9** **-10**	-8 -9 -10 -11	**-9** **-10** **-11** **-12**	-10 -11 -12 -13	**B** *8*
B- *80%*	-1	**-2**	-3	**-4**	-5	**-6**	-8	**-8**	-9	**-10**	-10 -11	**-11** **-12**	-12 -13	**-13** **-14**	-14 -15	**B-** *7*
C+ *78%*										**-11**	-12	**-13**	-14	**-15**	-16	**C+** *6*
C *72%*			-4	**-5**	-6 -7	**-7** **-8**	-9 -10	**-9** **-10** **-11**	-10 -11 -12	**-12** **-13** **-14**	-13 -14 -15	**-14** **-15** **-16**	-15 -16 -17 -18	**-16** **-17** **-18** **-19**	-17 -18 -19 -20 -21	**C** *5*
C- *70%*		**-3**		**-6**		**-9**	-11	**-12**	-13	**-15**	-16	**-17** **-18**	-19	**-20** **-21**	-22	**C-** *4*
D+ *68%*					-8		-12		-14	**-16**	-17	**-19**	-20	**-22**	-23 -24	**D+** *3*
D *62%*			-5	**-7**	-9	**-10** **-11**	-13 -14	**-13** **-14** **-15**	-15 -16 -17	**-17** **-18** **-19**	-18 -19 -20	**-20** **-21** **-22**	-21 -22 -23 -24	**-23** **-24** **-25** **-26**	-25 -26 -27 -28	**D** *2*
D- *60%*	-2	**-4**	-6	**-8**	-10	**-12**	-15	**-16**	-18	**-20**	-21 -22	**-23** **-24**	-25 -26	**-27** **-28**	-29 -30	**D-** *1*
NP *59%*	-3	**-5**	-7	**-9**	-11	**-13**	-16	**-17**	-19	**-21**	-23	**-25**	-27	**-29**	-31	**NP** *0*

SAMPLE FINAL TERM GRADE

Date: 2001 Qtr / Sem: First Period: 1 Instructor: Mrs. Smith		U N I T S	A	Football							Sum of A B C D E F	Use "*Unified Units Grade Scale*" to determine qtr/sem **FINAL GRADE**
			B	Soccer								
			C	Field Hockey								
			D	Basketball						No. of Units		
			E	Dance								
			F									
Roll	Class Roster		A	B	C	D	E	F			
1	Altman, Sara		8	9	0	6	3		5	26	C
2	Brown, Tony		11	11	11	11	11		5	55	A
3	Byers, Sean		12	11	12	12	11		5	58	A+
4	Clason, Sally		6	7	9	7	10		5	39	B

Directions:

1. Fill in all of the student names.

2. In column *A* record the first unit grade for football, in column *B* record the second unit grade in soccer and so on.

3. Next, record the total number of units in which each student received a grade in the *Number of Units* column.

4. Tally up the entire unit grade numbers and record this sum in the *Total of A+B+C+D+E* column.

5. Retrieve the *Unified Units Grade Scale* sheet. Find the number of units at the top and move down this column until the point total matches that of the *Total of A+B+C+D+E*. Move to the right *GRADE* column to reveal the final term or semester grade.

6. Lastly, record a *B* grade in the *FINAL GRADE* column of the *Final Term Grade* sheet.

7. Example: Sally Clason was graded in five units and received a 6 + 7 + 9 + 7 + 10 = 39. From the *Unified Units Grade Scale* sheet, go to the five (5) units column at the top, move down to 39, go right to B.

FINAL TERM GRADE SHEET

Date: Qtr / Sem: Period: Instructor:		UNITS	A B C D E F						No. of Units	Sum of A B C D E F	Use "*Unified Units Grade Scale*" to determine qtr/sem **FINAL GRADE**
Roll	Class Roster		A	B	C	D	E	F			
1											
2											
3											
4											
5											
6											
7											
8											
9											
10											
11											
12											
13											
14											
15											
16											
17											
18											
19											
20											
21											
22											
23											
24											
25											
26											
27											
28											
29											
30											
31											
32											
33											
34											
35											
36											
37											
38											
39											
40											

UNIFIED UNITS GRADE SCALE

Number of Units						
1	**2**	**3**	**4**	**5**	**6**	**GRADE**
0	0-1	0-1	0-2	0-2	0-3	**NP**
1	2-3	2-4	3-6	3-7	4-9	**D-**
2	4-5	5-7	7-10	8-12	10-15	**D**
3	6-7	8-10	11-14	13-17	16-21	**D+**
4	8-9	11-13	15-18	18-22	22-27	**C-**
5	10-11	14-16	19-22	23-27	28-33	**C**
6	12-13	17-19	23-26	28-32	34-39	**C+**
7	14-15	20-22	27-30	33-37	40-45	**B-**
8	16-17	23-25	31-34	38-42	46-51	**B**
9	18-19	26-28	35-38	43-47	52-57	**B+**
10	20-21	29-31	39-42	48-52	58-63	**A-**
11	22-23	32-34	43-46	53-57	64-69	**A**
12	24	35-36	47-48	58-60	70-72	**A+**

Directions:

1. The final grade is determined by averaging all of the activities for the semester/term.

2. Find the number of units at the top and move down this column until the point total matches that of the *Total of A+B+C+D+E* from the *Final Term Grade Sheet*.

3. Move to the right *GRADE* column to reveal the final term or semester grade.

ABOUT ACCOUNTABILITY STATEMENT

Objectives:

- ◆ Create student success in the physical education environment.
- ◆ Identify problem areas.
- ◆ Seek resolutions for the situation.

Essentials:

- ◆ Accountability statement form
- ◆ Pen or pencil

How to:

1. When a student is experiencing a problem in class (not following the rules for example), set a time for a brief meeting.
2. During this gathering, give the student the *Accountability Statement* form.
3. In your presence, have the individual write a short assertion of what the problem is and what is needed for the student to modify the behavior so that she/he may be more competent.
4. Collect the information and immediately evaluate it with the individual to ensure that positive results will occur.

Student Tasks:

1. Identify the problem on the paper.
2. How can the problem be alleviated?

Variations:

1. Put this information into a student contract if problems persist.
2. Involve councilors and parents.

ACCOUNTABILITY STATEMENT FORM

Date:

Name:

Identify the problem(s):

Method/s for improvement:

Additional instructor and student resolution(s):

ABOUT DEFICIENCY REPORT

Objectives:

◆ Provide an early warning tool that may promote and improve student success.

◆ Inform and involve the parents or legal guardians.

Essentials:

◆ Deficiency sheet

◆ Pen

Directions:

1. This form can easily be set up on a computer.

2. It is sent home whenever a student is averaging a "D+" or below after a few units. This allows the student plenty of time to raise the grade before the term or semester grade is recorded.

3. At the top of the form, fill in the date and the student's name.

4. For the unit information, copy the date, activity, iniquities, and grade from the Unit Grade Sheet.

5. Take the number of days that the student was present and multiply it by five. Place this number in the *Max Pts* section.

6. Write in all violations in the *Iniquities* column.

7. Tally the violation point values and subtract this number from the *Max Pts*. Place this result in the *Net Pts* box.

8. To determine the percentage, divide *Max Pts* into *Net Pts*.

9. Average the unit grades by using the *Unified Units Grade Scale*.

10. Finally, duplicate the sheet and send it to the student's home.

Example of Unit Information for a Deficiency Report
Unit Information

Date	Activity	Max Pts	Iniquities	Net Pts	%	Grade
Sept.	Football	50	Nd, Nd, Nd, Nd, = 20	30	60	D-
Oct.	Soccer	45	Nd, Pd, Pd, Nd, V, B = 16	29	64	D
Oct.	Swimming	50	Nd, Nd, Nd, S, = 16	34	68	D+
				Average		**D**

PHYSICAL EDUCATION DEFICIENCY REPORT

"Working together to ensure each other's success"

Date:

Dear Parent,

_____ has chosen not to be successful in P.E. Listed below are the former decisions that are constraining this student from reaching his or her full potential. Please verify the information with the student, check a preference or create a solution at the bottom, and return this form to me as soon as possible.

Thank you very much,

Physical Education Dept.
Phone # _____

Unit Information

Date	Activity	Max Pts	Iniquities	Net Pts	%	Grade
				Average		

© 2001 Parker Publishing Company

Key to abbreviations

Note: Each student begins class with no points and can earn up to five points each day present. Each unit grade is based on a percentage of the total points possible. (*A=90% B=80% C=70% D=60%*)

A = Arguing B = Belittling Bp = Bonus point C = Cut class D = Destroying property E = Lack of effort Ex = Excused F = Fighting H = Hazardous actions I = Insubordination Nd = Non dressed Nd3 = Non dressed active Pd = Partial dress T = Tardy R = Rules violation S = Sportsmanship U = Unexcused absence V = Vulgar language + = Bonus point (2 pts = one grade raise i.e. B+ to an A-

Parent/guardian response

Yes (please check one)
  a) When necessary, please keep this student during lunch.
  b) I will work with this individual at home.
  c) I will call and set up a conference time.

(Feel free to write on the back of this form any additional thoughts or ideas.)

TICKET TAKERS*

Objectives:

◆ Develop personal satisfaction for achieving outstanding behavior.

◆ Repeat this type of behavior to attain more chances at winning a prize.

Essentials:

◆ Roll of tickets (purchased at stationery store)

◆ 2 collection buckets (one in each P.E. office)

◆ 1 or more prizes (sports or entertainment articles such as a camera, portable compact disc player, bat, volleyball, basketball, sweat pants, etc.)

How To:

1. The prizes are either purchased from or donated by local merchants.

2. The instructor will issue a ticket to a student anytime she/he displays a commendable action or behavior.

3. Each teacher should always possess several tickets since it is important to issue one on the spot.

4. Tickets are not used as a replacement for bonus points.

5. Every student is given one ticket at the beginning of the school year so that everyone has at least one chance.

6. After receiving a ticket, the student will write her/his full name on the back and deposit it into the collection container.

7. The more tickets that are earned, over the course of the school year, the better the odds are of winning one of the prizes.

8. A ticket can be given for:

    a. Maintaining perfect attendance and no deficiencies.

    b. Making an outstanding play ("Play of the Day").

    c. Turning in something of value to the "lost and found."

    d. Helping organize and set up the playing area.

    e. Assisting another student to become better skilled or more informed.

    f. Making a creative suggestion that improves a game, unit, or the program.

    g. Introducing a new game that is eventually added to the curriculum.

9. One week prior to the end of the school year, the tickets are gathered from both offices, placed in a common container, and thoroughly mixed. A drawing is held to determine the winner/s for the prize/s.

Created by Julie Ponder, 1999.

Student Tasks:

1. Receive two or more tickets during the year.

2. Complete two or more of the above criteria listed in #8.

Variations:

1. Have several drawings throughout the year.

2. The ticket winner gets to choose the prize desired.

3. The last ticket drawn will win the grand prize.

4. The person that wins gets to draw the next ticket.

Illustration of Tickets for Ticket Takers

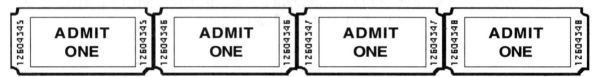

LUNCH BUNCH

Objectives:

♦ Create student success in the physical education environment.

♦ Displace a student from her/his desired social atmosphere.

Essentials:

♦ Room away from the masses

♦ Roster or muster sheet

How to:

1. The following information was obtained from a student survey:

    a. Detention can be a hindrance but it is no big deal when it is held during class time or after school.

    b. In the classroom, personal socialization is seldom allowed because of instructor assignments and activities.

    c. The best time to be with friends and interact is during lunch.

    d. The vast majority of students dislike losing social time.

2. A student who is having constant disciplinary problems in class is asked to join the "Lunch Bunch." Each teacher deals with her/his own students.

3. Our program works like this: The school has two adjoining lunch periods. We usually eat first lunch. Since our preparation period follows, we are usually available for both lunch periods.

4. Expectations:

    a. Students will have 10 minutes in which to eat lunch and then immediately report to the "Lunch Bunch" area (locker room).

    b. Homework or reading materials are advised but not required.

    c. Students must remain seated and quiet at all times.

    d. In exchange for a reduction of time, a student may elect to perform a duty such as sweeping the floor.

    e. Failure to show up or comply with any of the above expectations will result in additional "Lunch Bunch" time, or being sent to the Dean or principal for insubordination.

Student Tasks:

1. Follow the rules.

2. Volunteer to do something that can reduce the time.

3. Never return.

Variation:

1. Rotate the physical education teachers so that each teacher would supervise the "Lunch Bunch" for a week at a time. The other teachers would need to tell the duty teacher which students were supposed to show up.

2. Develop this program to encompass the entire school. A few logistics will need to be worked out. Each faculty member might have to do a short session once or twice a year or possibly an aide could be assigned to supervise the "Lunch Bunch" club.